DATE DUE

MECHANICAL & ELECTRICAL SYSTEMS FOR HISTORIC BUILDINGS

MECHANICAL & ELECTRICAL SYSTEMS
FOR
HISTORIC BUILDINGS

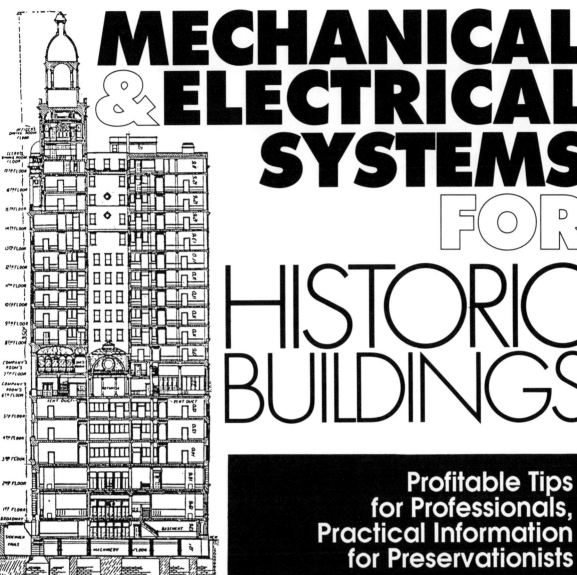

**Profitable Tips
for Professionals,
Practical Information
for Preservationists**

GERSIL NEWMARK KAY

Chief Executive Officer, M. Newmark & Bro., Inc., Philadelphia, Pa.
Founder/Chairman, Building Conservation International

McGraw-Hill, Inc.

New York St. Louis San Francisco Auckland Bogotá
Caracas Lisbon London Madrid Mexico
Milan Montreal New Delhi Paris
San Juan São Paulo Singapore
Sydney Tokyo Toronto

Library of Congress Cataloging-in-Publication Data

Kay, Gersil Newmark.

   Mechanical & electrical systems for historic buildings:
profitable tips for professionals, practical information for
preservationists / Gersil Newmark Kay.

        p.   cm.
   Includes bibliographical references and index.
   ISBN 0-07-033669-5
   1. Buildings—Mechanical equipment.   2. Buildings—Electrical
equipment.   3. Historic buildings—Maintenance and repair.
4. Historic buildings—Conservation and restoration.   I. Title.
II. Title: Mechanical and electrical systems for historic buildings.
TH6021.K29   1991
696—dc20   91-27319

1 2 3 4 5 6 7 8 9 0   HAL/HAL   9 7 6 5 4 3 2 1

ISBN 0-07-033669-5

The sponsoring editor for this book was Joel Stein, the editing supervisor was Stephen M. Smith, the designer was Susan Maksuta, and the production supervisor was Donald F. Schmidt. It was set in News Gothic by Arcata Graphics/Kingsport.

Printed and bound by Arcata Graphics/Halliday.

To the two men without whom this book could not have been done: my father, for his unfailing financial and moral support, and my long-suffering husband, who was the sounding board for all the versions of the manuscript

G.N.K.

CONTENTS

PREFACE

Some years ago, Charles E. Peterson, FAIA, then the architect of the restoration of Independence Hall in Philadelphia, complained that he had to put a 24-hour watch over the workmen, because they were punching holes in original fabric, whether they were needed or not! At that time, there was no practical reference book on how to install modern mechanical/electrical systems in pre–World War II buildings. Since I was an electrical contractor, Mr. Peterson suggested that I try to find a solution. This request started a worldwide search for ways to work on pre-1940 buildings which would be cost-effective *and* sympathetic to the original design.

The findings, presented in this book, show that the solutions to complex problems are often more simple than one might imagine. My objective is to show how to do the job with the *least cost and damage to original fabric.*

This book describes a *practical* approach to guide those not familiar with the historic methods of building construction. It will aid in the search for existing space available for the insertion of modern systems and make the search as effortless and as profitable as possible. Most of the information contained here is probably stored in the recesses of the mind of the reader, since it is common sense.

In researching this book, I traveled from Edinburgh, Scotland, to Shanghai, China, looking for answers, and was welcomed into offices and on sites everywhere by people proud of their industry and willing to teach future generations. The illustrations found here, most of which were taken from early (as far back as 1879) copies of the *Engineering Record,* show their age, but they still convey the message of how the structures were put together.

The list of those who graciously shared their expertise ranges from developers, financiers, architects, engineers, lawyers, accountants, contractors, craftsmen, architectural historians, interior designers, government agency workers, educators, apprentice-training instructors, museum curators, librarians, manufacturers, suppliers, inspectors, building superintendents, and consultants, to interested members of the public. Special thanks go to Craig Morrison, AIA, who meticulously went through the manuscript and offered excellent suggestions on style and content.

Therefore, this book is the product of many hands. I am merely the vehicle to deliver the message.

Gersil Newmark Kay

ACKNOWLEDGMENTS

Architects in the United States Tony Atkins, Donald Baerman, Penelope H. Batchelor, John Blatteau, John Bowie, Elliott Carroll, Henry J. Chambers, James Collins, Gerald Cope, Rudy D'Alessandro, Lewis Davis, Mary DeNadai, John Dickey, William Ensign, Max Ferro, Hugh Hardy, Alvin Holm, Harry Hunderman, Dan Peter Kopple, Russell Kuene, Herbert W. Levy, Henry J. Magaziner, John Milner, Craig Morrison, Hyman Myers, Lee Nelson, Charles E. Peterson, Robert Skaler, Bert L. Stern, Charles Stover, Watson & Henry.

Architects in Great Britain Ashley Barker, John Billingham, Charles Brown, Bernard Feilden, John Fidler, Michael Fishlock, Daryl Fowler, Ian Grant, Julian Harrap, Donald Insall, Charmian Lacey, Rodney Melville, Alan Parnell, James Simpson, Alfred Wood. HRH The Duke of Gloucester, himself an architect, is patron of Building Conservation International's The British Connection.

Engineers William Cornell, Salvatore Ferruggia, Nicholas Gianopulis, James Patterson, James N. Singer, David J. Stokoe.

Lighting designers Alfred Borden IV, Ray Grenald, LeMar Terry.

General contractors J. S. Cornell & Son, Haverstick-Borthwick, George Hyman Company, Turner Construction Company, Unkefer Brothers Construction.

Code experts Marlin Buckley, Jack Webster, William Wusinich.

Craftsmen Jerry Baker, M. Earle Felber, Jamie Kuryloski, Joseph C. Rudolph, Joel Westman.

Architectural historians Wim deWit, Robert Kapsch, Roger Moss, Satoko Parker, Timothy Samuelson, Deborah Slaton, Richard Tyler.

Electricians Don Bauer, Walt Burt, Randy Gould, Steve Lawrence, Andy Lynch, James Mackin, John Neilson, Irv Posten, Andy Pron, George J. Quinn Sr.

General Building Contractors' Association (Philadelphia Chapter, Associated General Contractors of America) Walter Palmer Jr., Walter Palmer III, James Sassaman, Judson Vodges.

National Electrical Contractors' Association, Penn-Del-Jersey Chapter Lawrence Bradley, Ellen Etter.

Mechanical Contractors' Association William Lindsay.

Pennsylvania Power & Light Company W. D. Singh, Frank Strauss.

Special thanks to Caroline Herd, Carl Nittinger, Richard Kennedy, Marion Dimitman, Marcus Binney, Desmond Guinness, and Monica Dance.

INTRODUCTION
IN A NUTSHELL

Perhaps the best place to start is to define *building conservation*. Simply, conservation is the action taken to prevent decay and prolong life. There are many types of conservation: energy, environment, and older technology, as well as architectural.

Every property, new or old, always needs *maintenance*. That is the very least expensive way to preserve real estate.

Because of local, state, or federal regulations, building and safety codes must be complied with, no matter what the age of the structure. The tenant also has specific needs. Thus, *retrofitting* is the major growth industry today. The cost of these upgraded systems constitutes the largest portion of the budget. Their presence and effectiveness determine whether there is profitable and useful occupancy. However, their installation, if not done sympathetically, can adversely alter the original architectural design of an historic building, to the owner's financial loss.

Properties of historical significance require *restoration* of missing or damaged components, in addition to maintenance and retrofitting. These three topics constitute building conservation. The criteria for good work are *minimum intervention* and *reversibility.*

However, there is a widespread myth that "Building conservation can't be done—it costs too much, takes too much time, and anyway, everyone who could do it is dead."

This is patently untrue, except for those who don't know how to do it. In 1847, John Ruskin, in *The Seven Lamps of Architecture,* put it more pointedly: "Know what you have to do, and do it."

Throughout the book, the reader may find certain remarks recurring in every chapter, but uttered by different people. This is not an oversight in editing; it is to reinforce the basic methods that everyone in every trade and discipline has discovered over the years.

Also, please note that this book is limited to work unusual to buildings from *1880 to 1940.* Since the systems being installed are new, their selection is referred to other sources. Likewise, their maintenance schedules would be covered by manufacturers' instructions delivered with the equipment. Because of the time between manuscript writing and publication, no prices are quoted since they would be hopelessly out of date and useless to the reader. The term *mechanical/electrical systems,* used throughout the book, will be shortened to M/E.

The author's comments, which are the result of much experience in educational programs with *Building Conservation International* (BCI), are found inside brackets within material from another source. BCI, a technical, nonprofit, educational organization, was created to act as the beacon to direct participants to the huge but yet unrealized market of building conservation. Its goal is to show how to do the job profitably and still be respectful of the original design of the building. Unless otherwise noted, photographs are by the author.

The reader is urged to persevere through the preliminary chapters before going directly to a specific system. If they become part of the reader's knowledge, these basics will help answer many questions that may occur in the field.

ECONOMIC REASONS FOR BUILDING CONSERVATION

In 1990, $200 billion was spent in the United States for scheduled maintenance, retrofitting to satisfy codes and tenants' requirements, and restoration of the over 1,200,000 commercial and institutional properties erected prior to 1940. In fact, building conservation, which constitutes 75 percent of construction, has been leading new installations for years. This huge figure simply cannot be ignored economically or culturally. Such a major segment of the market has proven very lucrative for those who know how to do it. It is *recession-proof,* and goes on continuously, with or without new building starts.

In order to retain the value and usefulness of real estate, some type of conservation must be done on a regular basis. Over *60 percent* of the $200 billion goes for M/E updating. This is because, while shelter is a basic necessity for all humans, today's occupants expect heating, ventilation, and air-conditioning as well as life safety, security, communications, lighting, elevators, and plumbing to exist in any structure, regardless of the age of that structure.

Investment tax credit   An added incentive for conservation in the United States is the 20 percent *investment tax credit* (ITC) that is available for rehabilitation of income-producing real estate. This was the only ITC retained in the sweeping tax revisions of 1986. It is a cash deduction from federal income tax, which is always most welcome.

HINDRANCES TO CONSERVATION

EDUCATION

Up to now, most courses, from trade school to university level, have virtually ignored the importance of M/E systems. Other subjects, such as colors of walls and treatment of masonry and windows, seem to have had precedence; however, this seems clearly illogical since none of the sophisticated tenant requirements would work without electric power.

What is more, since most schools for the professional, from architect and engineer to craft apprentices, have eliminated teaching the traditional earlier methods of *building technologies,* as well as studies in the *properties* of original materials, let alone *diagnostics* of existing structures, it is difficult for the uninitiated to learn how to accomplish the task so that it is cost-effective and sympathetic to the original design, unless old-timers will share their practical experience. Even the critical subject of *construction power electrical engineering* has disappeared from the curricula.

This woeful inadequacy in professional education is global and must be rectified, especially in times at the bottom of the business cycle. It is exactly at this time that people must know how to deal with both old and new structures, in order to remain employed.

ADVERSE EFFECTS OF ENVIRONMENTAL CONTROLS

Throughout the world, the improper introduction of modern heating, ventilating, and air-conditioning equipment has adversely affected traditionally constructed buildings and their contents. Where previously the existing materials had, over the years, accommodated on their own to the changes in temperature and humidity of their climate, they are now suddenly thrust into a new environmental condition which can cause serious accelerated deterioration. This phenomenon was first noticed in Europe, where ancient landmarks received central heating for the convenience of thousands of visitors. In the United States, where many historic properties have been renovated, some structures that had lasted for hundreds of years are now disintegrating at a rapid rate.

This means that in the decisions on equipment and installation, due consideration should be given to the effects of temperature and humidity on the original fabric.

EXISTING SYSTEMS

The question always arises as to whether to continue to use existing systems by renovating them or to pull them out and start over. Obviously ancient wiring must be replaced. However, if ornate lighting, plumbing, radiators, call boxes, or heaters can be made to work effectively, and if they contribute to the overall ambiance, there is no reason to dispose of them. *Old is not necessarily bad.*

LIGHTING

Intensity of lighting is another topic that requires thought. Unless needed for a purely commercial or institutional use, light in an historic space should approach the levels used at the time of construction. For example, the dining room of the 1920s Ritz Carlton Hotel in Montreal still has a ceiling unpierced by myriad downlights. The existing illumination from wall sconces and table lamps is most adequate for the atmosphere desired.

ELEVATORS

A more conservative approach would be less expensive and more effective historically. In a burst of imagined thrift, it is not necessary to convert perfectly good manually operated lifts to automatic. The old reliable mechanisms are simpler

Figure 1a. Styles of buildings: Fifteenth-century on left, seventeenth-century on right, eighteenth-century in center.

Figure 1b. Styles of buildings: Late-nineteenth-century in center, postmodern behind, 1912 on right, 1970 behind, Art Deco behind that.

YOU ARE CORDIALLY INVITED TO A PRIVATE SHOWING OF NEW YORK'S FINEST PRE-WAR BUILDINGS.

Figure 2. Contemporary ad in the Real Estate section of the *New York Times*.

and actually fail less frequently, if *properly maintained*. In addition, they are much less expensive to service and offer the added benefit of excellent security because of the necessary presence of the human operator, whose salary is much less than the cost of installating and monitoring high-priced equipment.

STYLES OF BUILDINGS (Fig. 1)

Any style of building can be retrofitted. In fact, it is much easier to work on those structures from 1880 to 1940 than those constructed after World War II. The decades of the 1950s and 1960s for the most part produced candidates for the wrecking ball because the design, materials, and construction were not selected for longevity. They are almost impossible to repair inexpensively, too.

Properties before 1940 had the three requisites for real estate: location, location, and location. Moreover, they offered the human qualities of windows that open (energy-conserving), high ceilings (better protection from smoke produced by fire), and decorative features pleasing to humans. The structures were built to last and *can be retrofit as many times as necessary*.

The high-tech approach has lately been decided "old hat." Traditional values are returning, and the ads in the sophisti-

cated *New York Times* now tout "prewar" buildings as the prestige purchase (Fig. 2).

NEW IDEAS

We, in the United States, should not be provincial. Other parts of the world may be using some new ideas that could be adopted here to great advantage. Previously used methods should not be ignored, either. Medieval stone churches were retrofitted in Victorian times with heating beneath the stone floors. They knew that it is senseless to heat the soaring vaults of cathedrals when the congregation was shivering at floor level.

CONCLUSION

There *can* be a bridge between construction and retaining architectural integrity for a cost-effective result. Moreover, the participants get greater satisfaction out of this type of job. This means that there is more productivity than on new work. This, of course, leads to better results for the client, and greater profits for the building team. If you follow what the original designer did, it will make your job easier. Keep it simple. *If it ain't broke, don't fix it!*

CHAPTER ONE
IN THE BEGINNING

DEALING WITH THE PRESERVATION COMMUNITY

A recent high-rise addition to an historic building suffered every plague but locusts. Preservationists were sure that this was a curse brought on by the "façadectomy" done on the Egyptian Revival structure, resulting in blank, staring, mullionless windows in front of the large new property (Fig. 3). Instead of keeping the entire building, only the front was retained, and the balance demolished. The original four-story building's façade had been dismantled with the pieces numbered like a giant jigsaw puzzle, and reerected in front of the new construction like a stage set. When the whole neighborhood objects to what is being done to "their" building, perhaps someone ought to listen.

Widespread opposition from even outside the area in question sometimes appears when the magnitude of the action affects many people. Since 1976, an affluent church faction has used up almost $12,000,000 in legal fees trying to demolish a portion of its holdings to build a secular and moneymaking high-rise. The fact is, they cannot enjoy nonprofit and non-taxable status while making money in competition with for-profit competitors. This is having it both ways, and has been most unpopular. Consequently, their plea of "economic hardship" has fallen on deaf ears. Certainly the legal fees, which they can afford, could have fed a lot of disadvantaged people.

Once the client has gained the approval of the community, the project will have a much smoother course.

Since 1981 and the introduction of the 25 percent investment tax credit, when restoration became the moneymaker for the "gut-and-sandblast set," bare bricks and wood, with scooped-out atria, have confused generations about what places erected 100 years ago really looked like. Considering

Figure 3. A "façadectomy," leaving only the original front.

that proper Victorians wouldn't even tolerate bare table legs, it is perverse to think that they would have had naked walls and woodwork.

Round air-conditioning ducts hanging like hemorrhoids from an ornamental ceiling are becoming less acceptable. Conduits running over ornamental surfaces like drunken snakes, and illogically placed sprinkler heads and smoke detectors, do not put their installers in the best light (Fig. 4).

There is a better way to handle M/E systems. Sometimes, it costs absolutely nothing to conceal them. Robert A. Lindsay, publisher of *Consulting/Specifying Engineer Magazine*, stated in the August 1990 issue, "It's often said the sign of a good mechanical-electrical system is that it's not noticed by the building occupants."

Writes Vincent Scully, professor of art history at Yale University, in the November 1990 *House and Garden Magazine*, "Architects who were less numerous than they are today, spent more time taking care of good old buildings than they did building bad new ones. This was true of most architects from antiquity into the nineteenth century. Preservation stood at the very heart of the profession, not on its periphery. . . . The premise of the modern movement, that everything has to be invented, is false."

In building conservation, as in everything else, there is nothing new under the sun. Somebody has always thought of a simpler solution before. Therefore, the more historic information you collect, the more workable tricks you will accumulate.

Figure 4a(1). Unacceptable installation: Conduits or wires on ornamental surfaces.

Figure 4b. Unacceptable installation: Poorly placed sprinkler heads.

Figure 4a(2). Unacceptable installation: Conduits or wires on ornamental surfaces.

Figure 4c. Unacceptable installation: Unsuitable smoke detectors—color and size wrong.

Figure 5a. A serious fault that must be corrected before work starts.

Figure 5b. Shoring up weak members.

Everyone knows about Egyptian and Sumerian engineering, Greek architectural design, and Roman running water and heating systems. The American Indians knew how to build high-rise structures over 1000 years ago. In the sixteenth century, Queen Elizabeth's godson designed a flush toilet for the monarch. Seventeenth-century India had the beginnings of air-conditioning. The ventilation ducts in the 1887 Carnegie Hall, New York, were more than adequate for use in the recent $70,000,000 restoration.

Really, there was nothing more energy-efficient than elegant nineteenth-century structures. They made superb use of the climate and location. Not recognizing the immutable rules of Mother Nature leads to building glass hotels in a known *tornado* area, which is not a good idea. It is also useless to install three sets of uninterruptible-power-supply (UPS) systems in a basement *below the level of an adjacent river,* which has a habit of overflowing. Energy-wasteful is an all-glass building in a hot climate which constantly needs massive air-conditioning.

Here are a few truisms that might be of use:[1]

1. There are few panaceas in building. Nothing lasts forever, especially if laced with cement.

2. The easy answer is often neither the right one nor the cheapest one.

3. It is never too late.

4. Who dares, wins.

5. A quality job will be economical and save time and hassle in the long run.

6. There are no hard-and-fast rules. A situation must be judged on its merits.

7. Like to like works best.

In building conservation, expensive mistakes can be avoided by an initial inspection which considers the building in its setting as a whole. At this point a correct diagnosis must be made.

Often, the first walk-through includes entry into dark voids above ceilings, in elevator shafts, or in other spaces. With a portable light, it may be possible to discover a ceiling or wall light. Follow the wiring or conduit from that light to a switch. If it works, and the area is now illuminated, you will be able to get the search done easier than by holding a lantern and groping.[2]

However, before anything else, so as not to wreck the structure or its contents, there should be an emphasis on *special housekeeping details* for historic buildings even during the first walk-through.

Moving furniture

Move office machines such as computers and typewriters on stands, *holding onto the equipment as well as the furniture.*

[1] Quoted from remarks by architect Peter Carey in *SPAB News* (Vol. 10, No. 3, 1989) on the revival of Lloyds Bank, Cirencester.

[2] Another practical suggestion from Michael Farinola, Otis Elevator.

Figure 6. Example of vernacular design, typical of a certain area.

Use at least two people.

Never drag a piece—it strains the carcass and marks the floor.

Carry fragile items such as glass and marble *vertically.*

Moving decorative pieces

Use two people, one for the front and one for the back, to move around corners, doorknobs, etc.

Plan the route from *A* to *B* to discover hazards *before moving.*

Carry a painting vertically by its shortest sides.

Take hold only by the frame, not the stretchers.

Do not lay statues, carvings, ornamental glass, wood, or metal on the floor where they will get dirty.

Failure to follow these procedures could result in irreversible damage even before the project is started. Therefore, these procedures must be communicated, understood, and used by *everyone* on the project *at all times,* because the structure is historic (i.e., at least 50 years old). Once this special watchfulness is instilled in the *team* (which is composed of everyone from owner to first-year apprentice), the actual operation can start.

Reduced to terms of lowest common denominator, we are looking for

1. Existing *interstitial* (between walls, floors, and ceilings) *space* available for the insertion of the modern systems, or repair of existing ones.

2. Lacking these, other methods of how to get the power,

water, air, steam, gas, or heat from the *source* to these *systems* so that the intrusions are concealed as much as possible.

Along the road to this destination, techniques will be discussed that apply not only to work on historic buildings but also for constructing new ones. It was found during research that vertical architectural sections were scarce as hens' teeth; they had been discarded as only working drawings, and for the most part, only façades and floor plans had been kept. However, they disclosed the spaces originally included in the buildings. Throughout this book, copies of such sections which were found will be shown, along with the descriptions of work done, as reported by the *Engineering Record* and its predecessors, and *The Builder,* an English publication of the same type.

It may be necessary to do some exploratory demolition to discover what is behind years of additions and changes. This should be done conservatively by a careful worker, under the architect's supervision, and preferably in a spot that can be easily and inexpensively refilled or covered.

Even after careful planning for new systems, there may be another pitfall awaiting. Too many landmarks, here and abroad, have been burned down accidentally by the very workers who were engaged to fix them. The contract documents must include stringent fire, housekeeping, and safety rules to protect life and property. Both the exterior and the interior must be adequately secured while under rehabilitation.

Every design professional should be familiar with procedures to follow after fire damage. Here is an opportunity, while walls and floors are open and exposed, to conceal the source of electric power, water, steam, gas, and air so that the site, when finished, looks as it did when first built. It may be 50 years old, but up to date. The test for a good job in conservation of a pre-1940 property is for the completed job to look as if the original designer just walked away from the opening ceremonies.

Because the concern here is historic buildings, the installation must be inconspicuous, to keep the original style which the owner purposely bought, or inherited. The choice of the project designer is, therefore, a serious one. There is a growing demand for singling out those professionals who have the specific education and/or practical experience in this specialized field. Identifying those who take continuing professional

Figure 7. Careless choice of 1950s modern fixture for Victorian interior.

Figure 8. Sullivan's dictum that form follows function: The office building has a base (entrance), middle (for offices), and top (for decoration and identity).

education in the subject is the simplest way to ensure competency.

Unless there has been a previous relationship, the client should review the latest three jobs completed. The level of various skills included in each design professional's office should be determined to ensure comprehensive coverage. It does not hurt to inquire whether the same staff will be put on the current project, if good results had been obtained from former customers. The existence of a stronger marketing department than design does not always guarantee the best job at the lowest price. In fact, occasionally it indicates a rocky road ahead with a difficult personality.

Perhaps one of the most significant statements made about the whole process of building conservation was uttered by Donald Insall, FRIBA (Fellow, Royal Institute of British Architects), the architect who restored the Houses of Parliament in London. At the 1988 Interiors Conference in Philadelphia, he opened his remarks by saying: "I am not the architect, but merely the leader of the TEAM."

UNIVERSAL PROCEDURES

Once the decision is made to do something to a building, several universal procedures should always be followed for best results.

1. Check for structural soundness (Fig. 5) It won't

matter what type of equipment is chosen, or what shade the floors are, if the building is liable to collapse on top of the construction team while working! Before anything is done, a structural engineer should check the soundness of the property to be sure that the members are not rotted, failing, or missing. Life safety is at stake for everyone on the premises. There have been cases where restoration was begun without this critical inspection, and the building suddenly fell on the workers.

The most obvious symptoms are slanting floors, questionable roofs, weak foundations, and supports to overhanging members. These all have to be declared safe before going further. Corrections may have to be done more wisely and less expensively after design studies are complete, when the entire condition is known.

2. Stabilize the building This means closing all openings where unwanted water can enter through roof, windows, walls, or foundations. The purpose is to stop continuing deterioration while under construction. *It is a toss-up as to which is more destructive—fire or water.*

Once these two factors are addressed, further steps are as follows:

3. Determining the type of building conservation Historic buildings are worked on to different levels of authenticity. Factors governing the level or quality of the job are the *time schedule* and the *building owner's budget*. The current condition of the property, the desires of the client, the expected profit or cost, tax advantages, financing, as well as the need for the new project, influence the design and scope of the work. While the owner and design professionals determine which level of restoration is to be achieved, the contractors should be familiar with the quality expected at each level.

a. Museum quality. Museum quality restoration is the most correct, and hence, most expensive type of conservation. The product is a close approximation of the building as it originally appeared when new.

In such cases, modern M/E systems must be concealed. An expert installation will look *as if nothing has been done.* It was said that on the work at Calke Abbey in Derbyshire, England even the cobwebs were retained!

b. Continued use of a purpose-built structure. A building erected to house a radio station, bank, school, hospital, or

Figure 9. A Georgian (colonial) building.

Figure 10. Classical Revival style.

hotel is purpose-built for that exclusive use. If the intention is to use it again for that purpose, the job may entail only updating M/E services and some cosmetics.

Because of constant code changes, some systems may have to be upgraded. The space for this equipment is already there, but extreme care must be given to removal and reinstallation (retrofitting). The original building fabrics cannot be ordered from the local supplier (they may now be unavailable from the source because the quarry for marble or the forest which produced the wood may be exhausted), or they may be too expensive to replicate, especially if they are ornamental. Here is where awareness training of the workforce can save money, lawsuits, and aggravation.

c. Adaptive use. When a structure is no longer used for its original purpose, but is sound and the location is profitable, alternative uses may be found. Adapting buildings for new uses is as old as time. Ancient Roman structures have been resurrected in many incarnations, from mausoleum to fortress, papal residence, prison, and museum. The Baths of Diocletian were recycled by Michelangelo into a church out of the main hall, and the rest is now a museum, cinema, and planetarium. Today, schools and factories may be converted to apartments. The M/E installations for these buildings can be extensive, and, in such cases, the design professionals and contractors must find innovative ways to use existing spaces.

4. Determining the style of the building Certainly this is not a treatise on architectural history. However, the team has to know the characteristics of the style being returned to in order to make the right selections, both inside and outside. Herbert W. Levy, AIA, advisor to the White House in Washington, D.C. on restoration, says that those who enjoy detective stories thrive on ferreting out just what was there in the beginning. Thus, a simple guide is offered here for those not already familiar with older types of structures.

The dates are approximate and meant only to illustrate the progression of design from High Victorian (when fortunes were made with speculative building) to pre–World War II. Fundamental earlier styles which influenced those from 1880 on are also shown, so that a better understanding of the subject is gained. The reader can then play the game of guessing the period simply by looking at every older property in the streetscape.

It is to be noted that in real life, there are very few pure architectural styles, because of the client's pocketbook and preferences. In addition, late-nineteenth-century design was often *eclectic,* mixing features from many sources and ages. Moreover, as buildings are used, subtle changes are made by the inhabitants to suit their uses.

a. Mixed styles resulting from subsequent additions. Often buildings have mixed styles, and the design team must decide which period should be kept and which removed. This is an important point in selecting lighting fixtures, ventilation grates, elevator doors, and other M/E equipment.

Example

George Washington's home in Mount Vernon, Virginia was, obviously, eighteenth-century, but no one would know it without the Victorian porch added in the mid-nineteenth century. The ladies of the 1850s who decided to restore the shrine thought the porch essential and kept it on. However, the interior was kept strictly eighteenth-century, including the latest installation—reproduction of the wall sconces, now in an electrical version.

Visitors are surprised, too, at the new color schemes introduced, which are supposed to be truer replicas of the original, but they are viewed with modern eyes, under today's light levels, and so appear startlingly bright, and almost garish.

b. Eclecticism. The exuberance of the Victorian architect Frank Furness on the 1876 Pennsylvania Academy of the Fine Arts in Philadelphia almost defies category. Oriental, Middle

Figure 11a. An example of early Victorian style: Greek revival.

Figure 11c. An example of early Victorian style: Italianate.

Figure 12b. High Victorian style—Venetian revival.

Figure 11b. An example of early Victorian style: Egyptian revival.

Figure 12a. High Victorian style—Renaissance revival.

Figure 12c. High Victorian style—Italianate (on right). This is a perfect example of a schizophrenic building. It was originally an Italianate brownstone, but the front façade was "colonialized" in the mistaken idea that everything historic was of the eighteenth century.

Figure 12e(1). High Victorian style—Victorian Gothic: Store on left; 1920s addition is to the right.

Figure 12f. High Victorian style—Richardsonian Romanesque.

Figure 12d. High Victorian style—Second Empire, with typical mansard roof.

Figure 12e(2). High Victorian style—Victorian Gothic: Office building with terra cotta façade.

Figure 12g. High Victorian style—early tall building, brownstone, Italianate.

Figure 13a. Early twentieth century—Beaux Arts.

Figure 13b. Early twentieth century—Renaissance revival.

Figure 13c. Early twentieth century—classical revival.

Figure 13d(2). Early twentieth century—period revival: Baroque.

Figure 13d(1). Early twentieth century—period revival: Tudor.

Eastern, medieval, and hybrid details leap out in a profusion that is dizzying. Even such an early candidate as this (built to celebrate the American Centennial) was brought up to twentieth-century requirements on time, on budget, and without loss of its exceptional historic features. It has air-conditioning, security, climate controls, life safety, specialized museum lighting, communications, computers, and new elevators cleverly tucked away in discreet places. Here is a job where the design professionals and contractors really did their homework, and walked away with many prizes to show for it.

c. Vernacular (Fig. 6). In every region and country, there are unique "vernacular" differences from the standard architectural styles, found only in that particular location. They should be retained wherever possible.

d. Anachronisms (Fig. 7). Features of the wrong style and time only advertise the lack of planning taken by the construction team and should be scrupulously avoided.

e. Older building technologies. The use of steel beams and terra cotta building components in the last third of the nineteenth century allowed larger amounts of space to be left between outer walls and inner plaster partitions than with previous methods. These allow insertion of modern systems with the least cost and effort. Early-twentieth-century building technology made use of mass-produced components, building standardization (originally decreed in China in 1103), and prefabrication, making the search for space more predictable.

Figure 13d(3). Early twentieth century—period revival: Fifteenth-century rusticated.

Figure 13d(4). Early twentieth century—period revival: Spanish colonial.

In the United States, everything from roughly the second third of the nineteenth century was called *Victorian.* Actually, Queen Victoria reigned from 1837 to 1901. The varied architecture designed during this period influenced the entire world. Many styles were used, reflecting earlier periods from many countries, but they have been lumped under the same all-encompassing term. The Victorians were past masters at reproducing previous types of buildings and decorative arts so skillfully that only experts could tell the difference. Keeping up with the Joneses was the thing to do, so even the Dowager Empress of China imported an electric chandelier to hang in

Figure 13d(5). Early twentieth century—period revival: Gothic.

Figure 13e(1). Early twentieth century—Edwardian: Arts and Crafts.

Even during the Great Depression of the 1930s, construction was for the most part exceptionally well done, and provided plenty of space for additions within.

Since building technology changes about every 10 years, studying a structure representative of a particular use and age provides a model to know where to look for usable space. The design "grapevine" is amazingly swift, and similar details can be seen across the United States within a very brief time. This makes it that much simpler for the construction team to know the methods of a particular time frame within a 10-year span in any geographic location. Of course, the news traveled faster to larger centers of population, so that older methods were still in use longer in more remote areas.

Figure 13e(2). Early twentieth century—Edwardian: Rusticated.

the Summer Palace when she heard that Victoria had installed one.

As the great fortunes were made in commerce, the properties erected by the newly rich reflected their affluence in increasing proportions until they reached the excesses of *High Victorian style*. At this point, many had had enough of opulence and sought older *classical* (from Greece and Rome) designs, or a return to nature via *Art Nouveau,* or still simpler handmade *Arts and Crafts.*

By 1906, the beginnings of what we now call *Art Deco* (a term derived from the 1925 Exposition des Arts Decoratifs in Paris, but not coined until the 1960s by Bevis Hiller) had already started on the continent. It was intended to make its debut in 1915, but World War I intervened. Everything was put on hold until after the Great War. The entire architectural period from the beginning of the twentieth century to the outbreak of World War II actually had many names, depending on the country, just as the earlier Art Nouveau was alternately called *Jugenstil, Liberty style,* and so on. Prior to 1914, there was a transitional period sometimes called the *secessionist movement* which could be recognized by geometric patterns in bold colors.

The skyscraper as we know it could only develop after the invention of steel cable (used on the Brooklyn Bridge) and the elevator, developed by Otis, in the mid-nineteenth century. When load-bearing masonry walls became too unwieldy because of the unmanageable thickness at the base, the use of steel instead of stone or earlier heavy timber allowed wider windows and lighter, higher construction.

A New York city ordinance in the early twentieth century which decreed light and air for the street and neighboring properties led to the *setback design,* creating a distinctive skyline.

However, the dictum of Mies van der Rohe in the 1920s was misinterpreted to mean the total absence of line or decoration, resulting in the elimination of crafts formerly used, and even worse, the change in architectural and trades education. The design of the new and the self-expression of the creator became the dominant features, instead of giving the student a comprehensive background based on the seminal architectural methods.

Where the great architect Louis Sullivan had preached "Form follows function," meaning that a commercial building had to have a base, a middle, and a finishing top, indicating its internal use, a one-piece monolithic look gradually emerged after World War II (Fig. 8).

Instead of Daniel Burnham's advice to "Make no little plans," insignificant or worse, inscrutable entrances and plain interiors with no extra interstitial space for expansion sprang forward in the 1950s, 1960s, and 1970s. Public interiors became mazes to be negotiated like the labyrinths of the mythological Minotaur.[3] The visitor is forced to use a series of doors, escalators, ramps, and stairs in order to reach the registration (if hotel), or auditorium (if theater) level, and then other elevators to ascend further. Retail stores employ nonconsecutive escalators to force prospective shoppers to wander around seeking the next conveyance up or down, in the hope that on their way, they will buy something. Lately, stairs leading to street level from places of assembly are eliminated altogether, requiring the bewildered occupant to squeeze on to narrow escalators or tiny elevators which present a serious problem in case of panic caused by emergency. Sometimes, fire stairs are locked for "security" reasons. What ever happened to a straightforward entrance with clear signage indicating the way out?

Somehow, too, the craftsmanship of everyone from architect to mechanic got lost in the shuffle. After 1945, construction was no longer intended to build for the ages, but to get it over with rapidly, cheaply, and for a limited lifetime. It was forgotten that many in the industry throughout the world made a great deal of money in speculative building in the past. At that time, those with expertise were relatively well paid, so that both entrepreneur and worker benefitted from the enterprise. So did the public, in gaining many handsome structures which became part of their cultural as well as economic legacy.

Not only was the beauty of design lost, but the materials were changed from natural ones, like stone and wood, to substitutes, frequently in prefabricated sections. Building became playing with a giant erector set, merely attaching parts instead of creating from scratch.

Architecture is by nature derivative, being based on antecedents from many cultures and periods. Even in the Ancient World, surprisingly, styles found their way across the miles. Witness the pyramids in both Mexico and Egypt, or the similarities within the entire Roman Empire, spread over most of the then known world.

Architecture before 1940 was to give a feeling of "place"

[3] A bull-headed man kept in a Cretan labyrinth and fed with human flesh.

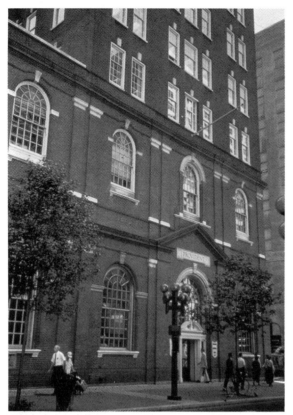

Figure 14a. Later twentieth century (up to World War II)—Georgian revival. It is interesting to note that last year, an addition was erected which was an exact copy of the style. *Plus ça change, plus la même chose.* ("The more things change, the more they stay the same.")

Figure 14b(1). Later twentieth century (up to World War II)—Art Deco: Setback (ziggurat style).

Figure 14b(2). Later twentieth century (up to World War II)—Art Deco: Façade containing symbols of the building's use (radio station).

Figure 14b(3). Later twentieth century (up to World War II)—Art Deco: Vertical style.

Figure 14c. Later twentieth century (up to World War II)—international style.

Figure 14d. Later twentieth century (up to World War II)—"Fascist" style. Note the flattened sculpture.

and also was expected to be elegant, just as ladies always wore hats and gloves whenever they left their residence.

Treading carefully through this aesthetic forest, the following are some simple ways to identify the basic period and the typical materials used (essentially residential styles will not be illustrated, in order to avoid confusion).

Georgian (1700–1775; Fig. 9) Americans call this period *colonial*. This style originated in Italy, and was brought to England in the seventeenth century and to America in the eighteenth century.

Materials: Brick, clapboard, fieldstone

Roofline: Hipped, pitched, or gambrel

Symmetrical

Decoration: Pedimented doorway, string courses

Classical revival (1780–1830; Fig. 10) It was thought that by reviving the architecture of the Greek democracy, it would reflect the attributes of being substantial and honest. That is why so many banks adopted the pillars outside their establishment as a visual sign of their trustworthiness to the then illiterate masses.

Materials: Brick laid in Flemish bond, plastered and painted surfaces, smoothly dressed marble, granite, or sandstone in lower courses

Roofline: Dome, cupola, hipped, pitched

Symmetrical

Decoration: Neoclassical style (from Rome); columned portico, federal fan-shaped light over door; Palladian motifs disappeared after 1820

Early Victorian (1820–1860; Fig. 11)

Materials: Ashlar masonry (granite, limestone, marble), brick, wood used to imitate stone; cast iron usage increased toward end of period

Roofline: Varied—towers and domes rather than shaped roofs

Symmetrical: Greek revival (from sixth century B.C.); Egyptian revival, with the graduated pillars and symbolism carved in stone

Asymmetrical: Gothic revival, from 1840; Italianate—round arch openings, richly profiled cornices, heavy masonry piers, massive vaulting, square towers

Decoration: Greek revival (from sixth century B.C.)—pillars, monumental porticos; Italianate—proportions taller and richer ornamentation

High Victorian (1860–1890; Fig. 12)

Materials: Different colors of brick and stone elaborately laid; cast-iron, including cresting (1870s); masonry replacing structural timber; decorative terra cotta; brownstone and granite; beginnings of M/E systems (steam heat, ventilating flues, etc.)

Roofline: Depending on style

Decoration:

1. From 1855
   a. Italianate
      (1) Large expanse of plate-glass windows.
      (2) Roofline flat with projecting cornice.
2. From 1870s
   a. Second Empire (originally French, seventeenth century); mansard roof.
   b. Queen Anne (English); picturesque roofline often with asymmetric round towers—mostly residential.
   c. Victorian Gothic (from fourteenth century); pointed arch windows with multicolored masonry.

3. From 1880s
   a. Richardsonian Romanesque
      (1) Monumental and massive with rounded windows, towers, turrets, and dormers (derived from eleventh to thirteenth centuries). Product of first professional training in architecture.
      (2) Totally asymmetric.
   b. Renaissance revival (from fourteenth to sixteenth centuries); rusticated masonry, richly detailed mouldings, heavy brackets, pedimented window caps.
   c. Venetian revival; even more colorful than Italianate, employing polychromy and Gothic elements.
4. After 1880
   a. Tall building; often base, shaft, and crown, depicting interior usages
   b. Art Nouveau; plantlike scrolls (1880–1905)—mostly residential and rare in North America.

Early twentieth century (1895–1920; Fig. 13)

Materials: Light marble, limestone, vitreous-glazed brick; bronze, brass, steel

Roofline: Top of the building making a statement with a crown of colonnade, cornice, or cupola

Decoration: Theatrical

1. Beaux-Arts classicism, in the baroque (seventeenth-century) tradition: festoons, cartouches, columns, wreaths, and figure sculpture
2. Renaissance revival (fifteenth century)
3. Classical revival—elaborate and grand (500 B.C. to A.D. 100)

4. Period revivals (1900–1940)
   a. Gothic (twelfth century)
   b. Tudor (fourteenth century)—half-timbered
   c. Renaissance rusticated (fifteenth century)
   d. Spanish colonial (sixteenth century)—tiled roof, wrought iron
   e. Baroque (seventeenth century)
   f. Mission: heavy oak "Arts and Crafts"; mostly residential
5. Edwardian (1901–1910): less florid than Victorian; beautiful craftsmanship; asymmetric
   a. Arts and Crafts
   b. Rusticated

Later twentieth century (1920–1940; Fig. 14)

1. Georgian revival.
2. Art Deco (1900–1933)—sometimes called Jazz Age.
   a. "Ziggurat"[4] setback skyscrapers (1911–1930).
   b. Decorated to illustrate building usage.
   c. Vertical style
   d. Decoration: formica, bakelite, colored glass and polished marble, neon tubes, decorative grilles; Mayan, Egyptian, geometric zigzags, symbolic of the client's business or governmental aspirations.
3. Moderne (after 1930)—Depression.
4. International style (1930–1940).
5. "Fascist" modern style, with flattened sculpture. Streamlined with spare surface ornament; horizontal lines, as opposed to earlier verticality.

---

[4] The name of the setback temples in ancient Mesopotamia circa 2500 B.C.

CHAPTER TWO
FIRST STEPS

HISTORIC RESEARCH

Many are of the opinion that the "fast track" or "design-as-you-go" method of construction is a contradiction in terms when dealing with older buildings. This is because of the need for *thorough planning*—to search for existing space, noting the many additions and changes made throughout the years, and determining the nature of the materials and the older methods originally used.

Advance research is much more efficient and eliminates many costly surprises. Systems installed as an afterthought will cost proportionately more, cause more anguish, and waste more time than if included in the original concept.

Information on how the building looked when new can be obtained from sources such as old photographs, sketches, surviving construction documents, wills, and insurance policies. Other sources of information for historic research are newspaper articles, historical society records, and early trade or professional publications such as *Inland Architect, The Builder,* or *Engineering News Record.*

Much information can be obtained at a local city hall or library. Even the advertisements can be clues to equipment or installation. In addition, retired workers with a good memory can offer a wealth of knowledge of previous jobs.

Neighborhood associations always have historic material. Aid can be obtained from the National Park Service, the State Historic Preservation Office, the Historic American Building Survey (HABS/HAER), specialized groups such as the Athenaeum of Philadelphia (a repository of Victorian architectural drawings), architectural storehouses such as the Boston Public Library and the Chicago Historical Society, museums such as the Art Institute of Chicago, educational institutions such as Columbia University's Avery Library, engineering associations, technical nonprofit educational organizations such as *Building Conservation International,* and labor union apprentice school files.

At first, the architect and engineers must do their research. Even in an architect's office, it is not possible to be totally acquainted with the entire panoply of crafts and historic data needed. It has been found that the cost of employing or consulting an architectural historian, trained to ferret out information, is far less than having mechanics floundering in the field. As soon as the contract is let, everyone else involved in a conservation project finds the need to do some historic research on their specialty, to a greater or lesser extent, depending on involvement.

Example

Even a year of research using a few key people is much less expensive than the cost of paying a whole construction crew of workers to stand around on the job site, unguided and unproductive. A large European government building, erected in the seventeenth century, needed major repairs. Modern mechanical/electrical (M/E) systems had to be retrofitted and, in addition, the elaborate but failing hardwood floors had to be reinforced. There were ornamental plaster ceilings and heavily carved marble mantlepieces to consider as well.

Close to 12 months of preconstruction planning was done by the architect and his staff. However, the entire time spent by workers on the job was only *3 weeks!* The work included slipping new steel beams between the floors. The savings in labor costs for this brief time were considerable. There was no need for "extras" because everything was anticipated.

PROPERTIES OF BUILDING MATERIALS

It is very useful to know about the properties of historic building materials (the *fabric*), because sometimes substitutions for

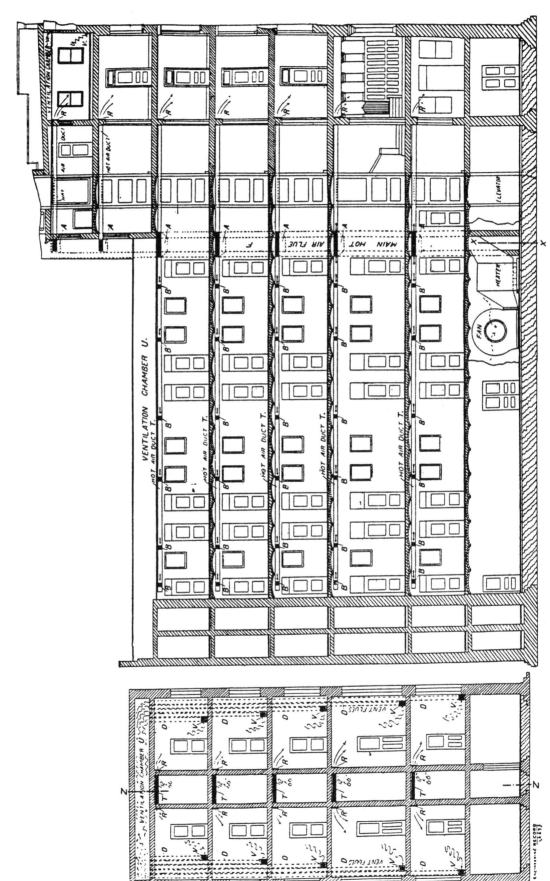

Figure 15a. Voids in the Walbridge Office Building, Toledo, Ohio, 1893.

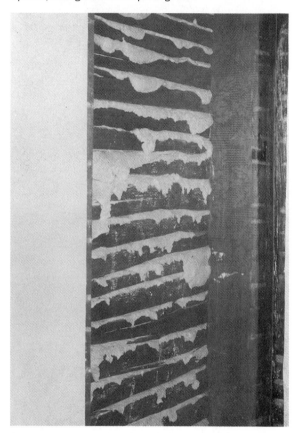

Figure 15b. An architect gaining entrance to search for space.

THOROUGHLY EXPLORING THE SITE FOR SPACE (Fig. 15)

Knowing how earlier buildings were put together will help find those existing interstitial spaces between walls, floors, and ceilings within which the modern systems can be concealed cost-effectively. Familiarity with old-style tools also explains how the work was originally accomplished.

Learning to interpret what your eyes *see*, combined with a little knowledge of how earlier construction was done, will save you endless hours and lots of money in preparing the contract documents, whether you are architect, engineer, contractor, consultant, or interior designer (Fig. 16).

The best way to start is at the bottom and follow the building upward, noting how it was put together.

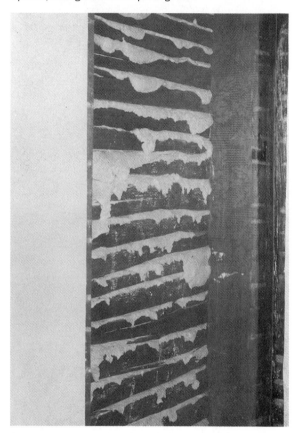

cost-saving or apparent work-saving may result in added expense and time, instead of what was expected.

Real plaster does not support combustion, has better sound properties, and is easier to patch than is drywall. Combinations of copper and aluminum may cause electrical short circuits. Plastic on fixtures can melt, whereas glass does not, except under extreme temperatures. A stone containing fossils is very difficult to cut, if holes have to be made for M/E devices.

Example

The owner of a famous concert hall wanted to save time and money by using fiber-glass ceiling ornamentation instead of plaster. After the first recital, the sound proved so dreadful that the space had to be closed and the entire decoration redone to rectify the acoustics. The client ended up paying twice—once to do it wrong, and a second time to remedy the situation.

Substitutions of modern architectural materials for antique ones should not be made before the new material has been tested for at least 10 years without failing. Otherwise, the contractor and design professions could risk their reputation and financial status. The law courts are filled with such suits. This conservative approach may not please manufacturers, but it will preserve the team's credibility.

Figure 15c. Space behind the wall of an 1837 house.

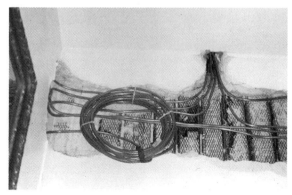

Figure 15d. Space in ceiling of a 1902 government building.

Figure 15e. Space in floor and wall for wiring in 1922 site.

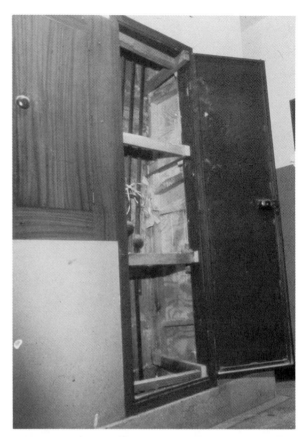

Figure 15f. Plenty of space in this 1924 wiring closet.

Figure 15g(1). During the search for space, the original lighting fixtures were discovered in a corner.

Figure 15g(2). The lighting fixtures of Fig. 15g(1), cleaned, rewired, and rehung.

Figure 16. Training the eye to see what is there: Is it a Greek temple, or trash cans with corrugated roof?

REUSING EXISTING SPACE

If, after an exhaustive search, you cannot find interstitial space, then use other spaces whose use has now changed. In physics class, this was called using "Finagler's constant"—you'd get the answer and work backward. Determine how much space you have available and design the system to fit.

Example (Fig. 17)

The always-occupied 1930 Merchandise Mart is situated on the edge of the Chicago River. There was no space for expansion. In order to improve delivery of air-conditioning to this 5,000,000-ft^2 building, the ingenious engineer took the now-unused coal bins. He placed a 200-yd-long pool for chilled water in the spot. The return-air registers were built into the wide corridors and when painted out, became almost invisible. Within only a few years, the entire project will be paid back, with continued energy savings and a 72°F temperature maintained in the hot Chicago summer. Just one operator is needed to monitor the entire system, and enlightened management is delighted.

Another example of creative use of space was in a vacant wine cellar in Kedleston Hall (Derbyshire, U.K.), a huge eighteenth-century mansion, now a museum. This was converted to the equipment room for heating, ventilation, and air-conditioning (HVAC) by Donald Insall (Fig. 18).

CREATING NEW SYMPATHETIC SPACE (Fig. 19)

In the absence of any existing space, innovative new ways to handle the M/E equipment must be invented. Extending the vertical wall to contain HVAC can be done, if it is camouflaged carefully. Creating voids between floors is another ploy.

DETERMINING THE SCOPE OF THE WORK

A very careful survey of every nook and corner has to be made to discover the many M/E installations and repairs performed over the years that were not likely part of an overall plan. The client should personally make the initial walk-through to become reacquainted with the building as it actually is, and then do it again with the design professionals consulted. Only after such a detailed analysis can the client decide what is to be done.

Like people, buildings start to deteriorate the day they are born. How long that aging process takes depends on

Design

Construction skill, techniques, and materials

Scheduled maintenance

The client will decide how lasting a monument is desired. The scope of the work should

Correct existing conditions

Make new installations

Provide for future needs

During this planning

Adjacent services can be coordinated

Zones of control can be established for economy and convenience

In addition, design professionals and contractors can render a great service to clients contemplating renewal by suggesting to check the HVAC *up front* to see if it has expired from old age or inefficiency. Here is a chance to advise that tending to the M/E system in a logical order, *before* decorating, would save a great deal of money and aggravation later.

Even if the job is to be done in phases as funds become available, a *master plan* must be in hand *before hitting the first nail.*

Since electric power comes first, it is important to consider the following.

1. *Corrections to existing electrical systems.* Even if the job consists of adding *one* outlet, the entire electrical system of an older building should be checked to detect hidden problems or insufficient capacity.

   a. To paraphrase Benjamin Franklin's saying that fish and guests spoil after 3 days, *electric wiring is a potential hazard after 30 years and is in need of evaluation.* In-

Figure 17a. The Merchandise Mart, Chicago—new chilled-water system: The entire 5,000,000-ft² building.

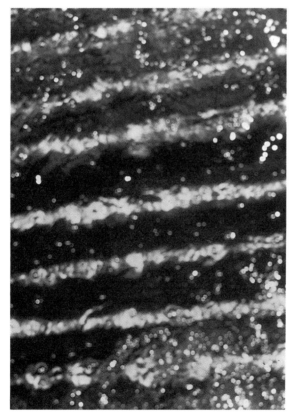

Figure 17c. The Merchandise Mart, Chicago—new chilled-water system: The chilled-water pool.

Figure 17b. The Merchandise Mart, Chicago—new chilled-water system: The new equipment in the old coal bins.

Figure 17d. The Merchandise Mart, Chicago—new chilled-water system: The return-air ducts built into corridors.

Figure 18a. Kedleston Hall, Derbyshire, England—use of former wine cellar for new M/E equipment: Exterior of building.

Figure 18b. Kedleston Hall, Derbyshire, England—use of former wine cellar for new M/E equipment: New equipment.

sulation may crack, dissimilar metals between connections and wire may "creep" and loosen, wire may break, or grounding may be faulty. There may be bad splices, or the load may be oversized for the wire used. An experienced electrical contractor should participate in this activity.

b. Is the electrical service capacity adequate to carry new loads, including HVAC and other additional systems?

c. Check this list of common sloppy additions or changes which should be corrected in the electrical system before doing anything else. (Figure 20 shows a selection of buildings on the National Register of Historic Places with thoughtless installations.)

(1) Is there conduit nailed over original fabric such as marble, ornamental plaster, or wood? Has it become such a familiar sight that these additions are now invisible to the tenant's eye (Fig. 20a)?

(2) Are there ancient fused panels that are constantly blowing?

(3) Are there loose wires running *under* the rugs?

(4) Are there totally inappropriate lighting fixtures, such as industrial fluorescents hanging from an ornamental plaster ceiling, or modern wall sconces in a Victorian setting (Fig. 20b and c)?

(5) Is there a proliferation of surface-mounted receptacles (Fig. 20d)?

(6) Is there a tangle of octopus outlets?

(7) Is there potentially dangerous aluminum wiring?

(8) Is the electrical system protected against dampness from leaky roof or pipes, wall penetration,

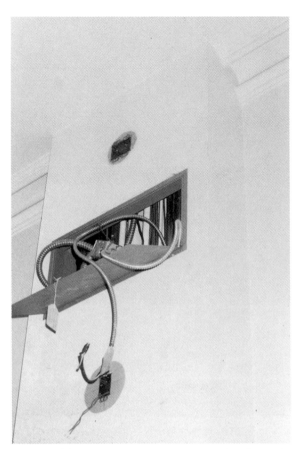

Figure 19a(1). Extending wall to contain power cables: Separately painted access panel.

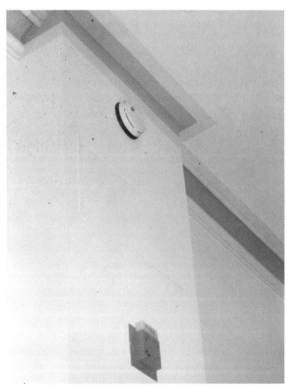

Figure 19a(2). Extending wall to contain power cables: Completed section with trompe l'oeil painting to make the newly created space look as though it belongs.

rising damp, and chemical, electrolytic, or rodent erosion?

(9) Is the lighting adequate for the task?

(10) Can the telephone and computer wiring be coordinated to neaten the "spaghetti" and expand service?

(11) Are there structural members such as I beams, and joists which have been reduced to Swiss cheese by holes drilled into them for wiring?

(12) Does the power panel with branch wiring look like a disaster waiting to happen [(Fig. 20g(1) and (2)]?

It is expected that at this point, the reader will have a knowing smile, recalling many of these conditions are in the surroundings at this very moment.

2. *Corrections to existing mechanical systems.*

a. Inspect the existing HVAC. Are the ducts creating drafts where they are now positioned? Would moving them improve airflow? Do half the occupants complain of cold while the other half are roasting?

b. Is the boiler or other heating equipment in adequate condition to last until the next major work is performed? If changes are needed, they should be incorporated into the original plans and not added as an afterthought, which might compromise the historic features to be retained. Sometimes, because of constricted original design, it might be necessary to break the pavement to extract old equipment in the basement. Less disruption will occur if this happens while construction is under way.

Figure 19b. New pillars to contain air-conditioning and lighting.

c. Are there too many window air-conditioning units that could be consolidated into a central system for cost and energy savings as well as aesthetic reasons (Fig. 20e)?

d. Can improvements be made to mechanical systems for better performance and energy saving?

There are many sources of information to check efficiencies in boilers, air-conditioning, fans, heat exchangers, filters, sound-

Figure 20a(1). Things which should be corrected in electrical system—conduit or cable over original fabric (interior): Over white tile in an historic kitchen.

Figure 20a(2). Things which should be corrected in electrical system—conduit or cable over original fabric (interior): Conduit exposed when the other side of the column was hollow.

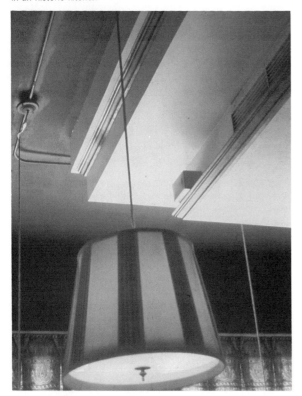

Figure 20a(3). Things which should be corrected in electrical system—conduit or cable over original fabric (interior): While the air-conditioning space in a recycled factory was well done, the conduit for lighting was not.

Figure 20a(4). Things which should be corrected in electrical system—conduit or cable over original fabric (interior): Wiring nailed to *travertine marble* walls!

Figure 20a(5). Things which should be corrected in electrical system—conduit or cable over original fabric (interior): Cables dangling over proscenium arch.

Figure 20a(7). Things which should be corrected in electrical system—conduit or cable over original fabric (exterior): After spending a lot of money for a new polychrome slate roof, this wiring was left as is.

Figure 20a(6). Things which should be corrected in electrical system—conduit or cable over original fabric (interior): Cables and emergency light do not enhance the pressed tin ceiling.

Figure 20a(8). Things which should be corrected in electrical system—conduit or cable over original fabric (exterior): The alarm certainly does not suit the terra cotta and metalwork.

Figure 20b. Things which should be corrected in electrical system—fluorescent fixture under ornate ceiling.

Figure 20c. Things which should be corrected in electrical system—a modern wall sconce in a Victorian room.

Figure 20d(1). Things which should be corrected in electrical system—receptacles and switches: Sloppy installation in an historic hotel.

Figure 20d(2). Things which should be corrected in electrical system—receptacles and switches: Poor choice of color and thoughtless workmanship.

Figure 20d(3). Things which should be corrected in electrical system—receptacles and switches: Contrast this unobtrusive placement with that of Fig. 20d(2).

Figure 20d(4). Things which should be corrected in electrical system—receptacles and switches: Why go to the trouble of cutting out the marble, when this switch and plate could simply have been installed above the wainscot?

Figure 20d(5). Things which should be corrected in electrical system—receptacles and switches: The culprit obviously *knew* this was wrong, because this ceiling plug was gilded to hide the shortcut.

Figure 20e. Things which should be corrected in electrical system—an "infestation" of window air-conditioners.

Figure 20f. Things which should be corrected in electrical system—boiler-room-looking ceiling ducts.

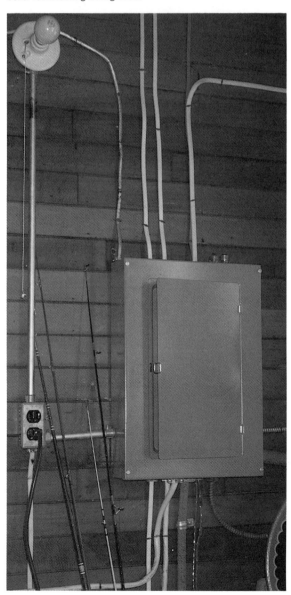

Figure 20g(1). Things which should be corrected in electrical system—a panel that needs help: Residential.

Figure 20g(2). Things which should be corrected in electrical system—a panel that needs help: Commercial.

proofing, controls, and similar, all of which are the same as in new construction.

    e. Is the exterior facade disintegrating because of condensation, or is water attacking structural elements?
    f. Are the building contents mysteriously self-destructing, indicating temperature or humidity problems?
    g. Have water leaks developed in ceilings and walls, undermining decoration?
    h. Are there too few bathrooms?
    i. Are there "boiler room–looking" ceiling ducts (Fig. 20f)?
3. *New electrical installations.* While you are at it, here are some items which are often overlooked:
    a. Extra doorbells.
    b. Extra security release buttons.
    c. Closed-circuit television surveillance.
    d. Provisions for additional computer terminals and telephone jacks.
    e. Grounded receptacles.
    f. Dedicated lines and surge protection.
    g. Floodlighting the exterior façade.

One of the best ways to enhance a city is to floodlight its important buildings. This increases tourism as well as the occupants' quality of life. It is also one of the best security solutions to deter crime (Fig. 21). Although lighting is by nature

highly visible, it does not consume the great amounts of energy imagined. Here is a large market just waiting to be tapped.

Example

A city that had fallen on hard times worked a partnership with the local utility and a large lamp manufacturer to offer reduced rates for all who participated in floodlighting major structures. Twenty-five properties were selected, and this action literally rejuvenated overnight a city center that had all but expired.

    h. If operations would be completely interrupted by a service outage, consider *emergency generators* or at least *uninterruptable-power-supply* (UPS) systems which shut down equipment in an orderly fashion. Their cost is small compared to the large losses for closing down a store, office, theater, or museum.

Example

In Great Britain during the coal strikes of the early 1970s, *every* establishment needing electricity kept going by very inventive means of producing power, from donkeys on a treadmills to generators air-lifted from foreign countries. On the contrary, during a similar earlier situation, New York City was brought to a standstill during a power outage.

Unfortunately, Manhattan did not learn a lesson, and in the summer of 1990, a break in service in the financial district virtually closed down Wall Street. Things did not get back to normal for almost 2 weeks. Much sophisticated equipment failed and could not be reinstated easily.

Example

A country club which made most of its revenue in the summer was struck by lightning not once, but three times during that period. Every wedding, graduation, and other event had to be transferred to another facility. They still would not spend the money for an emergency generator, so had to raise the member assessment because of the losses. That board was soon replaced.

The UPS system is delicate and heavy at the same time. It is said the installer needs industrial-strength kid gloves! *Proper grounding* at the originating power source is critical to avoid incompatibility of components, which include step-down transformers and standby generators, as well as the UPS units and other elements.

Figure 21. Example of European floodlighting of landmarks.

i. Investigate the building's lightning protection.

j. Upgrade life-safety systems.

k. Upgrade security systems.

4. *New mechanical systems.* The desire for additional plumbing facilities in older buildings is widespread. This installation presents a challenge to the team, and perhaps is one of the most demanding, if architectural integrity is to be preserved. If tiling is involved, sometimes it is easier to work from behind, in an adjoining room where only the plaster has to be redone.

HVAC inserted for the first time also demands imagination; however, buildings designed in the 1920s and 1930s often had plenty of interstitial space, anticipating more modern equipment.

Example

In 1928, when Schultz and Weaver were engaged to design the new Waldorf Astoria Hotel in New York City, they realized that within a few years, air-conditioning would be widely used. Although it was not originally provided, Schultz, in consulting with the Carrier Company, asked what additional space would be needed, and consequently left between $1\frac{1}{2}$ and $2\frac{1}{2}$ ft of interstitial space.

As an interesting sidelight, this 2000-room deluxe hotel was designed over the weekend, from Friday to 10:00 A.M. Monday morning! So much for long lead time. The contract was signed on the day the stock market crashed in October 1929, starting the Great Depression. This elegant structure filled with rooms of excellent routes of circulation, was completed in a year and 10 months, including a great deal of ornamentation. After 60 years, it remains a leading hostelry.

5. *Provisions for future needs.* It is prudent to *plan ahead.*

For just a little more money, larger-size wiring, piping, or ducts could be provided which would eliminate the need to disturb already-decorated spaces again if additions were needed later. The saving would more than compensate for the initial expenditure and would eliminate the subsequent aggravation and upheaval of an occupied space.

ENGAGING THE DESIGN PROFESSIONALS AND CONSULTANTS

In addition to those with normal construction expertise, there are other types of experts who should be included in the team to be selected.

THE ARCHITECT

The architect is the "general" of the team, or "conductor of the orchestra," and sets the tone of the entire operation. A "scaffold" architect, who gets in the field and talks to the workers, is much more effective on a restoration job than a "walkabout" one, who occasionally appears at the front door and quickly passes through to the back without concern for the details. Those who communicate with the mechanics learn a lot that can save time and money, simply because those skilled workers spend their entire lives in their field, and can often solve sticky problems, using past experience. It should be noted that while discussions with the crew on how to solve

a particular problem are important, *any changes* must flow through the central point of communication, whether the architect's office or that of the general contractor.

THE ENGINEERS

The engineers in various disciplines must work in concert with the architect to supply the M/E system or components without destroying the historic design. Occasionally, their strictly pragmatic plans may have to be tempered to accomplish this goal.

In addition to those with normal construction expertise, there are other types of experts who should be included in the team to be selected:

SPECIALIST IN CODE COMPLIANCE, COORDINATION, AND VARIANCES

This specialist is the member of the team who is familiar with all codes and arranges visits to review boards. Fire and life-safety codes are always being changed. If water sprinklers and the water tanks to supply them must be installed, where should they be located? Is the space compatible with the usage of the building?

Is the existing telephone system installed with nonrated cable? If so, how will this affect the present tenants? And so forth.

FINANCIAL AND TAX EXPERT

This consultant has to thread through the varied government regulations for the investment tax credit (ITC, a federal incentive of 20 percent to encourage rehabilitation of historic building stock), low-cost housing funding, and other tax inducements. If the client is nonprofit, where to find grant money is also crucial. Complete knowledge in all these fields is essential for ability to convince the owner to proceed, and to find the best way to comply with regulations. Design may depend on type of funding.

ARCHITECTURAL HISTORIANS/ ARCHAEOLOGISTS

If the architect's staff does not include historic specialists (architectural historians, research assistants, etc.), a second level of fees for outside consultants should be anticipated.

If these are merely historic and not construction-oriented, a third level of charges may be superimposed, increasing costs proportionately.

Example

A landmark restoration had hard costs of $250,000, but the bill to the unsuspecting and impoverished nonprofit institution was $500,000. The difference covered *three* general contractors plus consultants!

FLEXIBILITY OF DESIGN

It should be remembered that prior to 1940, buildings were erected mainly *by hand.* Therefore, dimensions may not be tight and absolutely square. You may be obliged to use existing openings wherever possible rather than determining positions arbitrarily in a vertical plane. A straight run may not be possible. This means that design must be *flexible.*

CHAPTER THREE
FURTHER ITEMS NEEDED TO PREPARE CONTRACT DOCUMENTS

DECISION ON JURISDICTIONS, TIME SCHEDULES, AND COORDINATION

JURISDICTIONS

Jurisdictional claims among trades are a fact of life. Who attaches electrical heat—electricians or plumbers? Who connects office partitions—carpenters or electricians? Even within the electrical trades, there are questions regarding who does the communications—construction specialists or telephone technicians. All of these politics should be ironed out ahead of time by the Solomon of the project, to avoid work stoppages later.

TIME SCHEDULES (Fig. 22)

These should be realistic, taking into account the long lead times on custom equipment usually needed on this type of project. Contingent plans should be in place if serious delays happen. Scheduling can be as sophisticated as Primavera Critical Path software, or as simple as a chart on the wall, but something positive must exist.

The electrical contractor must furnish light and power for all other trades to work and thus is one of the first on the site. From that point, since the structure already exists, the order of construction can be arranged to suit the team.

Example

In the interest of "saving money," a client scheduled plasterers to finish the walls 2 days *before* bringing in the electricians (no architect, engineer, general contractor, or other consultant was used). Obviously patching was needed after the electrical work was done, but the budget allowed for only 2 days of plasterers, so the holes are still there.

COORDINATION

Space has to be made available on scaffold and floors for adjacent trades. If there is no room for simultaneous installation, schedules have to be altered. As in new work, slower trades have to be urged along.

No project can be executed to best advantage unless there is someone in command over everyone, monitoring all progress. Problems can be nipped in the bud and conflicts resolved quickly if there is a leader in charge.

Example

In a 1930s train station, it was necessary for the general contractor to coordinate the metal finishers restoring the bronze heating grilles, the plumber repacking the valves in the radiators, and the asbestos remover taking away material behind the radiators. They all had to work simultaneously in a recessed space of 3 ft × 4 ft. Without the project coordinator, it would have been utter chaos.

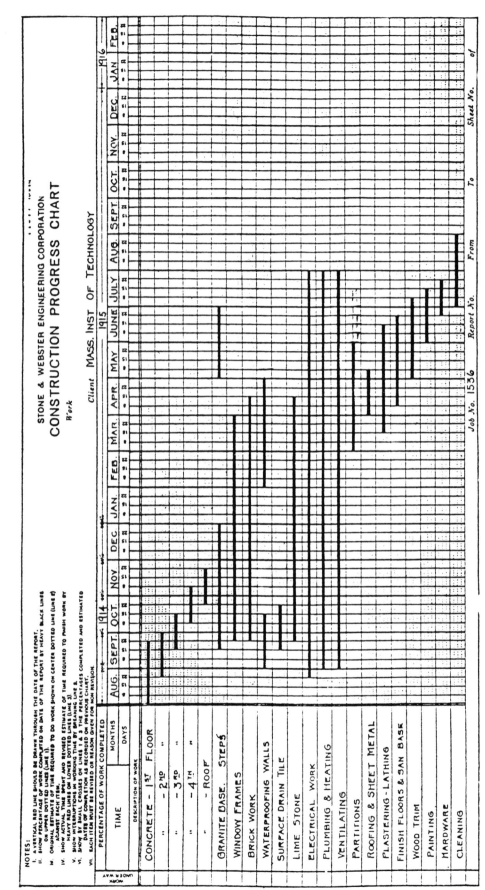

Figure 22. Example of a time schedule, 1914. (*Engineering Record, November 28, 1914, Vol. 70, No. 22, p. 580.*)

SPECIAL PRECONSTRUCTION REQUIREMENTS UNIQUE TO CONSERVATION WHICH MUST BE INCLUDED IN DOCUMENTS

PHYSICAL PROTECTION OF EXTERIOR AND INTERIOR (Fig. 23)

Specifications should mandate physical protection of the interior, especially if it is occupied while under construction. Unnecessary damage to existing materials could eliminate the expected profit, because of subsequent claims. Here is a checklist to follow.

1. Hands, clothing, and soles of shoes must be *clean* before touching original finishes.

2. For work on an ornamental plaster ceiling or other delicate surface, *clean white cotton gloves* must be worn.

3. Surfaces must be adequately covered with *protective material* and areas sealed off from dust and fumes.

4. All areas must be cleaned of refuse *daily* (Fig. 24).

5. Packing cartons and crates must not be discarded before checking quantity, condition, and catalog number of material or equipment.

6. No half-empty beverage containers are to be left to spill on finishes.

7. Ladders and long handles should not be propped against a wall or vertical glass without protection.

8. Require all workers to read instructions shipped with merchandise.

9. Ensure that there is adequate temporary lighting, such as movable quartz, for all trades (Fig. 25).

10. Scaffolding and lifts should be *padded* to protect building finishes.

11. Furnish usual temporary toilets, heat, drinking water, changing rooms, and other facilities as in new construction, but *away from areas which could be damaged.*

12. Follow all OSHA (Occupational Safety and Health Administration) health and safety regulations more stringently than on new construction.

13. Strict "No smoking" signs must be posted and enforced (Fig. 26).

14. If the structure is wood, ban playing radios, so that fire alarms can be heard in all parts of the structure.

15. Keep the local fire department informed on special conditions so that it can gain immediate access for life safety, without unnecessarily destroying irreplaceable architectural features, like stained-glass windows.

16. Protect surrounding shrubbery and landscaping.

17. Provide adequate *on-site storage space* convenient to the trades using the equipment, but not endangering the property.

18. If necessary, build a scale model of the building to demonstrate entrances and exits to be used for protection of life and property.

19. Keep a fresh supply of cornstarch in the nail bag or a work apron to avoid marring of surfaces by fingertips.

SCAFFOLDING

Both interior and exterior scaffolding must be padded or otherwise insulated from original fabric or fragile items. Cantilevered systems may be necessary for special architectural features. The team must be continually advised to maneuver rolling lifts with care.

Example

In a 1930s railroad station, a 50-ft × 60-ft × 100-ft high rolling scaffold was custom-designed and furnished by the general contractor[5] to allow a number of trades working on a high coffered ceiling to get one portion completed at the same time. The scaffold was moved with two come-alongs on early Sunday mornings to its next spot. It accommodated the plasterers, ornamental painters, flat painters, electricians, and laborers. The area below was a busy waiting room, filled with passengers, yet this arrangement allowed the project to proceed overhead.

SPECIAL SAFETY AND FIRE PRECAUTIONS

Safety   Because of the special hazards of dry, brittle materials, OSHA regulations must be carefully adhered to. Contractor organizations will perform "house calls" at the job site for members to familiarize the team on how to protect themselves and the property. Each project supervisor should give weekly 5-minute toolbox safety talks. These few minutes spent during a coffee break or pay distribution time, can save money on claims for property damage or personal injury. Each trade should have a safety officer on the lookout for dangerous conditions, and report them for correction.

Example

In a preliminary inspection, an architect walking on the roof of an early-twentieth century site fell through to his death. Structurally unsound members, rotted wood or metal could be hidden behind subsequent additions. The specifications should contain caution to look behind walls or false flooring.

Insecticides   Often workers are called on to enter properties which have been abandoned or poorly maintained, so there may be insect infestation.

Some insecticides are flammable, so great care must be taken not to spray wiring, outlet boxes, or anything hot, such as lit bulbs or lamps. Also sufficient ventilation must be provided to avoid having the tradespeople falling over with the bugs.

Example

A very famous seafood restaurant contracted for some work. On entering the basement, the electricians had to throw their channel lock pliers ahead of them to scatter the thousands of cockroaches in their path to the panelboard. They had to

---

[5] George Hyman Construction.

Figure 23a. Protection of the building and its surroundings: Interior items which are immovable.

Figure 23c. Protection of the building and its surroundings: Walls and floors.

Figure 23b. Protection of the building and its surroundings: Interior items which are in the way.

Figure 23d. Protection of the building and its surroundings: Exterior protection, especially after a fire (allow the building to dry out).

crunch their way along, and should have gotten combat pay.

Accidental fire How many fires are started by a careless match thrown into uncollected debris on the site, or by a stray spark from welding or acetylene? Fire on the job certainly affects the bottom line.

Example

A large commercial tax act job went up in smoke because demolition procedures created a giant flue in the center of

the structure. The wooden floors of the late-nineteenth-century factory destined for office use were oil-soaked from their previous manufacturing use. A spark caught the updraft and quickly flared up through the highly flammable materials to a height several stories above the roof.

Adjoining properties were caught in the blaze, and the apparent lack of regular job fire drills caused the entire building to be leveled, in spite of heroic efforts of the local fire department. Although there were no fatalities, instead of ex-

Figure 24. Refuse which can cause fire or accident.

pected profits, the client ended up with a vacant lot, losing all the fees paid for construction documents and financing. Contractors lost the cost of estimating and a chance to make a good profit.

A proper fire crew should be in attendance during working hours. Some projects employ retired fire fighters to monitor dangerous procedures.

Example

On an all wooden 1,000,000-ft² structure, a four-member team was used whenever welding was done: a welder, a laborer to rake the floor for sparks, a retired fire fighter as overseer, and a laborer with a hose at the ready.

Asbestos   Sixty years ago, every American school had asbestos roofing, soundproofing, floor tiles, pipes, and insulation. However, the statistics on the dangers of this material were based on heavy-smoking asbestos workers, not the general public, leading to an entire new industry of asbestos removal. The fact is that unless the asbestos is rendered *friable,* that is, in microscopic pieces flying about in the atmosphere to attach itself permanently to human lungs, it can be left alone, or at least encapsulated.[6]

The process of removing asbestos is very expensive because it entails cumbersome equipment which makes the work excruciatingly slow and tedious. Specialists have to tend to this matter as well as to disposal of polychlorinated biphenyls (PCBs) in transformers and ballasts. Their costs must be added in to the bid. Here is another situation where knowing how the building was put together, along with the type of materials used, is a necessity, because there could be many otherwise uncounted voids filled with asbestos.

REQUIRED DAILY PRACTICES

1. At the end of each day, a brief conference among contractors working in the same area should be held, to adapt to rapidly changing conditions. This conference should be required in the contract documents.

2. *All construction pieces should be saved;* that one piece of old glass, lighting fixture part, or other building material might be needed later. *Do not remove or damage material without consulting the architect.*

SECURITY

A property erected prior to 1940 may be irreplaceable because of historic significance or rarity of materials or type of construction, so it may be necessary to have round-the-clock personnel in attendance to guard against theft, vandalism, and arson.

Unfortunately, it has become the habit not to provide security after hours on a construction site. Consequently there are few contractors who have not lost expensive tools and equipment to clever thieves who often spot items requested by their clients. Just so much can be reported on insurance claims before the rates are increased. In addition to the cost of the lost items themselves, there is a loss in labor costs incurred while the crew is waiting for replacements to arrive. This can escalate costs considerably.

Because of the proliferation of theft and vandalism, it would be prudent to secure ladders and scaffolds leading into a building against intruders while the site is unoccupied. There are people who "find" desirable pieces of a building before they are "lost." There have been many cases of marble mantels, lighting fixtures, elaborate woodwork and doors, and stained glass disappearing off a project since there is a heavy traffic in antique architectural components.

Figure 25. One type of temporary lighting.

---

[6] In its June 1989 issue, the *New England Journal of Medicine* published a comprehensive review of recent asbestos international research that challenges the conventional thinking about pliable chrysotile fibers, as opposed to the needle-like amphiboles.

Figure 26. Typical "No smoking" sign on an historic project.

MATERIAL AND EQUIPMENT STORAGE

Careful planning can save effort here, too. An air-conditioning contractor had to relocate the position of the HVAC equipment to the roof of a train station. Until his turn in the schedule to work on the material, it had to be kept somewhere close on the site. He used a helicopter to make 20 lifts to bring up the piping, condensers, fans, and other equipment onto the roof for storage. Since it was to be used there, anyway, there was a minimum movement of the materials. He accomplished two more things—there was no convenient available space on the ground, and he avoided risk of theft or damage of the cartons in its elevated location.

REQUIRED DOCUMENTATION OF WORK DONE

From the very moment you meet the participants of the project, a complete project history should be compiled:

1. Dates, names, places, estimates, takeoffs, computations, drawings, and meeting minutes must be recorded and filed *where they can be found for future reference.* All worksheets should be stapled to the subsequent order or correspondence.

2. Change orders with backup data must be tracked.

3. Lost time days, weather conditions, changed work conditions, or delays must be noted.

4. Daily logs, time and material accounts, and section or team supervisor's daily work reports must be accurately maintained.

This practice will not only engender careful record-keeping for a more profitable job but could also stand you in good stead in case of later disputes.

For future repairs or expansion, a record of what has been done should be kept daily. A small, inexpensive 35-mm automatic camera can be used for before-during-after shots of ingenious methods devised to solve problems. This practice is invaluable on future projects that are similar but have different teams. Photographing site details also trains the eye to see what previously might have gone unnoticed.

Contractors can also protect themselves from liability by

taking pictures of the area before start of work, so that subsequent claims of damage to original fabric can be avoided.

In addition to slides or photographs, other pertinent facts to keep on file include

Indication of access to each trade's equipment (especially if concealed)

Routes of power, water, gas, air, and steam lines to avoid accidental cutting

Correct labeling of panelboards, switches, piping, and all other controls

SUPERVISION

Some owners and governmental agencies procure individual prime contracts without hiring an overall project supervisor. This practice often proves counterproductive. Ideally, the architect's representative, project manager of a general contractor or construction manager, or another in authority representing the client should be on the job daily to coordinate.

The cost of this person more than pays for itself by facilitating completion on time and budget. Even when only the M/E portion of a building is done, there should be one designated supervisor on the job to eliminate bottlenecks and delays.

TEMPORARY LIGHTING

Silly as it seems, if the provision for temporary lights for the trades is not mentioned in the specifications, the crafts may find themselves working in the dark! This situation is especially unacceptable in restoration, if marble cleaners, painters, plasterers, carpenters, sheetmetal workers, and anyone else trying to replicate existing fabric can't see what to do.

OTHER NECESSARY REQUIREMENTS

CODES

Throughout the United States there are major building codes plus plumbing, fire, structural, and electrical guidelines to be followed. Large cities such as New York and Chicago have written their own versions. Any out-of-town design professional who works in another area must know the *local codes* as well as the national codes. Daily long-distance phone calls to solve constant emergencies can thus be avoided.

A proposed change to the National Electric Code required that the workers read the instructions provided for equipment installation. This may appear unnecessary, but mechanics are sorely tempted to rely on their natural ability to "make things work." Sometimes, this tendency can cause trouble.

Example

Plugging appliances into a receptacle placed over an electric baseboard heater could cause the cord to burn up, creating a fire hazard. The instructions warn against this practice, but they are often thrown out with the wrappings without ever being read.

Similarly, failure to read how to operate new expensive sophisticated tools could cause unnecessary damage and loss of time.

Example

A word on *diamond drilling:* the concrete floors with rebar in older industrial properties are much harder and more difficult to drill into than contemporary ones. Make sure that the operator is shown how to do the operation, otherwise you will end up with a $500 diamond bit stuck firmly in the floor, or have water dripping down on an ornamental ceiling below.

VARIANCES

Inspectors will give variances if it is proved that the intent, if not the letter of the law, is followed for life safety. The mere fact that the properties have survived for so long is not just luck, but evidence of practical design.

The contractors who encourage salespersons and manufacturers to make presentations of new lines to inspectors' associations make it easier on themselves. Then when they wish to use new products, they are already known to the officials.

The BOCA[7] code used in the eastern part of the United States does have a clause which mentions certified and listed properties or those in an historic district. In such cases, inspectors are able to grant variances as long as life safety is retained.

It would simplify matters if all other codes could eventually contain the same wording. Everywhere it is up to the construction team to prove that the installation is safe.

PENETRATION OF ORIGINAL FABRICS

Craig Morrison, AIA,[8] counsels: "Just say *no*" if someone suggests making unsuitable holes in historic fabric, indoors or out. This also applies to positioning thermostats or other controls on decorative marble, wood, or metal surfaces.

It is better (and cheaper) to determine *in advance* the best way to get electric power, water, air, steam, or gas to the new systems without punching unnecessary holes in decorative surfaces or nailing conduits or ducts on top of them.

If holes are required, they should be as small as possible, so that the damage can be, ideally, hidden by the new installation alone (fixture canopy, smoke detector, receptacle, fire alarm station, etc.).

Where it is necessary to penetrate the original, unique, or expensive materials (marble, wood, plaster, glass, or metal), the specifications should carefully spell out *who* is to do the cutting and subsequent filling in. Anyone can punch a hole, but it is the aftermath that matters.

When cutting fine wood floors or wall coverings for ductwork insertion, it should be done neatly, saving the square cut pieces, in case installation is removed at a later date and the hole is to be eliminated.

Every member of the team must be firmly aware that working with original fabric is different from working with new materials.

Figure 27. A neat opening for air-conditioning in a 12-inch-thick solid masonry wall.

It is that much more important, profitwise, for them to take extra care when making holes for any trade.

Example (Fig. 27)

A worker made a perfectly square opening through a 12-inch solid masonry exterior wall for an air-conditioning duct in an 1868 townhouse, now an office building. It did not take that much, because instead of having to make unattractive patches around a jagged edge, he could go right to work in installing the duct as soon as the aperture was made. The outside looked much better, too.

The challenge of making an acceptable opening which indicates the ultimate skill of the tradesman, usually arouses a feeling of pride of skill rarely found in new construction. This attention to the problem at hand increases production, because members of the team are thinking about their impact on the older building. Everyone on the restoration of the Statue of Liberty in New York Harbor, referred to the project as "The Lady." This gift from France took on almost human dimensions for those in charge of rejuvenating it. The same affection existed for Union Station in Washington, D.C., which was called "Burnham's Baby" after Daniel Burnham, the architect.

DETAILS

A checklist for facilities normally needed for a particular use should be consulted every time. Forgetting details such as

---

[7] Building Officials Code Association.

[8] Chairman of the Preservation Committee, Philadelphia Chapter, American Institute of Architects.

venting the carbon monoxide fumes from a basement garage, making provisions for gas and water jets in a laboratory, and placing small electrical transformers *over* slop sinks in a museum are clues that the specifications were not carefully written.

Where there is a choice, material with all parts *attached,* rather than loose bits and pieces should be selected. This eliminates the delay in reordering the inevitable lost crucial bolt or screw.

FINAL DEVELOPMENT OF PLANS AND SPECIFICATIONS

A MASTER PLAN

Even if the entire job is to be done in phases as funds become available, the *master plan* must be in hand *before hammering the first nail.* Subsequent work, if not prepared for in advance, may cause problems later. Otherwise, newly finished sections may have to be torn out and redone if they are in the way of additional work not anticipated.

Example

A prestigious museum agonized over the selection of a proper paint conservator and experts to replicate the marbling on the existing paint scheme. After it was completed, they realized the electricians had to make holes in the wall plaster for lighting sconces. When last seen, 6 months after construction, the newly marbled mouldings were covered with a row of clocks telling worldwide time! This is certainly a case of the left hand not knowing what the right hand was doing.

DOCUMENTS SPECIFIC TO THE PROJECT

Contract documents for buildings over 50 years old cannot be copied from the design professional's ordinary stock of specs. They must pertain to the particular property and provide enough information for the contractors to convey the intentions of the client. A vague phrase such as "conceal the wiring" is not sufficient, especially with less-than-qualified personnel. Many contractors have teetered on the brink of bankruptcy when they finally discovered what was behind the walls had not figured in their bids. A look at the finely detailed drawings made prior to the 1940s would astound today's viewer. Practically every nail was included.

CONTRACTOR'S RESPONSIBILITY

Each contractor should ensure that the work is in accordance with all applicable codes and should also check the plans to verify that the M/E lines are not inadvertently routed through the same location. The use of three-dimensional *computer-assisted-design* (CAD) systems may finally eliminate this reoccurring mistake. Electrical wiring cannot go in plumbing pipes!

SUBSTANTIAL COMPLETION

Agreement should be reached early on as to what constitutes *substantial completion.* This is particularly important for comprehensive multi-million-dollar restoration projects which last several years. If one portion of a heavily trafficked building is finished and opened to the public while work continues elsewhere, a decision should be made when the client accepts the first segment. Otherwise contractors may suffer financial losses not of their making.

WARRANTIES AND GUARANTEES

Warranty information from the supplier as well as from the installing contractor should be requested. A walk-through to acquaint the new owners with proper maintenance procedures is essential.

It should also be mentioned that provision is made for the contractors to return soon after completion and check that the equipment is being used correctly, before problems arise within the warranty periods.

Example

A textbook case of how not to operate took place during the restoration of a utility's historic property. The contract obliged the electrical contractor to receive, store, redeliver, and install equipment ordered by the mechanical contractor. The riggers accommodated their customer by holding it without charge. Their insurance policy lapsed just about the time of a snowstorm, when the cartons got wet. From past experience, they assumed that the contractor's insurance covered the property, but this was a different situation not communicated to the rigger. When the machinery was delivered to the site for installation, the customer, seeing the damp packing, refused it. He sent it back to the manufacturer, who checked it, and returned it, but declined to extend the year's guarantee.

Since the electrical contractor's insurance did not cover items not purchased by him, he was out $35,000 for the unit, and guilty of delaying the job.

Here is a case where the project manager should have read the specifications, informed his office of this clause, and obtained special insurance coverage.

CHAPTER FOUR
AWARDING THE CONTRACT AND ACTUAL CONSTRUCTION

Once the preliminary procedures of thoroughly thinking out the project ahead of time, investigating the building and its spaces completely, and preparing the documents to respect the integrity of the structure, to give direction to the team, and to design the means for continued maintenance (see Appendix A for detail) have been accomplished, awarding of the contracts and actual construction to a *competent,* experienced team can begin.

AWARDING THE CONTRACT

On agreement among clients, professionals, contractors, and consultants on completed documents, the job is either put out to bid or negotiated.

BID PROCESS

In this method, general and subcontractors, after either seeing notice of the project in trade publications, or direct invitation, obtain plans and specs. Quantity takeoffs for labor, material, and subcontracting items are made.

In Europe, quantity surveyors do the takeoffs, which are distributed to all bidders, so that everyone is using the same figures. In the United States, everyone's interpretation of the documents is different, so that coverage of the particular trade may not be similar, and the finished product is not what was expected. This partially explains the wide variances in prices which sometime occur.

In some cases, the lowest bidder is awarded the contract regardless of whether that individual is in fact competent and *qualified* for restoration work. This is looking for trouble. Other times, high and low bids are discarded and the one in the

middle is chosen. Whatever the methods, a team is created.

This team concept is absolutely essential in building conservation. It may not be as important in new construction, but its absence in this type of project could lead to a disaster because there is such a close interrelationship among the trades.

Example (Fig. 28)

A municipality wanted to recycle a 300-year-old building for museum and office use. They let prime contracts to the lowest *unqualified* bidders and made no provision for overall supervision. The electrical contractor was told to channel out the original plaster walls for a 1-inch conduit.

On visiting the job, the architect—who had no jurisdiction over the various trades—saw $65,000 worth of damage to the walls! The inexperienced and unsupervised workers had gone wild with their mallets. The volunteer building committee, none of whom knew anything about construction, let alone restoration, halted the work, fired the contractor, and started to look for more money to repair the damage and complete the job. Not having given the architect control over the contractors, the board could not look to that individual for responsibility.

The point is, no member of the team can wake up one morning and suddenly claim to be a conservation expert. It takes education and experience. Few owners are willing to allow neophytes to practice on their buildings, either.

The term *lowest qualified bidder* refers to the contractor who can best perform the job competently for the least cost. Lee Nelson, former director of preservation services for the National Park Service, agreed that even governmental agencies can weed out prospective bidders who are not equipped to do the job and insist on *prequalification of bidders.* In coor-

Figure 28. Damage caused by the incompetent low bidder.

dination with the design professionals, the client may use any or all of these means to decide qualifications:

1. References from the design professionals and general contractors, on firms previously used successfully.

2. Inspection of the three latest projects completed. Comments from the previous owners should be sought.

3. As in new construction, requirements for proof of license, certification (if any), adequate public liability and property damage insurance, and Workmen's Compensation Insurance.

4. For new or unknown firms, financial statements and proof of bonding capacity.

5. A list of those taking approved professional continuing education courses.

The client can undermine the expected results by insisting on hiring merely the lowest bidder, whose workforce may be ill-trained and unconcerned. Inexperience, inattention to details, unauthorized substitutions, and attempts to make an inordinate amount of money at the expense of both the owner and building are the risks of choosing a contractor based solely on price. The unqualified contractor can make any work difficult, but is even worse on older existing buildings.

In addition, unqualified low bidders are often financially weak, and may constantly ask for money in advance to buy materials and pay labor. A cash poor firm generally cannot buy to best advantage, and cannot get prompt deliveries, which can lead to costly delays in the schedule.

Moreover, in mechanical/electrical (M/E) work, no matter what size the job, all applicable codes must be met. Those not fully familiar with regulations would be a further detriment to the rest of the team.

NEGOTIATED CONTRACT

In large restoration jobs, effort is made to recreate a successful construction team from a previous project. The breaking-in period is eliminated, and the strong points of each member are already known. Especially in working on existing buildings, negotiated contracts can provide substantial savings while giving superior results. This type of arrangement allows the chance for contractors to verify site conditions prior to the agreement and even offer suggestions for the plans.

Any time unexpected problems can be discovered in advance, their cost can be covered lessening the stress of change orders or lawsuits. It is also more protective of the historic features of the building.

There is motivation for the specialty contractor to offer "value engineering" recommendations during the negotiating process. These ideas can result in savings while retaining quality and desired effect. This process also saves the client fees of consulting engineers or other design professionals who would otherwise have to be called in when the initial bids prove too high.

Selection of skilled workers Most apprentice-training schools usually teach techniques for new construction, not conservation. One of the reasons for this is that a brand-new structure is so conspicuous in the landscape as to be regarded as the major portion of the market.

However, if young people are made aware of the older methods, they are intrigued and eagerly participate. The Philadelphia Chapter of the Associated General Contractors of America has created a Building Conservation Advisory Team. This body goes into craft training schools to acquaint the students with this large segment of the industry. In areas where there is open shop, some business associations have courses for preservation to expand their business opportunities.

A contractor with workers who can handle both old and new construction should make every effort to retain those members in the crew. Sometimes a client may actually request specific skilled workers, and the contract may depend on furnishing them.

Whether these specialists are developed by training apprentices from scratch, recalling retirees, or retraining existing workers, this pool should be constantly increased to take care of additional work in this field. There are future generations to be educated for this significant phase of the industry.

Concerned professionals and contractors sometimes have to hire and fire until they get the proper team. In Europe, the architect can request candidates from specially trained sources of the traditional trades. Thereafter, the architect and the contractors can concentrate on solving the construction problems instead of running an "employment agency with a revolving door."

Ultimately it falls to those in the front lines (the crew) to make or break a job, so no project, new or old, can be successful without skilled workers as part of the team.

Example

An exclusive private club located in an historic building decided to "fix up." They immediately received over $1,000,000 from affluent members for the work, but decided to eliminate the architect, engineers, consultants, or even proper contractors. They thought they could do it themselves, hiring untrained day workers. This is tantamount to being your own brain surgeon—while reading the instruction book during an operation, you could die of a misprint!

The air-conditioning ductwork ended up looking like a python that swallowed a cow. The ornamental ceilings were ruined. Instead of changing obsolete electrical work, they blithely painted around it. Even the colors selected were totally wrong for the period of the clubhouse and made this formerly elegant space look like a sporting house. Members considered resigning in droves when union pickets, protesting the type of unqualified workers engaged, marched up and down the entrance.

Equal Employment Opportunity (EEO) requirements Requirements for employing minorities and women can be satisfied more easily if small portions of work are initially given to these contractors as on-the-job training. Workers can be carefully supervised while gaining experience. On completion of this breaking in period, they will be able to work with less monitoring and can be given progressively larger shares of the project.

Here is where an improved system of education reaching out to those eager to learn is needed. For over 20 years, the Academy Program, developed as a joint venture of the private sector and public high schools in Philadelphia, has been in operation. It seeks out disadvantaged and/or minority students and places them in a school within the school. Remedial reading and arithmetic are taught along with the work ethic. Jobs are found for after school so that the students can afford to attend classes. (Many do not have carfare or proper clothing without this money.) Every subject is geared to the trade so that aspects such as vocabulary, how to calculate, how to appear for a job interview, and how to perform on a project become familiar.

In high schools with 40 percent attendance, the Philadelphia Academy Program segment has 98 percent. Almost all graduates either continue on in companies where they are employed, or seek higher education. In place of "throwaway" children, solid citizens with bright futures are produced, because someone simply extended a hand to help. Instead of looking forward to the bleakness of a life of illiteracy and no skill, Academy students are sought out for employment on the basis of their training.

ACTUAL CONSTRUCTION

Once upon a time, there was a game hunter who went up to the North woods annually. After several visits, he instructed his favorite guide to build him a lodge to be ready on his return the following season. The guide did not think this big-city fellow would know the difference, and so selected some used materials which were not very good to begin with, and slapped the structure together without much care.

On his return to the woods the following fall, the hunter enthusiastically met his guide and announced that because he was so pleased with previous service, he had planned a surprise for the native. It was, of course, the gift of the lodge to its builder.

The moral here is to *build as if you were occupying the space yourself.* You never know—as in a recent case where the escalator collapsed in a hotel, injuring the mother of one of the workers who installed it—whether it will return to haunt you.

Every member of the team, from architect to apprentice, must follow the prescribed guidelines for building conservation, in order to keep every link of the chain which is the team strong. To ignore them could cause irreversible property damage or personal injury, both adversely affecting the outcome of the project, economically and culturally.

GENERAL TIPS

A caveat for all trades is: *Look before you dig!* There may be electric, gas, water, or telephone lines buried below the surface. You can avoid red faces and legal claims if you check with the utility companies before sinking a shovel or back-hoe blade into the ground. Make sure that everyone on the team is aware of this procedure.

Individual systems will be covered in subsequent chapters, but here are some suggestions for all M/E trades.

Good use of interstitial spaces for concealment of systems Any unused space, once discovered, may be considered.

1. Unused heating grates can conceal fire-alarm equipment.

2. Wiring for stair lighting can often be run up under banisters (Fig. 29a).

3. Power conductors and receptacles can be hidden behind flaps in baseboards or door surrounds.

4. Unused closets or balconies can house electrical panelboards and ductwork, with proper ventilation.

5. A great deal of work can be laid in temporarily opened spaces (as after a fire), provided future access panels are furnished.

6. Ornamental ceiling moldings, if deep enough, can conceal ambient lighting, if heat can be dissipated adequately.

7. In tin or plaster ceilings, smoke detectors and sprinklers can be inserted unobtrusively within the center of a decorative feature (Fig. 29b).

8. An air-sampling system can be used instead of smoke detectors. Only a small ceiling hole is required. The pipe ending in that opening takes 30-second samples of the room air, monitoring its quality for heat and smoke. Very little space is needed in the ceiling for the narrow pipe.

9. Sprinklers need about 18 inches of clear space above the ceiling. Most older commercial properties contain this amount of room, so that visible pipes for sprinklers are unnecessary (Fig. 29c).

Figure 29a. Wiring run up banister.

Figure 29b. Available space above ceiling for sprinkler pipes.

Figure 29c(1). Unobtrusive location for sprinkler.

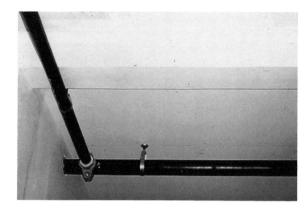

Figure 29c(2). Unnecessary placement of sprinkler pipes below a ceiling.

Figure 29d(1). Feeding fire-alarm conduits from behind a wall.

Figure 29d(2). Fire-alarm unit simply nailed on column [compare with Fig. 29d(1)].

Figure 29e. Trompe l'oeil painting.

Figure 29f. Linear diffuser for air-conditioning at window of 1837 house.

Figure 29g. Real or mock furniture used to disguise ducts.

Figure 29h. Ducts under stairs.

Figure 29i. Antique furniture over duct—fatal!

10. Wall-mounted light switches, fire alarms, and other controls can be fed through the back of ornamental wood or marble walls, so that unsightly conduit is not nailed onto these decorative surfaces (Fig. 29d).

11. In some applications, wireless fire-alarm systems can eliminate conduit and wiring altogether.

12. If an experienced painter is available, the *trompe l'oeil* technique can be used to hide modern intrusions. In this technique, (French for "fool the eye") paint is used to create three-dimensional views. An irregular ceiling can be made to look square by this method (Fig. 29e).

13. Shallow false floors can hide M/E systems.

14. If ceilings are too low, vertical sections built out a few inches from the wall can contain ducting and equipment.

15. Linear diffusers can be concealed within ornamental plasterwork or wood on the walls or on the floor at the window (Fig. 29f).

Figure 30. Even in the eighteenth century, access panels were provided for ducts.

16. If the stone or wood floors can be picked up, underfloor heating will eliminate need for radiators.

17. Victorians were so proud of having water pipes within a building that they gilded them to be more noticeable. If that is the period of the property, the piping does not have to be concealed.

18. Unused fireplaces can be used as return-air ducts.

19. Permanently placed mock furniture can disguise ducting (Fig. 29g).

20. Vacant space under stairways can be used for ducts (Fig. 29h).

21. Be sure to have all access panels and switch or receptacle plates painted separately, so that they can be removed without cracking the surrounding paint.

22. If all else fails, use curtains or drapery for disguise.

23. *Never* locate air-conditioning ducts if valuable furniture or collections are to be placed over or under them. The artifacts will self-destruct in no time! Consult with the interior designer first (Fig. 29i).

24. Never leave the job without providing adequate access to the system (Fig. 30).

25. Horizontal sidewall automatic sprinklers are low-profile units which do not deface an ornamental ceiling.

Innovative tools, equipment, and instruments   Enterprising workers have often invented special tools on the job to achieve greater production with less effort, even without direction from others. Alertness and an open mind offer endless possibilities for experimentation.

Example

On a very large restoration job, the electrical contractor fashioned a tool to chase long runs of marble, granite, and brick with controlled width and depth. This obviously reduced labor costs tremendously, and the cut was neat and uniform throughout. *Any tool* that will do the job is useful, even if it is not of the particular trade in question. A plumber's plunger can remove a wood panel for the electrician. Medical examination tools have been adapted for looking behind walls and under floors. Whatever can see down throats and stomachs, works for buildings, too.

It would not be a bad idea to convince manufacturers to offer the best-selling tools of 100 years ago. It would make it a lot easier to replicate the work, if the original tool were available. An item such as the one to lift up a tongue-and-groove flooring would be very useful.

John Fidler, Superintending Architect for Properties in Care of *English Heritage,* has traveled the world seeking out the latest methods to avoid unnecessary destruction to original fabric while trying to discover space or determine causes of problems. *Radar* and *radiography* (*x-rays*) have been used abroad to find out what is behind stone walls. *Infrared heat-detection equipment* can point out hot spots in the electrical system. It is also useful in energy conservation. *Photogrammetry* enables every crack and stone to be graphed accurately. It enables irregular objects and those whose access is difficult, to be plotted.

Cordless electric tools enable workers to get into formerly inaccessible places. In fact, the selection of implements to get the job done is limited only by the person's imagination.

Provision for convenient access points   Over the years, many access points are covered over with additional services or construction. If the plumbing has to be disassembled to get to the electrical equipment, or vice versa, that had better be corrected. If the panelboard door cannot be opened all the way because of some barrier, that has to be tended to, also. If the access opening is so tiny, only a small child can manage it, that has to be dealt with in another way. At some point, the equipment will have to be maintained, repaired, or replaced, so provisions should be made up front, to avoid disarranging decoration or structure later.

Make mock-ups in difficult situations Mock-ups of everything from finishes and lighting fixtures to methods of cabling sometimes can save considerable time and money on the actual site, especially if building access is confusing or interior configuration must be shared by many trades. In the seventeenth century, most architects used models rather than drawings because of the visual clarity of three dimensions.

Make provisions to operate even with loss of primary power Sophisticated equipment for communications and computers are ultrasensitive and can cease operation for reasons from a particle of dust to a power surge. Alternate means of reaching the outside world should be in place, even if it means a messenger on a bicycle. A single-line phone or a cordless instrument should be available for emergency use.

CHAPTER FIVE
ELECTRIC POWER

GETTING ELECTRIC POWER FROM SOURCE TO SYSTEM

Nothing will work unless it is energized. Wiring makes it happen. Even before the advent of electronics, British hotels installed wiring which could control radio and lights from the bedstand. This was done in even the older buildings, dating from the nineteenth century. Flicking one switch at the room door could extinguish all the lights, or turn them on again, indicating once more that the "smart" telephone controller of today is just another version of creative wiring.

One of the first considerations for the power source is the reliability of the utility delivering electrical service. If there is a history of outages, additional methods of obtaining electricity might have to the introduced, depending on how critical the need for continuous power is. How the power is delivered can seriously affect the historic "look" of the building; therefore, it is imperative to use methods that do not substantially alter it. When working with older structures, it is doubly necessary for every trade to become familiar with techniques of an adjacent craft because of the interaction of the existing systems.

SOME PRACTICAL SUGGESTIONS

1. Masonry walls can often be cut into for concealment (Fig. 31a). Openings necessitated by fire damage offer opportunities, also (Fig. 31b).

2. To run electic conduit in an ornamental ceiling, look for the smooth, unadorned portions to channel out. These spots are easier to replaster later than the decorated ones (Fig. 32).

3. If it is impossible to conceal ceiling conduit, follow the

Figure 31a. Concealing electrical work: Channeling into solid masonry walls.

Figure 31b. Concealing electrical work: Making use of floor openings after a fire.

Figure 32a. Cutting and plastering: Channeling on the flat, not decorated, surfaces.

Figure 32b. Cutting and plastering: It doesn't take much time to plaster over.

Figure 32c. Cutting and plastering: Completed concealment.

creases of the decorated ceiling and go at right angles. Pipe or wire staggering across the ceiling does not enhance the installation.

4. When threading flexible metal-clad cable through walls and ceilings, make sure the materials are suitable for the particular situations: heat, cold, impact, direct burial, chemicals, fire alarm, control, home run, water, oil, insects or animals, or sunlight.

5. To install receptacles in scagliola or marble, use wood

block backings behind the hole cut in the decorative material to bring the fitting flush with the wall.[9]

6. Many items can be concealed behind wood paneling, or even under permanent furniture.[10]

7. The use of window sash chain instead of a steel fish tape is especially valuable when installing new flexible cable or wires in an existing hollow wall. This eliminates completely cutting open the walls. Only a small entry hole is needed.

[9] Suggested by M. Earle Felber, master plaster craftsman.

[10] Items 6, 7, and 8 suggested by a 35-year veteran electrician-inspector.

8. A "horse's tail" made from unbraided hemp rope makes it possible to pull wires in a confined area without damage to wires or cable. This is made from unbraided hemp rope approximately 30 ft in length and $\frac{5}{8}$ inch or larger in diameter. Unbraid approximately half the length of the hemp rope and tie a knot at the junction of the unbraided and braided rope. Separate the unbraided section of rope into two strands, and braid a basket onto the exposed cable or wires that are to be pulled between the conduit opening and the pulling machine. Hold the two ends of the unbraided rope and start the pulling machine with the rope attached to it. The braid will slip slightly on the cable or wire being pulled. Using this technique, move the unbraided rope along the cable or wires as much as needed to pull enough into the confined area.

9. To install new electrical outlets in an existing ceramic tile wall without damaging the surrounding tiles, lay out and mark the desired opening. Using a standard electric drill with a high-speed machine drill bit, drill holes of approximately $\frac{1}{4}$-inch diameter in a close pattern with the open layout just deep enough to cut through the ceramic tile glaze. The drill bit should then be changed to one with a carbide tip to complete the hole through the tile. After all the holes are drilled around the perimeter of the opening, use a $\frac{1}{8}$- to $\frac{1}{2}$-inch steel chisel to gently cut the tile between the drilled holes. Do *not* use a hammer drill. It will crack and damage the surrounding tiles.

10. Low-voltage (12-V) wiring with the smaller, more precise fittings, is well suited for accurate beams needed in museum quality lighting. This takes up less space and uses less energy.

11. European-style fiber-optics lighting fittings are even smaller than low-voltage fittings. This system, with remote source, does not throw heat or ultraviolet rays, consequently protecting fragile organic materials. The length of the wire is still problematical, however.

12. Metal-clad cables take the place of conduit and wire and can be fitted into the walls of older buildings. The only drawback is that once buried in the walls, replacement of broken wires is inconvenient.

13. Flexible conduit can be inserted in irregular spots where conventional metal thin wall or heavy wall may not work.

14. Chases and channels in solid masonry are more of a mind-set than an actual difficulty for the mechanic. If there is a great quantity of this to be done, production methods can be found to standardize the size of opening and speed up the job.

15. For the undercarpet system, the floor must be cleaned of dust, dirt, and debris before installation. Power comes first, then voice (communications), and finally data (computers). The flat tape floor wiring systems may be useful, but only if carpet squares applied over them are in suitable period design (Fig. 33).

Many other ways to accomplish the task will present themselves if an open-minded approach is made. At all times, however, the worker must remember to use a drop cloth, or any other protection for the surroundings, before starting. It is to

Figure 33. Undercarpet system in a seventeenth-century building.

be remembered that a *structural engineer should always be consulted before drilling holes in structural members.*

CONSTRUCTION GUIDE AND WIRING MANUAL[11]

It is important that the individual doing the wiring understand how buildings are put together. This knowledge will help choose the easiest and most direct way of wiring. *At all times, wiring should follow the mouldings and ornament of the structure.*

Normally early twentieth-century commercial buildings have telephone, plumbing, and electric chases (open spaces running between floors in which building plumbing and electric wiring is run), so wiring between floors is not difficult.

Wiring in most cases is limited to interior walls or normal construction (studs, paneling, etc.) and above ceilings. If the ceiling will not support a great deal of weight (workers, conduit, equipment, etc.), the wiring is then run to the chase area and run from floor to floor.

The chase area can usually be located by following the ducts, piping, or electric wiring. These services normally spread across each level of the structure like a spider web, with the chase at the center. If local codes permit, an elevator shaft can be used to run wires from floor to floor.

ELECTRICAL WIRING

Never drill or excavate before checking to see if power, gas, water, or telephone lines are in the way.

Drill holes as a last resort. Seek the advice of a structural engineer before piercing structural members.

Also check with the mason, carpenter, or plasterer before drilling.

Receive approval from the architect before proceeding.

After holes have been drilled, check with a tape measure for proper clearance and depth. Be sure to use some form of fire stop to close up floor or wall penetrations.

[11] Courtesy of Ademco, copyright 1975 by Honeywell Inc.

If the walls are solid masonry, they can be chased out *neatly* to the depth desired. Good electricians can plaster them up again with dispatch, being sure to protect original surfaces from dropped broken plaster and any water or wet plaster that may spill.

(Fig. 34 contains illustrations on wiring from 1975).

COMMENTS RIGHT FROM THE HORSE'S MOUTH

The following are the actual remarks of mechanics from around the country who were involved with important conservation projects.

WIRING TECHNIQUES

GENERAL INFORMATION

NOTE: All wiring must be in accordance with local codes, ordinances, and regulations.

Because of the partitioning effect of the studs in a frame wall, wire runs are usually limited to vertical routes, up or down, inside the wall. Using a flexible bit, it is possible to cross a maximum of three wooden studs if necessary. Normally the wire will have to be run through either the attic or the basement to get from one part of the building to another.

NOTE: Many commercial type buildings use metal studs and plates for partitions and party walls.

Unfinished attics may have no floor boards. The installer will have to use planks to walk on if he intends to run wire through the attic. Four to six 1 x 10 boards, six or eight feet long, should do the job.

Generally, the basement provides the best possibility for running wires from one part of the house to another. Access to the outside walls of a building can usually be gained from the basement.

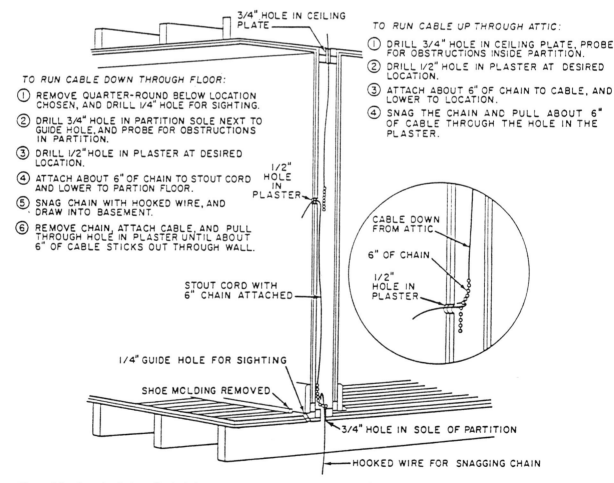

Figure 34a. Example of wire-pulling technique.

RUNNING WIRES TO BASEMENT

METHOD 1

If it *is* possible to drill up into an outside wall from below, use the following procedure.

1. Locate the hole in one of the following ways:

   a. Measure from some object such as conduit, pipe, heating duct or electrical wires that go into the same wall.

   b. Remove the shoe molding from the baseboard. Drill a small guide hole (1/4 inch or less) through the floor at the selected location or

drive a finishing nail through the floor as a guide. Use this hole as a guide to determine the proper location at which to drill the hole from below.

   c. Replace the shoe molding when finished.

2. Drill up through the floor boards and sole plate into the wall.

3. Run fish wire through hole into wall and pull signal wires.

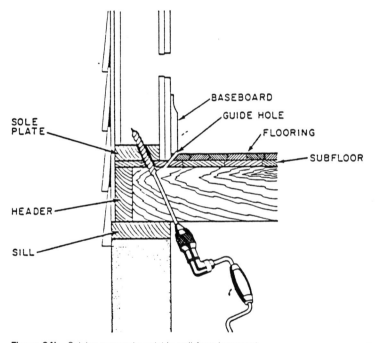
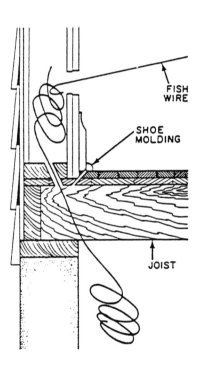

Figure 34b. Gaining access to outside wall from basement.

Andy Lynch, a fifth-year electrical apprentice working on an 1868 building, compiled the following list for his fellow apprentices:

1. Three times a day meet with the other trades to discuss work to be done—once first thing in the morning, right after lunch, and at the end of the day.

2. Any cutting, drilling, or chopping should first be discussed with the carpenter or mason.

3. It is a good idea to get the main service established first. Then go room to room one at a time and complete everything possible in each room before moving on to the next.

4. Save all pieces of molding, brick, or finished material that has to be temporarily removed. Mark it!

5. In spots where switches are needed, try to use that area of the wall to get as many wires in as you can for that room and/or any adjoining rooms above or below.

6. It will be necessary to obtain plenty of wood spade bits and extensions for them. Also have *plenty* of hole saws on hand.

7. For any wired controls such as keypads, doorlocks, alarms, or television equipment, pull multiconductor cable with *plenty of spares.*

If it *is not* possible to drill into an outside wall from below, use the following procedure.

Use the flexible bit to drill down from the mounting hole through the sole plate and floorboards. Connect wires to bit and pull wires up through the wall.

CAUTION: Be sure that the flexible bit enters the floorboards at the proper angle so it will emerge in the right place. Before drilling a hole, check area the bit will cross and emerge for pipes, conduit, or wiring.

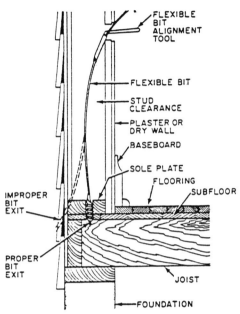
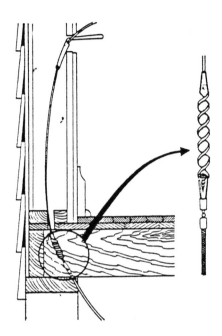

Figure 34c. Proper and improper use of flexible bit.

METHOD 3

If it *is not* possible to drill into an outside wall from below, use the following procedure.

1. Remove the baseboard and drill through the plaster into the wall. Also drill down through the floor into the basement

   a. Cut a channel in the plaster or back of baseboard to accept the wire.

   b. Run a fish wire through the wall from above. Signal wires can be pulled up from, or down to. the basement as desired.

   c. Pull the signal wires to or from the basement, routing it through the channel in the plaster or baseboard. Replace baseboard.

2. In a similar manner. the signal wire can be routed behind the baseboard to an interior wall and then to the basement.

Figure 34d. Gaining access to outside wall.

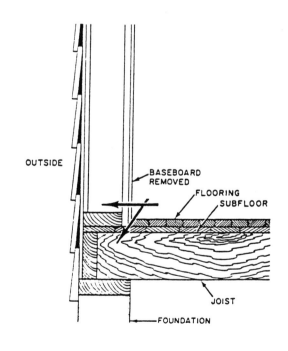

8. If possible, eliminate all knob and tube wiring with switched neutrals. This older wiring method should only be retained for single-circuit application.

9. When fastening anything to the lath, sheetrock screws hold best.

10. Have plenty of temporary light on hand, and lots of batteries for flashlights, because you use them *all* the time.

11. A voltage scanner is a helpful tool. It makes it easy to follow circuits you can't see.

12. When removing old existing circuits, if possible, remove them *all the way* to the panel. Do not just cut them off and leave them. It will only add to the confusion.

13. Try not to work or occupy areas that have already been completed, except for storage of material.

14. Any furniture that requires wiring should be wired, assembled, and finished by a *qualified* electrician. (An entire shipment of office partitions arrived with receptacles installed at the factory backward. They had to be rewired on the site.)

15. Do not assemble any finish lighting fixtures until all the work in that area is completed. They might get damaged.

METHOD 4

Use the following procedure to run signal wires from a device, such as the control, through an interior wall to the basement. When possible, use the flexible bit since it is usually faster than separately drilling the hole and fishing the wire.

1. From the basement, drill a hole through the floor boards and sole plate into the wall. Locate the hole in one of the following ways.

   a. Measure from some object such as conduit, pipe, heating duct, or electrical wires that go into the same wall.

   b. Remove the shoe molding from the baseboard. Drill a small locating hole through the floor at the selected location or drive a finishing nail through the floor as a guide. Use this hole as a guide to drill a hole from the basement into the wall.

   c. Replace shoe molding when finished.

2. From the basement, push a fish wire through the hole and into the wall. At this point you may either—

   a. Hook a cord to the fish wire and pull it to the basement and then pull the signal wire from the basement up to the device being installed, or

   b. Hook the signal wire to the fish wire and pull it from the device location to the basement.

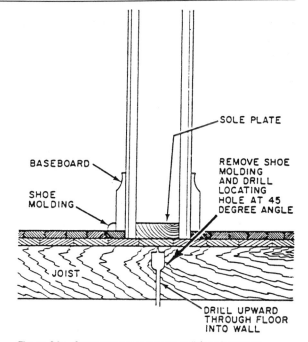

Figure 34e. Gaining access to interior wall from basement.

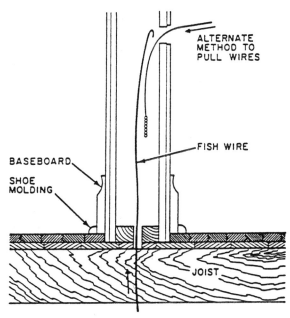

Figure 34f. Fishing wire through wall to basement.

16. Break 20 minutes early to clean the workplace, because any dirt can be very damaging to a finished area. You can't let debris build up.

17. At the end of the day, discuss any changes that occurred that day as a result of the work in progress. Sudden changes can happen at any time. *Communication* is the most important aspect. *You have to be able to adapt to the building.*

18. If at all possible, find craftsmen with restoration *experience.* That is invaluable to the younger people.

A 35-year veteran electrician-inspector says: "Electrical renovation in an existing building is a very demanding art, requiring special skills in the removal of existing electrical systems, the installation of new ones, and the integration and reuse of suitable parts of the existing electrical system. In historic structures, it is important to assure minimum impact on the original fabric."

There is always another way to accomplish the task. Here is a suggestion by P. Wutz, of Olmsted Township, Ohio, who writes in the May 1990 issue of *Electrical Contractor Magazine:* "I have found that when trying to snake wires through drop ceilings, you encounter many unseen obstacles. By attaching the cable to the back of a four-wheel-drive remote control toy truck, I was able to maneuver through or around all obstructions. I snaked telephone and coax cable through 100 feet of ceiling in a matter of minutes at a cost of only $50. [*Author's comment:* And he, or his child, got to play with the toy afterward.]"

Here is an innovation from Steve Braddy, of Warren, Michigan, reported in the November 1990 issue of *Electrical Contractor Magazine:* "While trying to use a vacuum system to install a pull wire, I ran into difficulty trying to get the mouse to suck into a long run. I went to a local party store and purchased a package of balloons. I blew up the balloon to the size of my 4-inch pipe and tied my fish to it. The vacuum sucked the balloon right through my long run without getting stuck. The nice thing about this method is that you can blow the balloon up to fit any size conduit you're working with and if there are any left, you can take them home to your kids."

At the same time this idea appeared in the magazine, John Ashurst, the British architect who specializes in masonry conservation, was telling, during his lecture tour, of how very narrow spaces between stones could be pointed by squeezing the mortar through a small hole cut in a condom stretched over a lamp armature attached to a plastic container.

This proves that there is no geographic or cultural limit to ways problems can be surmounted if a little thought is given.

Here are the comments of an electrician supervisor well-skilled in fiber-optics and other sophisticated systems:[12] "Many times, there are no original prints or specifications for the building existing. Inspection of the building, starting at the incoming service and lower levels of the property, is the key to good planning for proper installation and updating of the electrical system.

"Older buildings may have basements or sub-basements, including crawl spaces, where electrical feeder and branch circuits and control wiring systems can be installed. Smaller

[12] Andrew C. Pron, Local Union No. 98, IBEW.

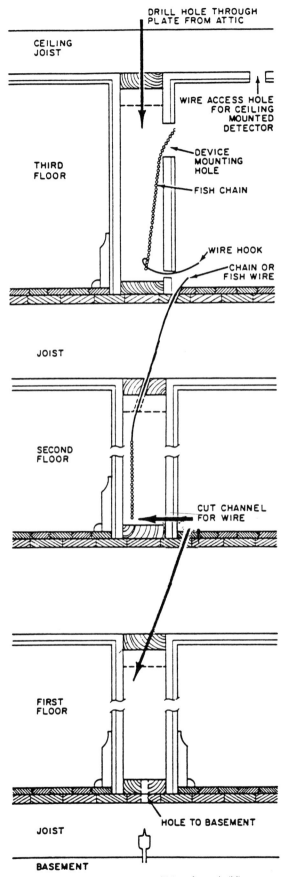

Figure 34g. Running wires in a multistory frame building.

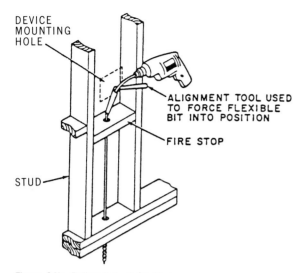

Figure 34h. Drilling through firestops.

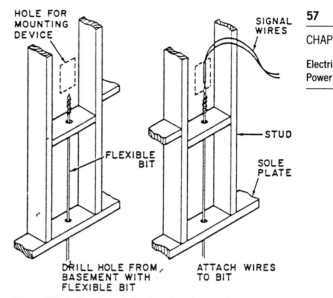

Figure 34i. Drilling through firestops from basement.

3. If the brace or fire stop is close to a door, it may be possible to bring the wire out to the door and then continue below the obstruction.

   a. Remove the door stop (molding) on the side of the door frame closest to the wire run.

   b. Drill holes through the door frame and studs above and below the obstruction.

   c. Chisel a channel in the door frame between the two holes to accept the wire.

   d. Drill into the wall space next to the door from the basement.

   e. Wire the upper part of the wall from the access hole for the device being installed or the attic. Wire the lower part of the wall from the basement.

   f. When desirable, the wire can be run behind the door stop all the way to the floor and then to the basement.

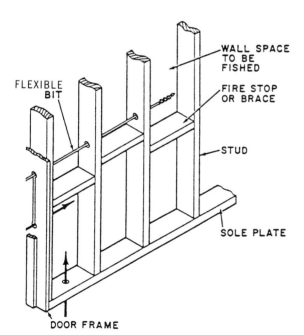

Figure 34j. Drilling around firestops.

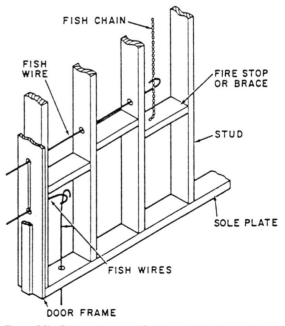

Figure 34k. Fishing wire around firestops and into basement.

SOLID PARTITIONS

There are several types of partitions which allow quick and easy rearrangement of interior walls. Some of these partitions are solid and do not allow the routing of wires through them. However, the supporting frames are hollow and provide a good area for running system wires.

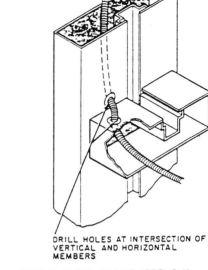

CAUTION: IF ARMORED CABLE IS NOT USED, RUBBER GROMMETS MUST BE FITTED INTO ALL DRILLED HOLES.

4/C #18 ARMORED CABLE

DRILL HOLES AT INTERSECTION OF VERTICAL AND HORIZONTAL MEMBERS

WIRING AFTER FRAME ASSEMBLY

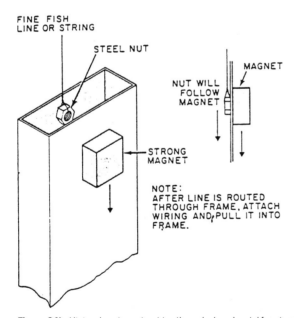

FINE FISH LINE OR STRING

STEEL NUT

MAGNET

NUT WILL FOLLOW MAGNET

STRONG MAGNET

NOTE: AFTER LINE IS ROUTED THROUGH FRAME, ATTACH WIRING AND PULL IT INTO FRAME.

Figure 34l. Hint on how to route wiring through closed metal framing.

4/C #18 ARMORED CABLE

DRILL HOLE IN VERTICAL MEMBER AT INTERSECTION WITH HORIZONTAL CROSS MEMBER

WIRING DURING FRAME ASSEMBLY

Figure 34m. Wire routing in partition or door frames.

buildings, as well as large office type buildings, may have shaft and pipe chases where feeders and the main riser to sub-panel can be placed. In some cases, feeders are installed in the new pipe chases with access doors. It is always a top priority to check and re-check the building for the best route with the least amount of demolition to the surrounding structure.

"The modern day materials on the market make rewiring and updating to electrical codes a lot easier. The use of flexible metal conduit, electrical metallic tubing and service entrance cable help meet installation requirements. The National Electrical Code lists the different types of wiring methods available to the installer for use in the building.

"A typical older office building has plaster walls, and in some cases, marble on the wall. Plaster walls can be cut and refinished to install feeder and electrical panels yielding power needed for modern offices. Modern power tools are a great help.

"Once the main power is put in, the next job is to plan the branch circuit installation. This will feed the general convenience outlets for typewriters and computers. In order to do this, plaster walls must be cut and branch wiring and outlet boxes inserted. With the wall still open, other systems including computer cables, telephones and other anticipated future needs can be roughed in conduits or other raceways. This important thing to remember is *not to miss anything while the walls are open.* Once the walls are replastered, the job should be finished.

"Power needs in small buildings with wooden beams and floors may offer a challenge. Wooden floors may have to be removed in part to establish cables for power and communication. Plaster walls with wood lath may have horizontal support in the wall, thus preventing easy installation.

"Life safety systems are a must in older buildings. The wooden structures are a real fire hazard and must be protected. The use of low voltage flexible rated cables makes fire zoning

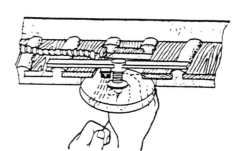

1. Mark location and then cut away plaster to size of a shallow box. Remove center lath.

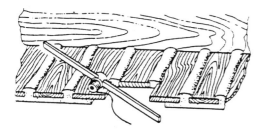

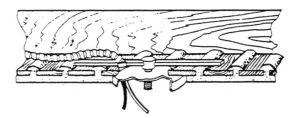

2. Insert hanger (remove locknut and attach wire inside threaded stud).

    NOTE: This procedure could be used to surface mount small boxes or other items.

3. Connect cable to shallow box. Slip wire (on hanger) through the center knockout of box and install locknut on threaded stud.

Figure 34n. Shallow box and hanger installation.

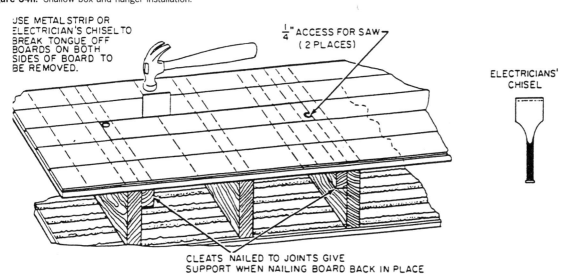

USE METAL STRIP OR ELECTRICIAN'S CHISEL TO BREAK TONGUE OFF BOARDS ON BOTH SIDES OF BOARD TO BE REMOVED.

$\frac{1}{4}$" ACCESS FOR SAW (2 PLACES)

ELECTRICIANS' CHISEL

CLEATS NAILED TO JOINTS GIVE SUPPORT WHEN NAILING BOARD BACK IN PLACE

Figure 34o. Removing floor boards.

easier. The moulding along the floor and around the doors may have to be removed *carefully* prior to cable installation. Drilling floor and roof joints is feasible with the use of wood bits and extensions. Once the drilling is finished, the cables can be pulled to their locations. A fish wire or a string and small chain can be used to help work the cables around the walls.

"Although these buildings may require more time and attention to historical detail, the end result is always worth the effort."

ELECTRICAL SYSTEMS AND DISASTER[13]

[*Author's comment:* Historic buildings exist in many locations. Some are found in sites over faults in earthquake-prone areas. Certainly, they need special attention.]

To most technical people, the term *seismic* implies an immediate connection to the building structure *during an earthquake* with little or no consideration to the elements within. Logically, this is correct, if the structure fails, there is no point of argument. If the structure survives, and any of the nonstructural elements, like the electrical, air-conditioning, water piping, architectural, or life-safety systems fail and cause fatalities, then a whole series of problems will be generated.

[*Author's comment:* Taking into account the additional hazards, such as the dynamic forces from bombings and gas explosions, which occur in today's world], the electrical engineer can no longer work on the electrical system without thinking about the *type of structure, interior architectural rendition,* and *electrical conduiting system* that should be used. It is necessary to identify the essential portions of an electrical system which must survive a worst-case scenario, that is, the emergency backup generator and the emergency distribution system.

Of the methods used in interior wiring, use of *metal conduit* [thin wall (TW), heavy wall (HW), or intermediate conduit (IMC)] has proven the most reliable in survival of a catastrophe. The method of installation is the essential element of its success. Conduit can be installed by being clamped or supported by pipe hangers bolted to the ceiling slab and routed downward, concealed in the walls.

Even though there are various methods of conduit installation that work, the application at the end load, as in the connection from conduit to ceiling-mounted lighting fixtures, also must be considered.

The behavior of electrical installations during earthquakes was presented as a background to formulate a more understandable design criteria which will help to expand the requirements stated in Section 1807(K) of the Uniform Building Code.

The first part of this criteria concerns interior installations. The conduit, fixtures, and boxes used in an interior system should be installed in such a manner that they will *move in the same way* that its supporting structure is anticipated to move. If the conduit, bus duct, or system component are extended to a portion of the structure which moves differently, then the transition point between the two structures should

be bridged by a *flexible connection.*

The second part of the criteria concerns the interior electrical distribution components of a structure. Since we expect a particular group of electrical systems to remain operating after the event, this system and its components should be designed as a *separate system,* with the emergency generator treated as the prime power source. The only interconnection to the normal utility supply should be the *transfer switch* which provides utility power for these electrical systems under normal operating conditions.

To extend these criteria further, the switchboard and transfer switch that are used to feed to the emergency system should be a *separate assembly* and installed on a different pad from the normal switchboard.

Despite the failure of some portions of the electrical systems during the Alaskan earthquake of 1964, the underground distribution system feeding the building switchgear, and the switchgear itself, did not fail. Concrete-encased conduit from the utility company tap point to the building switchgear was the standard method of installation prevailing at that time, and is still being used, with the exception of changes from technological improvements such as direct-buried cable.

It was also observed that the switchgear units in service were prefabricated single assemblies, bolted down to their own concrete slabs or foundations. The only point where failure occurred was when an additional device or section was installed within or additionally to the switchgear and connected by a solid copper bus connection. Such a failure occurred in a high-voltage switchgear section and has been corrected by means of a copper braid connection.

Surprisingly, no fires could be attributed to the electrical system in either the Alaskan or the 1989 San Francisco earthquake. In both cases, installation requirements were rigidly enforced by the agencies concerned, especially in the area of *grounding.*

The point of concern regarding the grounding system is that the protective devices (circuit breakers and fuses) are sensitive to high-level current for satisfactory operation. If the grounding does not provide a low-impedance return path, these devices will not sense the fault and will not operate. This will then create a definite fire hazard. Therefore

1. The portions of the electrical system that survived the earthquake were either bolted to a very strong portion of the structure or moved in the same way as the supporting structure moved.

2. Adequate grounding of the electrical circuits prevented further structural damage from fire caused by electrical arcing.

3. Electrical system survived when the fixture or electrical device moved in the same way as the supporting structure.

4. When the electrical device can move independently from the supporting structure, then a flexible connection is used between the two.

5. Close cooperation among architect, structural engineer, and electrical engineer is needed to determine the strongest structural members of the building where electrical

[13] Adapted from Arthur T. Owen, Frederick Russell Brown & Assocs., "Electrical Design that Stands up to Shock Treatment," *Electrical Systems Design Magazine,* June 1990.

equipment and risers can be located: along the core walls (near the elevator shafts) or in stairwell shafts.

Risers and ducts.   For risers and ducts which pass through floor slabs, *blockouts* are recommended with sufficient allowance around the conduits or bus ducts so that these will not be damaged because of slab movement. However, this may run counter to regional fire laws. In that case, the use of *flange* or *sleeve-type fittings* for the upper and lower portions of the slab which gives the conduit group or bus duct sufficient allowance for movement. *The fitting will have to maintain the fire integrity of the floors on and below the point where the slab is pierced.* For horizontal runs, the problem has been solved in terms of air-conditioning duct requirements; flange and sleeve-type fittings are used. Normally the load-bearing (shear) wall should not be pierced. However, if there is no choice, a *blockout* should be provided or the wall should be pierced with *flexible conduit*. To recap:

1. Run risers along the core so the conduit or bus ducts can move with the core. Since the conduit and bus ducts are made of metal, they are capable of more deflection and will therefore sustain little or no damage during the movement of the building.

2. Horizontal runs below the structural slab will be subjected to more scrutiny because of situations where load-bearing walls are pierced and difference in the way the conduits are supported. Where load-bearing walls are pierced, blockouts need to be provided.

Proper anchoring to foundation

1. Location of a building's distribution system (depending on requirements)
   a. At the building exterior
   b. Nearest the core
2. Total centroid (electrical equipment and foundation) should be as close as possible to the centroid of the foundation to lessen overturning.
   a. Make the foundation as wide as possible.
3. Transformers, switchboards, and generators
   a. Single assemblies preferred
   b. Interconnections by conduit, cable tray, or trenches
4. Engine-generator sets
   a. Integrated units complete with day tanks and auxiliary equipment to lessen the problems of piping damage.

Emergency lighting systems.   The first priority is to get people out of the area. This requires lighting to define all paths out.

1. Floor or low-level wall-mounted directional strip lights and low-level exit signs best suit a fire situation when smoke causes poor visibility for ceiling-mounted signs.
2. In event of fire, there should be an emergency power source for
   a. Pressurization (see Chap. 7)
   b. Smoke evacuation
   c. Fire pumps
3. In the absence of an alternate power supply
   a. The fire control panel is connected before the service protective device.
   b. Water pump motors are provided with nonfusible dis-

connects. Both actions are to provide uninterrupted operation under extreme conditions.

The behavior of electrical installations during earthquake conditions was presented as a background to formulate a more understandable design criterion which will help to expand the requirements stated in Section 1807(K) of the Uniform Building Code.

1. Interior installations
   a. Conduit, fixtures, and boxes should be installed so that they move in the same way that the supporting structure is anticipated to move.
   b. If the conduit, bus duct, or system components are extended to a portion of the structure that moves differently, then the transition point between the two structures should be bridged by a flexible connection.
2. Interior electrical distribution components
   a. Since a particular group of electrical systems is expected to remain in operation after a disaster, this system and its components should be designed as a separate system, with the emergency generator treated as the prime power source.
   b. The only interconnection to the normal utility supply should be the *transfer switch,* which provides utility power for these systems under normal operating conditions.
   c. The switchboard and transfer switch that are used to feed the emergency system should be a separate assembly and installed on a different pad from the normal switchboard.

COMMUNICATIONS AND SECURITY

Inasmuch as the critical component in security as well as telephone and computer systems is the wiring, the same techniques used to conceal conduits, cables, and ducts previously discussed can be used here. The most important thing is to ensure that the installer works *cleanly* and *neatly* in an already completed or occupied area. Every installer should be cautioned to insert wiring *in the valley* of two vertical walls, meeting at right angles, and not where it is highly visible. Use the proper tools and the right-colored staples and wire for the background. A black wire with gold staples against a white wall is not acceptable, especially if there are no plans for repainting after the installation.

Some telephone systems appear to be constructed to self-destruct within a few years. Their manufacturers go on the instant obsolescence theory, to force users to have to upgrade constantly, "because the parts are no longer available." There are newer systems which are flexible, can be relocated by the customer personally, and can do more things than simply carry communications.

These fittings take up much less space than conventional ones. Their installation can be done by a full-service contractor who handles construction as well as communications, expediting the entire project, and removing one more layer of workers the owner has to deal with. Wiring can be done either in copper or fiber-optics, which offers endless possibilities in usage. Here is an opportunity to consolidate a bird's nest of wiring into a neat package which will do a better job.

COGENERATION[14]

Quite simply, cogenerators provide useful heat and electricity at the same time from a single engine. This is the sequential use of energy from a primary energy source, such as natural gas, to produce two useful energy forms: power and heat. [*Author's comment:* Thus, a single fuel source is fed into an engine that turns an electric generator. At the same time it produces electricity, its excess thermal energy is used to produce hot water or steam for heating.] The incentives are reduced cost and reduced energy utilization.

The ability to use the rejected heat from a prime mover for useful work, rather than wasting it to the environment, is the economic attractiveness.

1. Operating options
   a. To handle a specific load; no tie-in with the power company (least-expensive option)
   b. Cogeneration plant in tandem with the electric utility
      (1) Base-loaded with additional power supplied by utility as needed
      (2) Used for peak shaving of the electrical demand
      (3) Either receive power from or deliver (sell) to the utility (for large installations)
   c. Supply all power with no physical tie-in with utility (least-often selected)
2. Available equipment (from under 10 kW to several megawatts)
   a. Complete packaged systems (PCS) may not be customized.
   b. In larger units, a basic engine-generator-control package
      (1) 100 percent hot-water heat recovery
      (2) Combined hot-water and steam heat recovery
      (3) Primarily steam heat recovery

Units may be as small as a refrigerator. Anything that pushes up the rates for purchased electricity, while natural gas, used for fuel for PCS, remains cheap, could dramatically increase sales of PCS.

Stiffer air-quality standards and regulations aimed at acid rain could also make a difference.

ENERGY CONSERVATION

There is much good advice available on this vital subject. However, energy conservation should be briefly mentioned here because of the critical interaction among architectural, engineering, and construction factors which impact especially hard on historic buildings.

Because of their older methods of construction, and the more logical selection of the site vis à vis the local climate, historic structures are actually easier to work with than those of the 1950s, 1960s, 1970s. Space, materials, and workmanship make the difference.

[14] Adapted from *Heating, Piping, and Air Conditioning,* July 1990.

To save energy, *always start with the most obvious and least expensive procedures,* then work up to the more expensive ones. Failure to use the natural thermal characteristics of a building (ventilation and permeable materials) is the most extravagant waste of energy. Here are some suggestions:

Use shutters, sun-blinds, or curtains.

Use dust covers to protect objects subject to fading.

Install interlocking weatherstripping on windows.

Fit windows with ultraviolet filters.

Repair windows (rather than replace).

Install a revolving door at the entrance (for twentieth-century structures).

Point and repair the facade *correctly.*

Use energy-saving lamps and ballasts.

Install *zoned* environment and lighting controls for areas used intermittently.

If feasible, install interior storm windows with *adequate provisions for condensation control.*

Check and replace, if necessary, cast-iron expansion joints.

Replace obsolete HVAC equipment with smaller, more efficient units.

Repair or replace failing pipes and ductwork.

Wrap pipes and ducts with insulating material.

Use reduced-water plumbing fixtures (which require less energy). *Note:* Never install pressure-reducing valves which will hamper the fire department in putting out a fire. Great care must be taken not to reduce the pressure below the needs of normal and fire use. A disastrous blaze resulting in many fatalities and extensive property damage occurred because of this apparent overzealous economizing.

Open the windows during spring and fall when neither heating nor cooling is necessary.

Make use of low-peak electric service at night (for chilled water systems, etc.) This is a common usage in Europe.

Variable-speed motors consume less power when less work is needed than do larger, constant-speed units. They are a better choice than the larger motors, whose excess capacity must be controlled either with brakes or by reducing their flow by forcing them to strain against a valve.

Maintain negative pressure at the outer skin boundary of a building, to prevent the escape of heating or cooling.

During the cold-weather months, find a method to recycle heat to augment the building heating system.

For larger properties, consider *cogeneration.*

At all times, monitor the effects of new environmental controls installed in an old building which never had them before.

Example

A 26-story office building built in 1927, containing 185,000 ft^2 of space, was to be the subject of energy conservation,

Figure 35a. A very poor job of pointing—the mortar is the wrong color and is applied too wide to match the existing. What is worse, Portland cement was used, which, during the freeze-thaw cycle, will destroy the bricks.

Figure 35b. This poor work is visible across the street.

since it was owned by a utility company. It had a large exterior/interior ratio in that it had seven hundred and forty 8-ft × 4-ft single-glazed windows.

In 1973 it had been insulated according to the procedures of that time, but only 5 years later, it was not in good shape. The engineer who designed it originally was called back and was distressed to see the property was not working as he had envisioned.

His philosophy was to extend the life of this Art Deco symbol of its city by tuning it up like an automobile. He created a scheduled maintenance program, in addition to the following:

1. Interior storm windows were installed.

2. Ultraviolet film was placed on windows.

3. Two 2000-kW boilers were replaced with one 12-kW high electric boiler, reducing the demand to 620 kW.

4. No heat source was needed above the thirteenth floor because of the convection principle.

5. All façades were pointed where needed (Fig. 35).

Note: As in all conservation work, there has to be a close cooperation among all disciplines. A specialist in masonry was required to test the existing mortar to reproduce it in color and makeup so that it was indistinguishable when applied.

It is a mistake to slap on Portland cement. This has a *coefficient of elasticity* so different from stone or brick that during the *freeze-thaw cycle,* it will crack anything around it. Also, if the new pointing itself can be seen from across the street, it is a bad job. In fact, if anything sticks out like a sore thumb, it is probably the wrong thing to do.

6. Revolving doors were returned to their original location.

Figure 35c. These windows need fixing to save energy.

7. Energy-efficient lamps and ballasts were used.

8. Plumbing was repaired or upgraded to reduce water flow.

Since this project was completed several years ago, the engineer has been looking into further methods of saving energy while retaining the historic image of the building.

Note: Reducing water flow or airflow by 50 percent reduces the energy requirement to 12 percent. Reducing heat by 50 percent reduces the energy requirement to 30 percent. This correlation between air, water, heat flow, and energy needs is another example of what is best described by that old song "The knee bone is connected to the thigh bone."

Energy conservation does *not* mean turning off the air-conditioning and lighting at 4 p.m.! That is counterproductive. Humans have a way of using a building at odd hours contrary to what systems are set for; therefore, flexibility of control is necessary.

Cost and availability of fuel source are the impetus for effecting savings. However, some tactics that are taken may cause environmental problems injurious to not only buildings but also their contents and occupants. At all times, it must be remembered that a building, like a person, must be able to *breathe.*

LIGHTNING PROTECTION

Lightning *does* strike twice, and sometimes even more than that. In the electronic world we live in, not only the buildings and occupants, but the expensive electrically operated equipment contained in them has to be protected from this natural phenomenon.

The following is a quotation from Sir Bernard Feilden's book, *Conservation of Historic Buildings* (Butterworths, London, 1982):

"When lightning strikes, the total energy can be many thousand megawatts, most of which is dissipated as heat, so that any moisture present is flashed into steam with explosive force. This steam is what splits trees, shatters stones and causes most of the damage.

"The degree of disruption depends on variables such as differences in resistance and moisture content. Another way of causing damage is by setting fire to timbers, by melting and cracking metal and by causing overloading of electrical wiring and devices through inductive effects. Some means of interior protection include transient voltage surge protectors, wiring protection directly from the panel, and uninterruptible power supply units (UPS).

"A tower with a flat top and parapet should have a ring conductor around the top with four terminal spikes, as well as a single terminal if there is a tall central flagpole which can carry the terminal. If there is a metal roof and no parapet, a single terminal will suffice, provided it is bonded to the roof.

"Chimneys are especially vulnerable, as a column of hot smoke during the summer is much more conductive than the surrounding air and doubles the effective height of the chimney as far as lightning is concerned. A single terminal on the chimney top will give the necessary protection.

"[*Author's comment:* Attention must be taken to where the exterior wiring is installed, so that it is *unobtrusive.* Routes must be planned with a specialist, but the architect must have final approval. Cable should be inserted where two 90-degree vertical planes meet, instead of out in full view on one of the sides of the building (Fig. 36).]

"The main down-lead must go by the most direct route possible and avoid all sharp bends, particularly loops such as might be needed around a cornice. It is better to drill through a cornice and line the hole with a lead or plastic sleeve. Otherwise lightning can leap across a loop by the shortest path.

"When a tape has to pass from interior to exterior, it should go through a hole of at least 150 mm (6 in) diameter, sloping downwards to keep out rain and wired to keep out birds. Metal roofs, structural steelwork, bells and metal bell frames should be connected to the conductor system; so too should minor metal items (flashings, gutters, etc.) if they are close to the down-lead or bonding tape and form a possible alternative route to earth. Gas and water pipes, electric conduit, metal sheathing and earth continuity conductors should be connected to the main down-lead if possible.

"The point in an installation most vulnerable to neglect is the connection between down-lead and earth terminal. If possible, this should be contained in a small chamber with a removable cover, so that it is easy to inspect and repair. Earth terminals are usually sectional copper rods with the capability of extension when necessary to improve earthing.

"It is the moisture in the ground which provides the conductive path for lightning strikes, as the minerals making up the soil are poor conductors in themselves. In summer, sandy soils sometimes become so dry that resistance to earth is very high just when the conductor system is most needed. When this happens, matters can be improved by putting rock salt in the terminal box or in the soil and watering the ground with a hose. If there is a high resistance to earth from the terminal, the conductor will still operate—although less effectively than normally—but there will be a risk of great disturbance of the ground and possible damage to the foundations.

"Where protection is necessary and has been installed, it is essential to maintain the original electrical performance. If joint continuity is lacking, for example, the conductor can be more of a liability than an asset, as the lightning discharge might leave the conductor halfway down and possibly cause more damage than if it had struck directly.

"A specialist firm should service the system at one-year to, at the most, five-year intervals; some valuable high-risk buildings need annual inspection. All connections on tapes and elevation rods should be remade every 20 years, however difficult access to them may be (as on a tall spire). After a lightning strike has taken place, it is wise to have the installation checked."

HARMONICS

Few organizations, either for-profit or nonprofit, exist today without some computerized equipment. Because of the proliferation of systems using the same wiring, a new phenomenon has developed from overloading. Harmonics[15] can cause difficulties, especially with computers. Nonlinear electrical loads have led to serious, often severe overheating of full-sized neutral conductors. When odd-order harmonics are present (third, fifth, ninth, etc.), the return currents remain in phase with one another and are additive. As a result, the sum of the three (third, fifth, ninth) harmonic phase currents and all odd multiples of the third, ninth, fifteenth, twenty-first, etc. harmonics combine for a possible neutral current of 1.73 times the phase current! The resulting adverse effects are

Figure 36. The route of the wire is too obvious. It should have been positioned where the two right-angled walls meet.

1. Overstressed and overheated insulation

2. Malfunctioning electrical devices and computer equipment

3. Meter error

4. Lamp flicker

5. Machine vibration

6. Auxillary equipment burnout

When an end user connects a nonlinear load drawing short pulses of current, that is, the load current is not continous, but rather switched on and off for part of the cycle, the current wave becomes distorted and harmonic currents begin to flow. Load-generating harmonic currents include

1. Power supplies for computers, etc. and similar electronic equipment containing AC-to-DC converters (rectifiers)

2. Switching-mode power supplies (SMPS) controlling incoming voltage and switching at high frequency for computer- and microprocessor-based electronic equipment.

3. Electronic discharge lighting

4. Solid-state heating controls

5. UPS equipment

6. Electronic and medical test equipment

7. Variable (-frequency) speed motor drives

[15] Harmonics are currents (or voltages) at integral multiples of the fundamental frequency, which in the United States is 60 Hz. Thus the third harmonic would be 180 Hz, the fifth harmonic 300 Hz, and so on

To correct this condition, many engineers are specifying cables with neutrals 1.5 to 1.73 times the ampacity of the phase conductors, and for simplicity, some engineers have gone to neutral conductors two AWG (American Wire Gauge) sizes larger than the phase conductor. For complete system protection, many design engineers require, in addition to the oversized or multiconductor neutrals:

1. Filters—to reduce harmonics and eliminate resonance conditions. (It is possible to filter or reduce one harmonic only to increase another.)

2. Installing isolation transformers as close as physically possible to the load.

3. Derating equipment such as motors, generators, and transformers.[16]

[*Author's comment:* Harmonics are also the reason why an army breaks step when marching over a bridge; unless this is done, the structure will begin to sway and pitch like the famous Galloping Gertie Bridge in Washington State.]

---

[16] Information courtesy of Wayne Miller of AFC, New Bedford, Mass.

CHAPTER SIX
LIFE-SAFETY SYSTEMS

Life safety should be of primary concern in any building, new or old. However, some may view it as a ticket to great wealth, and stay up nights looking for ways to make systems increasingly complicated and costly, with little improvement over less sophisticated but well-maintained schemes. Here is an opportunity for overkill, by uttering the battle cry "Safety!"—much like the other buzzwords "motherhood" and "apple pie."

Mechanisms, electronic or not, can go wrong or be misinterpreted, and they still cannot take the place of human beings who have the capacity to think. Historic buildings, because of their irreplaceable nature, need that extra surveillance that can be provided only by people. An internationally distinguished museum lost part of a unique collection the day after the guards were eliminated and a life-safety–security system went into operation. The employee who was at the monitor honestly did not understand the signals he was viewing (the robbery). The guards are now back, but the stolen items are not.

Example

A brand-new posh hotel's marketing department worked overtime to secure luncheons and dinners from every major organization in the city. However, at each event, the automatic fire alarm recorded message broke into the most crucial point in the honored speaker's talk, not once but five or six times. The frustrated employees simply could not silence the repeated "This is a test" and then "This is not a test." The audience first stunned, was reduced to laughter. If there had been an emergency, everyone would have stayed in place, having heard "wolf" cried too often. Now, very few business functions are booked there, and even mention of the hotel's

name brings a smile to the face of anyone who witnessed this recalcitrant machinery's actions.

Therefore, before tearing apart an historic building for "state-of-the-art" (rapidly becoming a pejorative term) systems, think of the most practical and simplest methods to protect life and property.

FIRE-PROTECTION DESIGN[17]

1. Sprinklers [*Author's comment:* This necessary item must be positioned so that it does not adversely affect historic decorative features such as ornamental plaster, woodwork, pressed-tin ceilings, and marble. Nor should it detract from the symmetry of the space. Consider the use of horizontal sidewall fittings.]

a. Sprinklers can be used alone for fire suppression or as backup to Halon systems. Sprinklers are heat-activated and thus slower to operate than are systems using smoke detectors for actuation. Consequently, more damage occurs before suppression takes place.

b. There is also the fear of accidental water discharge from broken or defective sprinkler heads. A *pre-action* sprinkler system does not discharge until a sprinkler head operates by activation from a detection device (heat or smoke detector). Only then is the piping charged with water.

2. On/off sprinklers An *on/off* sprinkler system cycles water flow in response to heat detectors. Flow stops when the fire is under control.

---

[17] Adapted from D. Peterson, P. E. Schwalbe, and K. Schwalbe, "Preventing Fire Disasters in Computer Rooms," *Consulting/Specifying Engineer Magazine,* September 1990.

3. Early detection Early detection is most desirable. However, from a suppression viewpoint, little is gained by using smoke detectors to activate pre-action sprinkler valves automatically, as a fire must be sufficiently intense to generate the heat needed to open sprinkler heads. If used, detectors often are *cross-zoned* to avoid pipe draining from premature operation. However, this method may delay activation because random airflow patterns may trigger more than one detector on the first initiating circuit before activating a detector on the second circuit.

4. Halon Halon 1301 (bromotrifluoromethane) is a colorless, odorless gas stored as a liquid under pressure. It leaves no residue and has low toxicity at concentration levels effective for fire suppression. However, it has been linked to atmospheric ozone depletion and is currently under restrictions. There is noise, turbulence, and impaired visibility on surprise discharge, causing occupants to panic. This necessitates notification and/or evacuation procedures.

Halon prevents oxygen from combining with fuel. At volume concentrations of 5 to 7%, there is still adequate oxygen for breathing. Even so, NFPA 12A mandates personnel exposure be limited to 15 min at concentrations of 7% and less.

Halon 1301 decomposes into toxic products when exposed to flame. Therefore, the gas must reach design concentration rapidly (10 seconds, per NFPA 12A) to suppress fire before significant decomposition takes place. The room must hold a sufficient Halon 1301 concentration for a 10- to 15-min "soaking time."

Halon leaks at low levels in the area are a main concern:

1. Propped-open doors must be released prior to discharge.

2. Doors should be fitted with sweeps or gaskets to prevent leaks and outside air infiltration.

3. Piping or conduit penetrations must be sealed.

4. HVAC ducts should be fitted with tight dampers that close on system activation.

5. Porous masonry materials should be sealed.

[*Author's comment:* Whenever Halon is installed, the area to be protected must have as few opportunities to leak as possible. This means that after installation, even the addition of a floor receptacle means a plug of some form of fire-stop material to keep the gas within the space.]

The turbulence of the Halon 1301 discharge also warrants precautions. Furnishings should be sufficiently heavy to withstand discharge force. Pendant lighting fixtures should be avoided if possible. If not, nozzle locations should be coordinated to prevent the discharge from sending fixtures (*and anything else*) flying across the room.

Designing the detection portion of a Halon 1301 system involves balancing:

1. Earliest possible activation, and

2. Prevention of unnecessary discharge.
   a. Smoke detectors sense a fire earlier than do heat detectors.
   b. Airflow pattern rather than detector spacing is crucial.
   c. If a large number of smoke detectors is required, a graphic annunciator would be helpful in investigating alarms.
   d. At least two smoke detectors should be required to alarm regardless of location, before the system activates.
3. Manual overrides are common and manual discharge capability is a code requirement.
4. An abort capability is a common client requirement. Abort stations must be "deadman" types, requiring continuous pressure, rather than maintained-position switches. The insurance carrier may place restrictions on this feature.
5. The final design consideration is clearing the air of the gas and its decomposition products. A mechanical ventilation system that vents directly outside may be required.
   (End of section adapted from Peterson et al.)

A nineteenth-century advertisement for fireproofing materials (Fig. 37a) and diagrams from the same era (Figs. 37b and 38) indicate the construction methods of commercial buildings of the time. The ornamental ceiling was not expected to be obscured by pipes, wires, and fittings (Fig. 39).

Case history: York Minster, York, England[18]

This venerable building was the first that drew the writer's attention to the entire subject of building conservation. This case history of such an ancient structure was particularly chosen to illustrate that work can be done effectively on property of any age. The then Surveyor of the Fabric, Sir Bernard M. Feilden, came to the United States in 1972 at the invitation of Charles E. Peterson, FAIA, who had convened the national conference on "Building Early America."[19] Extraordinary measures were taken to preserve this huge medieval structure, including space-age discoveries using computer techniques.

After a fire on July 9, 1984 which destroyed the thirteenth-century vaulted-roof structure and severely damaged the stained glass of the sixteenth-century Rose Window (part of the largest and most comprehensive collection of stained glass in Great Britain) of the York Minster, elaborate lightning protection was installed.

Dr. Charles Brown, FRIBA, Surveyor of the Fabric, wrote: "No one could have wished the disastrous fire upon the Cathedral. Nevertheless, after acceptance of the calamity, an opportunity was given to the skilled craftsmen of today to show that reconstruction was possible. During the exercise of that skill, much has been learnt about timber technology and fire precaution techniques. For those reasons alone, many historic buildings besides York Minster will benefit from the studies made and the techniques applied, and it can be hoped that painful adversity has been turned to profitable advantage.

"York Minster has had a tragic history of fires ever since

---

[18] The architect was Dr. Charles Brown, Surveyor of the Fabric, Hinton Brown Langstone. Dr. Brown graciously loaned the original drawings of the building to the author along with the specifications. The technical information given here is from the proposal by Gent Limited for the fire alarm system, prepared by N. Moss and G. Wentworth, June 1986.

[19] The title of the book by Charles E. Peterson.

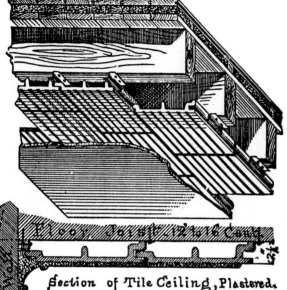

Figure 37a. A late-nineteenth-century advertisement shows how a typical building is put together. This can aid in determining the routing for wires and ducts. (From *The Inland Architect.*)

the eighth century and the lessons of this latest calamity must ensure that all known precautions are taken to avoid another one.

"Apart from the new lightning conductor system, now completed, other measures to be undertaken are

1. Compartmentation of roof voids

2. Creation of more access points to roof voids

3. Laying of fire blankets over vaults

4. Creation of emergency fire vents to roofs

5. Installation of advanced fire-detection system

6. Installation of new locking system for all turret doors

7. Still under consideration is the installation of a dry sprinkler system and in some voids a Halon gas system."

In 1986, the following advanced fire-detection system was proposed for the York Minster.[20]

1. *Addressable.* This is one in which each system component is individually given a form of identification. The address is often simply a number. The Gent System 3400 automatically addresses all devices when commissioning, or recommissioning after system alterations. It takes addressing one stage further by allowing the user to give each device a 32-character label in addition to its address. This means that the display will show clearly the location of the incident.

2. *Analog.* This describes the type of information supplied to the control panel and also provides an explanation for the difference between *detectors* and *sensors*. In a traditional system, the detector monitors the level of smoke, heat, or other variables in the room. When a preset threshold is reached it will trigger, informing the panel of a fire condition. The information itself is presented in an "on or off" fashion and therefore the fire decision is taken at the detector. In an analog system the room sensor monitors the relevant condition and constantly relays the reading to the control panel. This continuous stream of information is termed analog data. In this case it is the panel that makes the fire decision and therefore the room device is termed a *sensor* rather than a *detector.* System 3400 uses a microprocessor in every sensor to continuously monitor its own system status, and therefore specific events such as the triggering of a manual call point can be identified and acted on within one second. The combination of analog sensors with the fast event response ensures the minimum possible delay in fire signaling with the minimization of unwanted false alarms.

Many systems that are both addressable and analog claim to be "intelligent." System 3400 reaches a higher level of performance and is therefore on a higher level of advanced fire detection.

Optical scatter smoke and heat sensor combined head This apparatus has an exceptionally high signal-to-noise ratio. A full spectrum of fires, from burning solvents to low-energy smoul-

[20] Taken from the specifications prepared by Gent.

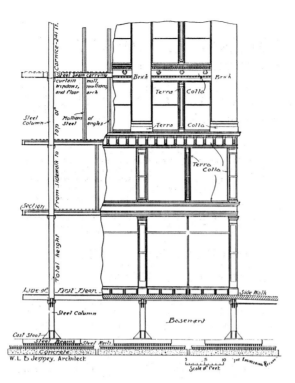

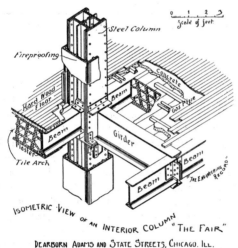

Figure 37b. A late-nineteenth-century diagram shows how a building is put together. This can aid in determining the routing for wires and ducts.

dering fires, can be met. The optical sensor can be totally disabled during certain hours. Alternatively, the sensitivity can be adjusted. This permits the advantage of smoke sensors to be effectively realized even in those environments in which conventional smoke detectors would not be considered suitable, such as in kitchens, laundries, staff rooms, and loading bays.

Heat sensor   This can be configured as a genuine rate-of-rise heat sensor, or as a high-temperature heat sensor. As such, it is ideally suited for locations requiring rapid response to temperature rise, as in rooms with high ceilings or cold stores. Configured for the high-temperature specification, it is suitable for boiler rooms and similar locations.

Ionization smoke sensor   This sensor shows a very low susceptibility to known causes of false alarm, such as wind, insects, temperature, and humidity extremes. Its use is recommended for the most rapid detection in areas with a particular risk of free-burning fires, as in warehouses. It should also be mixed with optical plus heat sensors in areas where the earliest and most comprehensive fire detection is desired, as in computer suites and roof voids.

Beam sensor   This is infrared, suitable for path lengths to 328.1 ft (100 m). Its low consumption and unique synchronization feature for the transmitter and receiver allows low-cost installation on the same circuit as the other sensors and peripherals. The transmitter and receiver are largely self-aligning within a wide field of view, without risking interference between adjacent sensor units. Its base compatibility with the other sensors permits units to be unplugged for cleaning. The detection criteria can be adjusted for specific path lengths if required. An extra level of sophisticated microcomputer processing is incorporated in each receiver head, leading to a much lower false-alarm rate than for conventional beam detectors.

Flame sensor   The sensor will use the output of a flame 4.3 nm in the infrared band as the sensing mechanism. An extra level of signal processing will be added to the sensor to enable the recognition of the characteristic modulation of many of the common causes of false alarms in conventional detectors. The range will be up to 82.025 ft (25 m) and it will have a wide field of view. The sensitivity can be adjusted, depending on conditions and usage of the areas being monitored, from the fire-alarm panel.

Call points   Conventional manual call points can be utilized with System 3400 being wired from the base of the nearest sensor. This eliminates the need to take the two-wire loop to and from each call point. Alternatively, system call points can be wired directly to the loop, having a unique address and label.

Wiring integrity   The ability to wire a circuit as a complete loop results in a tolerance to a single open-circuit fault. The use of a sub-loops can further increase the fault tolerance. A short circuit can be isolated, generally within 0.5 second, with all the loop-wired hardware remaining functional. The location of both short- and open-circuit faults can be indicated within 10 seconds.

Sensors can be unplugged without disabling other sensors, sounders, system manual call points, and other hardware on the same circuit. Where malicious removal is likely to occur, the use of the integral locking device is recommended. Where it is necessary to disable a sensor, because of maintenance work leading to the risk of a false alarm, the facilities available within the fire-alarm panel should be employed.

Some causes of false alarms

1. Contamination

2. Wind

3. Insect infestation

4. Radio-frequency interference

5. Electrical transients

6. Vandalism

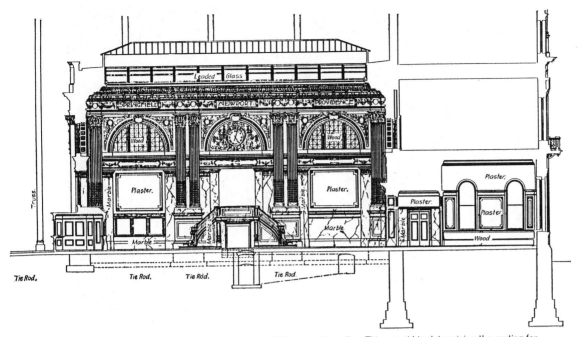

Figure 38a. A late-nineteenth-century diagram shows how a building is put together. This can aid in determining the routing for wires and ducts.

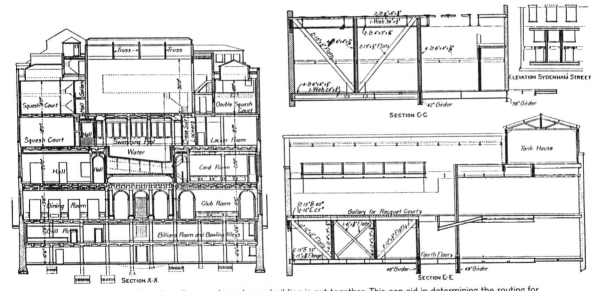

Figure 38b. An early-twentieth-century diagram shows how a building is put together. This can aid in determining the routing for wires and ducts.

[*Author's comment:* One drawback of *wireless fire alarms* is their susceptibility to radio-frequency interference. There have been cases where a police patrol car drove by, setting off an alarm. Even heart pacemakers could affect either the wearer or the system. The frequencies must be carefully chosen to avoid conflicts.]

System installation   System 3400 can permit significant reductions in installation costs when compared with conventional and other new-generation systems. This is because of the ability to wire a large number of sensors, sounders, interface units, and repeat panels on one circuit. However, the number of sensors and peripherals on one circuit can be limited for a number of reasons, including

1. The total number of addresses required

2. The electrical load on the circuit, particularly the number of electronic sounders

3. The maximum cable length

4. Other geographic considerations

Fixed extinguishing systems   Halon 1301 fixed extinguishing systems are included to the M. V. Room and organ loft. Both systems operate on a "double-knock" principle, the operation

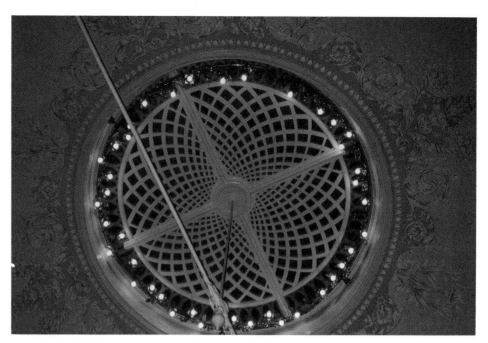

Figure 39. The sprinkler pipe ruins this ceiling. Another method could have been used.

of any two individual sensors occurring before the extinguishant release cycle can commence.

Each area is provided with a mixture of optical and ionization smoke sensors to give protection from the full range of fire types from slow smoldering to free flaming. At the entrance to each area a status unit is sited, giving visual indication of the system state, manual release, and manual and automatic switching facilities.

The fixed extinguishing system to the M. V. Room will utilize Halon cylinders sited within the anteroom adjacent to the boiler house, the extinguishant to be piped to discharge nozzles throughout the M. V. Room.

At the site meeting a central bank extinguishing system was also proposed for the organ loft; however, on closer inspection of the area a modular system is offered, giving a more effective means of protection to the area and cutting the system cost.

The modular system will consist of cylinders sited below the organ loft area, the system providing an initial discharge of extinguishant giving a 5% concentration by volume and then a subsequent gradual discharge of a further 5% concentration to maintain the concentration for a period of 10 min and compensating for losses occurring through fixed openings within the area. The second discharge would not be available with a central bank system.

It should be noted that at no time would the concentration reach a level beyond that allowable by the health and safety executive for discharge into an occupied area. Also both modular units would be situated in the space directly below the loft, hence being completely hidden from view.

Future developments   Future consideration may be given to

egress control for the purpose of the automatic opening of hatches to roof spaces, for example, whenever a fire condition occurs. [*Author's comment:* This installation may be necessary where there is fear of arson or insurrection.]

Maintenance   This fully comprehensive maintenance contract is recommended for the Gent System 3400 in the York Minster:

1. Four routine visits per year, where all equipment will be checked.

2. All emergency visits, whether in or out of normal working hours, free of charge.

3. All parts replaced free of charge after normal wear and tear.

4. All smoke sensors cleaned annually.

[*Author's comment:* This extremely complicated restoration of the largest church in Great Britain took less than 4 years, and actually was finished 1 year *ahead of schedule.*] (End of section taken from the specifications prepared by Gent.)

"The complete work,[21] with the exception of the lead sheeting and craneage, was carried out by the Stoneyard—the Minster craftsmen, consisting of stonemasons, glaziers, carpenters, plasterers, electricians, and decorators. The work nevertheless was administered as a *contract* with priced bills of quantities, progress schedule, and monthly valuations."

On all drawings, Dr. Brown has the legend: "If in doubt, ask." This would be a very helpful addition to every print.

[21] Article printed in *Structural Survey,* Vol. 7, No. 3, 1989.

CONTINUING ON LIFE-SAFETY EQUIPMENT IN EUROPE

Alan C. Parnell, FRIBA, is the acknowledged leader in life safety throughout Europe. His book[22] has been published in many languages, including Russian. He is also familiar with American laws and practices and has been a pioneer in *smoke control*. The items which are excerpted or adapted below from Mr. Parnell's book include detection, alarms, emergency lighting, and fire-fighting equipment. Obviously, all of these subjects require electric power as well as water sources.

Because of the cultural and economic value of pre-1940 buildings, every member of the team must be constantly on the alert to avoid fire and if it occurs, to minimize its effects. The most common excuse reported in the media for cause of fire is usually "faulty wiring," even if the incident was really caused by an employee sneaking a smoke in a closet filled with flammable materials.

Mr. Parnell states: "The design, construction and subsequent maintenance of systems must be directed toward a common goal of Life Safety. These goals are not easy to attain. Many factors work at cross purposes to make achievement more costly and troublesome than necessary."

1. There are many local, state, and federal laws (*and codes*) which sometime do not correspond to each other, creating uncertainty.

2. [*Author's comment:* The experience and education of inspectors varies considerably, so that codes are not interpreted equally, even in the same geographic area.]

3. [*Author's comment:* The codes themselves can be likened to the Delphic Oracle of ancient Greece—the answer can be yes, no, or maybe, depending on the Sibyl[23] in charge. Most codes emphasize new construction and show very little consideration for the older existing properties which make up the major segment of the market. It is, however, possible to acquaint inspectors with the latest techniques, materials, tools, and equipment in the ever-growing industry, so that they will be willing to accept changes to retain original design, *as long as life safety is uppermost.*]

[*Author's comment:* Some codes have "grandfather" clauses which allow maintenance work to replace like with like without restriction. New work, if not affected by exemption, usually has to comply with regulations.

Clearly, the choice of oil- and gas-burning appliances and the associated storage of fuel is very important.]

PROBLEMS AND CONFLICTS WITH LIFE-SAFETY INSTALLATIONS

The physical effects of legislation as applied to mechanical/electrical (M/E) installations with respect to life safety in historic buildings are as follows.

1. Structural problems
   a. Physical difficulties in making the building (or part) stable
   b. Interpretive or enforcement problems of agreeing what constitutes adequate stability
2. Dimensional problems
   a. Headroom, insufficient window/floor-area ratio for daylight or ventilation
   b. Stairways, need for additional, or existing height/width
   c. Any problem of fitting new measures into an existing building where physical dimensions were a constraint
3. Architectural or historic character
   a. Introduction of new elements
   b. Removal or covering up of old elements
   c. Spatial matters as well as details
4. Additional cost
   a. Direct costs of the requirement
   b. Indirect costs due to the delay or disruption

The most problems arise from building regulations; the next, from fire precautions; and the third, from housing acts.

1. Problems with automatic detection Unsightly surface wiring (*and piping*), expense of installation, and/or inconvenience and loss of confidence due to false alarms.

2. Smoke detectors [*Author's comment:* It is hoped that soon manufacturers will offer a better selection of shapes and colors of fittings which would fit into older design more appropriately. The ungainly and frankly ugly units now on the market are the bane of many an owner. Unfamiliarity with better units already available is another hindrance.]

3. False alarms Heat detectors, being relatively less sensitive, have an acceptable record. The ratio of false alarms to genuine fire alarms for smoke detectors is put at between 5:1 and 20:1. [*Author's comment:* If outside parties, other than the installing contractor, fiddle with the system, without knowledge of those responsible, all kinds of trouble, including breach of warranty, can be caused.

Where the client insists on having the fire alarm system put in very early in construction, so that this delicate mechanism is prey to dust, dirt, and general abuse, neither the manufacturer nor the installer can guarantee the product or installation.

Likewise mischievous pranks, or even deliberate changes made to the system by tenants, can be a source of real concern, especially when it comes to final payment to the contractor.]

4. First-aid fire-fighting equipment Hoses and extinguishers can cause more serious visual and financial problems in historic buildings than elsewhere, because the interiors are more sensitive and the measures needed to accommodate the equipment have to be more elaborate for concealment.

Any historic buildings with fabric or contents of high artistic, architectural, or historic value also rely to a great extent on the ability of their occupants to subdue fire in its earliest stages, as critical fire or smoke damage can be caused before the

---

[22] Alan C. Parnell, FRIBA, *Building Legislation and Historic Buildings*, English Heritage Architectural Press, London, 1987. (This section is adapted from this book.)

[23] One of the women who in ancient Greek times acted in various places as reputed mouthpiece of a god.

professional fire fighters arrive. The water damage resulting from the full-sized 2.73-inch (70-mm) hose with its 0.741-inch (19-mm) jet used by the fire brigades can be as grave as that of the fire itself.

5. Signs Signs should be posted directing occupants to an exit and/or giving warnings or instruction of some kind.

[*Author's comment:* Even though dictated by code, there should be an attempt to coordinate their form, finish, or mounting with the historic surroundings. In Europe, they consider red the color of danger, and normally use green for exit signs.

Sometimes designers lose sight of the need to evacuate large numbers of occupants during an emergency in their quest for the unusual space. Some of the newest theaters and recycled shopping centers resemble a Chinese puzzle with their unorthodox versions of entrances and exits. Bewildered people need instant visual guides, not a series of unrelated escalators, locked stairs, blind corners, dead ends, and unmarked doors that open onto padlocked yards.]

6. Housekeeping and management System *maintenance* is essential on a regular basis.

APPROACH TO HISTORIC BUILDINGS

Sometimes, there is a lack of guidance on how fire authorities should balance historic or architectural interests against those of fire safety. At the moment, this is done in the form of adversarial debate:

1. The fire officer responds to the building or proposed works from the fire safety point of view.

2. The architect or owner makes a case for not doing as suggested, either because of some conservation interest or because of the cost.

What is needed is a code of practice for historic buildings that discusses the issues, sets out basic principles, and gives examples. Usually a material change of use precipitates the controversy.

ESTABLISHING STANDARDS FOR HISTORIC BUILDINGS

When standards were set in matters such as health and safety, it is unlikely that historic building factors were taken into account. Standards are concerned with the protection of people. People are considered to warrant the same protection whether they are in old buildings or new ones, and the fact that it might be difficult to achieve this protection in old buildings is not a consideration when the standard itself is set.

With the increased and widespread interest in historic buildings, various steps have been taken to protect these properties. Most listed building controls have power to stop standards being applied where they do harm in historic building terms, but these, of themselves, do not solve the problem where alteration, extension, or change of use is required.

Here there should be encouragement to those who enforce legislation to make ad hoc adjustments to the standards.

HEAT AND SMOKE GENERATION CALCULATIONS

Smoke and toxic products of the fire are the most common killers. Therefore, *smoke control* should be of primary concern. Instead of traditional space-dividing methods of fire precaution which can spoil historic buildings, *the partial substitution of smoke control by pressurization* could be of considerable benefit.

As yet there is very little use of this practice in historic buildings. The prime reason for its rarity is that very few architects or engineers have either experience or knowledge of smoke-control systems.

Case study (shops): The Central Market Building, Covent Garden, London (Figs. 40 and 41)

This three-story building (including the extensive basements) was erected in 1830 for the Covent Garden fruit and vegetable market. In its original form, it consisted of four parallel rows of vendor stalls with aisles between them. At the east end the buildings were linked by a stone terrace. In 1875 and 1890 the south and north aisles were covered by cast-iron and glass roofs whose structures are independent of the original buildings. [*Author's comment:* The entire space takes up more than a city block.]

The traders' accommodation consisted of basement storage, reached through floor "shop" spaces with access from both sides. First-floor (American second) offices above the shops were reached by steep timber stairs. The basement was something of a warren. Two fire fighters had been killed in fires there since World War II.

When the market moved out of central London in 1974, the need for fire-safety improvements was one of the many factors involved in the selection of a new use for the building. It was decided to create a shopping arcade with allied facilities such as restaurants.

Sprinklers were required throughout. It was considered that the cast-iron columns in the shops and first-floor rooms required protection from fire. An external drencher system was avoided by positioning some of the sprinkler heads close to the windows.

Smoke vents were required from the basement and from the new stairways to the first (American second) floors. The pavement vents are breakout panels, and the stair vents have been designed as openable rooflights. Neither type is visually intrusive.

Case study (museum/art gallery): Kenwood House, London (Fig. 42)

Kenwood is a large house of two stories, with an attic and basement, set in park land and built in about 1770 to an Adam design. The house is run as a museum and art gallery, with ancillary offices and a curator's flat all within the main building. The need for fire-prevention measures has been increased by the very valuable collection of paintings housed within. It has been hard to define which measures were taken for statutory reasons and which were insurance and security requirements.

There is automatic detection throughout and the alarm system is linked by landline to the fire service. A hose-reel, required in the southwest stairway for fire fighting, has been disguised by enclosing it in a low, glass-fronted cupboard on floor runners

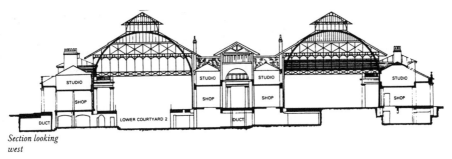

*Section looking
west*

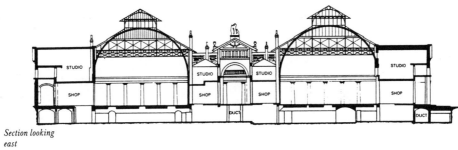

*Section looking
east*

Basement plan

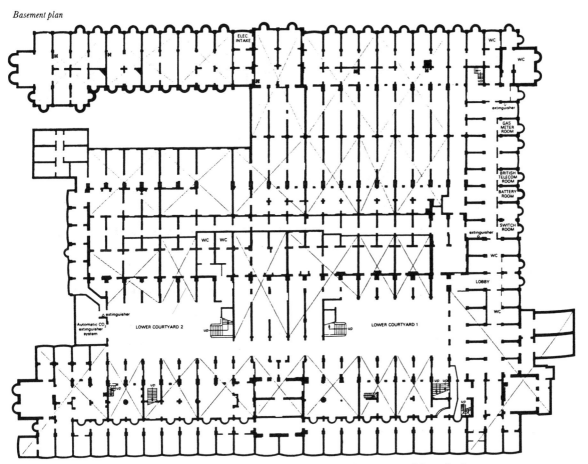

Figure 40. The Central Market Building, Covent Garden, London. (*Reproduced with permission of the author.*)

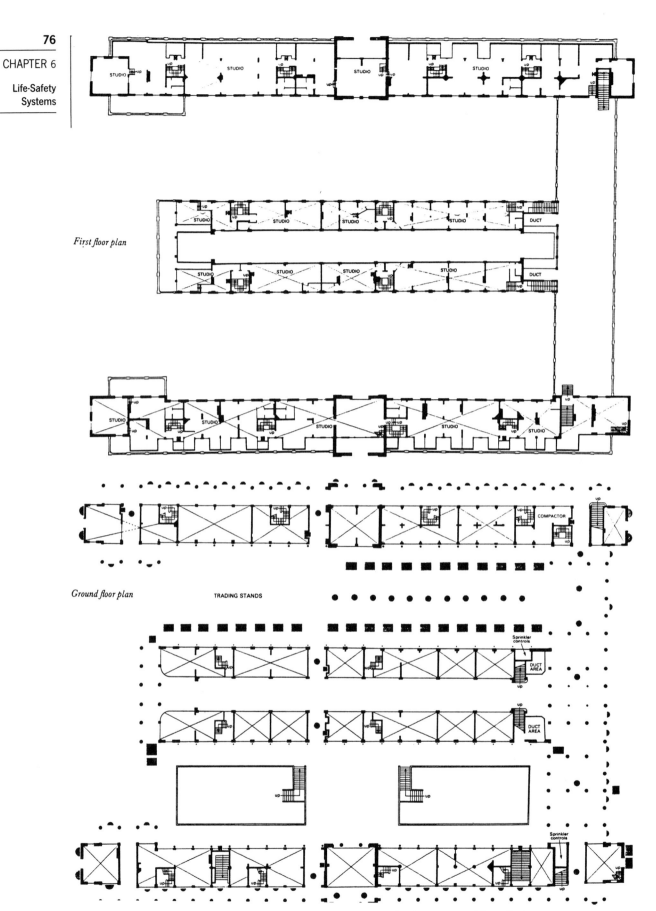

First floor plan

Ground floor plan

TRADING STANDS

Figure 41. The Central Market Building, Covent Garden, London. (*Reproduced with permission of the author.*)

Second floor plan

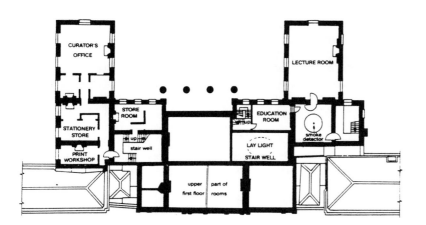

Mezzanine floor plan

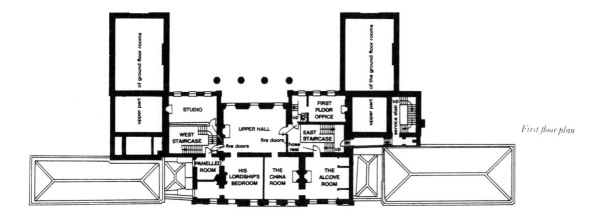

First floor plan

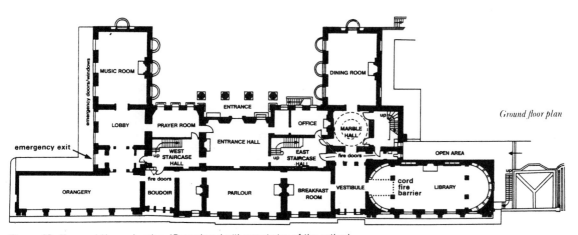

Ground floor plan

Figure 42. Kenwood House, London. (*Reproduced with permission of the author.*)

which can be rolled sideways for rapid access to the hose-reel.

Case study (house museum): Hardwick Hall, Derbyshire, England

This three-story house is one of the most splendid and least altered of all Elizabethan houses. It was built by Smythson for Bess of Hardwick[24] between 1591 and 1597. Its design was revolutionary, consisting of a compact H-plan and an exterior elevation in which the windows increase progressively in height from the ground upward. The house contains the country's finest collection of Elizabethan embroideries and tapestries dating from 1600.

It is provided with a comprehensive fire-detection system consisting of either a mix of ionization, smoke detector units, or rate-of-rise heat detectors. In addition, there are manual *break-glass* fire alarms linked with the detection system.

An *autodialer* is provided whereby a taped message is sent via the 999 (911 American) telephone circuit to the fire service. *The entire system is serviced and tested twice annually.*

Forty hand fire extinguishers and seven hose-reels are located within the building, which is surrounded by nine fire hydrants, and all the façades are accessible for ladders and fire appliances.

These arrangements are supplemented by a detailed fire procedure, including the evacuation of visitors from the building and the prohibition of smoking except in the restaurant and shop areas.

Independent consultants were brought in to see whether alternative ways could be found of ensuring that visitors and staff could escape from the premises without risk from fire or smoke, while maintaining the character of the interior.

Of the alternative approaches which can be adopted to achieve this objective, the most important is based on a comprehensive fire-engineering appraisal. The aspects which have a bearing on this approach include

1. The fire load of the contents, surface, and structure.
    a. In determining the fire load, two features, listed in order of priority, were considered to reduce significantly the fire risk:
       (1) The height of the individual rooms.
       (2) The relatively low fire load of the contents.
2. The speed with which escape routes could become smoke-logged.
    a. As the ceilings are so high compared with the doorway openings, a deep smoke reservoir would be formed, delaying the spread of smoke to other areas of the house.

It has been possible to indicate the potential fire size based on the type of furniture and furnishings within the building. This, in turn, has allowed an evaluation to be made of the smoke emission, the temperature, and the depth of the smoke layer. Evaluation of smoke-layer level has made it possible to show how quickly conditions in individual rooms will become unsuitable for sustaining life.

The fire authority requested that the house be divided into a series of fire zones and that the majority of doors serving the route used by the public should be provided with *self-closing doors,* with a half-hour standard of fire resistance. The doors to any room or space other than those which are entered by the public are kept locked shut. Locked doors may not have a full standard of fire resistance, but as the areas behind them are monitored by the automatic fire-detection system, they are ensured an early warning of fire. This approach, taken in conjunction with the fire-engineering analysis, would appear to be satisfactory for a building of this type.

Case study (hotel): Cliveden Manor, Buckinghamshire, England (Fig. 43)

Cliveden is one of England's great country houses, with a magnificent setting on the River Thames. The original house was designed by William Wind for the Duke of Buckingham in 1666. Unfortunately, a large part of the house was destroyed by fire in 1793, and in about 1850 the Duke of Sutherland employed Sir Charles Barry to design the present mansion.

In 1984 it was leased to Blakeney Hotels, who required considerable restoration and conversion work. The architects were Messrs. William Bertram and Fell.

The premises consist of a central mansion of three stories 150 ft long with two wings of two stories, united by a common basement and served by link corridors at ground and basement levels.

Because of the elements of structure and the surface finishes of walls and ceilings, it was apparent that it would be virtually impossible to comply with the regulations in the normal way without destroying many of the historically or architecturally important parts of the building. It would have entailed removing almost every ceiling and applying protection to the wrought-iron beams which support the upper floors.

The property did have, however, the following:

1. Substantial floors

2. Voids between ceilings and floors range from 1.08 to 1.64 ft (0.33 to 0.5 m) or more

Figure 43. Cliveden, Buckinghamshire, England.

---

[24] Bess of Hardwick (the Countess of Shrewsbury) was a friend of the first Queen Elizabeth. She married successively richer husbands until most of England was owned by these two women. She was an innovative client and commissioned many structures which changed the look of architecture from then on. Large windows and wide, sweeping staircases were some of the features which brought the Renaissance to medieval Britain.

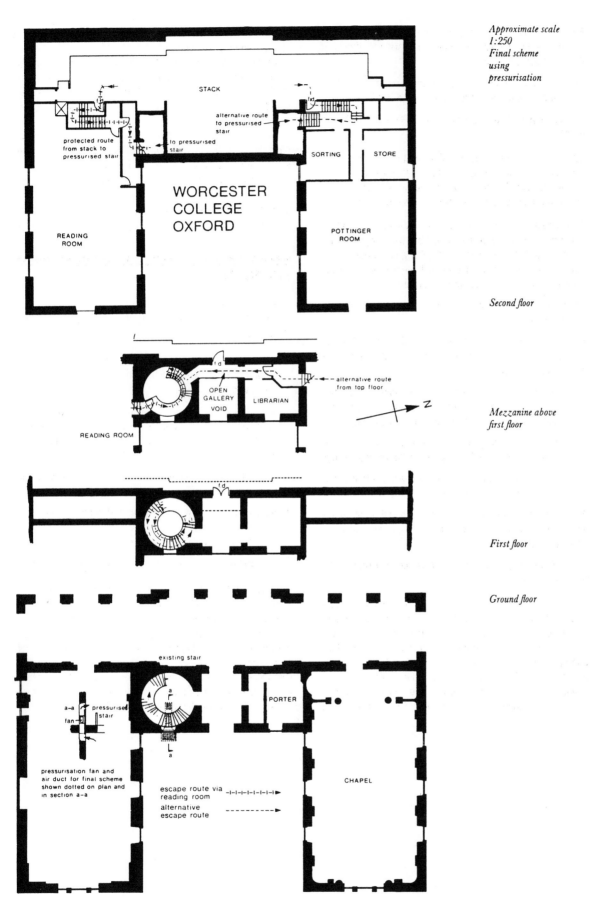

Approximate scale
1:250
Final scheme
using
pressurisation

79

CHAPTER 6

Life-Safety
Systems

Second floor

*Mezzanine above
first floor*

First floor

Ground floor

Figure 44. Worcester College, Oxford University, England. (*Reproduced with permission of the author.*)

3. Beams of heavy construction, together with the timber floor and the ceiling beneath, which would resist the effects of fire and heat for a long time

4. Corridors on the upper floors with a height of 9.8 ft (~3 m) and width of 9.2 to 9.8 ft (2.8 to 3 m)

5. Ceiling height on the ground floor in excess of 19.6 ft (6 m)

Again, a fire-engineering appraisal was required. It was found that if a combination of compensatory measures were introduced, it was possible to carry out the conversion without impairing the character of the house. These included

1. Reducing the fire load on the premises by installing furniture and fittings which were incombustible to a degree compatible with hotel use, such as providing hardwood tables and chairs, and curtains and other hangings of inherently nonflammable or durable flameproof fabric

2. Providing separate storage facilities for spare furnishings and bedding

3. Extending the fire-detection system to include all bedrooms, suites, and function rooms and connecting it directly to a central alarm depot

4. Providing hose-reels on escape routes adjacent to stair enclosures, and fire extinguishers in kitchens, boiler rooms, electrical intake rooms, and other special risk areas

5. Sealing up all openings where ventilation ducts, service piping, and cables passed through walls, floors, and ceilings

6. Installing magnetic handles on many of the doors that would *fail-safe* when the fire-alarm system operated

7. Ensuring that all staff received instruction in fire drill, keeping a log book and displaying plans of all floors at each ground-floor entrance

Case study (library): Worcester College, Oxford University, England (Fig. 44)

The object of the project was to provide adequate means of escape from the extended library within the roof space. The drawings show the rather complicated layout of the new stack area above the main library. Fire service advice had been to provide an alternative escape stairway from the north end near the Pottinger room. The problem was to find an acceptable path down through or past the chapel below. The first proposal faced very strong opposition from The Victorian

Society because of the damage it would have done to the chapel's internal decorations.

Therefore, a specialist fire engineering consultancy, Fire Check Consultants, was engaged, and with the cooperation of the fire service, demonstrated that an *air-pressurization system* could be used to prevent fire or smoke from spreading into the existing spiral stair.

The fan and motor for the pressurization system are in a pit below the spiral stair and the only visible sign of their existence is a grille in the ground floor of the stair.

A stair through the chapel was not required because, as a result of the use of pressurization, the independent routes from the second floor could be brought together at first-floor—mezzanine level and permitted to share the single staircase.

SUMMARY

Where any question of measures to save life are concerned, in particular fire safety and structural measures, the emphasis should be on

1. Requirements being expressed in terms of *performance standards* to allow *flexibility* in the ways whereby unavoidable needs may be met

2. Research, including case studies of fires that have occurred in historic buildings, to check the effects of upgrading to meet the requirements and the result of failing to take action

3. Tests on historic building components to see how far they meet requirements

4. Research in to new techniques and, where these prove suitable, their recognition by the authorities concerned as a means of meeting specific requirements

5. Preparation of a code of practice for historic buildings

Behind all this lies a need for new attitudes and greater understanding. These imply better education and closer liaison or cooperation among everyone concerned.

[*Author's comment:* Although everyone must know this, it does not hurt to repeat again that smoke detectors or sprinklers *must not be painted in situ.* If special colors are needed, samples should be given to the factory which will bake on the paint. Painting these fittings after installation renders them *useless.*] (End of section adapted from Parnell.)

CHAPTER SEVEN
HEATING, VENTILATING, AIR-CONDITIONING

Figure 45b contains vintage diagrams of heating-ventilating equipment schemes in historic buildings, constructed from 1881 to 1930, many of which are still in existence today. Since they show how the property was put together, they should be of help in figuring how to insert modern systems (or make existing ones operable) in similar structures (Fig. 45c to f).

INTRODUCTION

There are two problems: either to *introduce* a modern air-conditioning system into an existing building which was not constructed for it originally, using interstitial spaces and camouflage, or to *upgrade* the existing systems within the given spaces, without destroying the integrity of the interior.

Proper design of an air-conditioning system will control humidity, heat, condensation, ventilation, pressurization, and air pollution, while extending the life of a beautiful historic structure.

As mentioned earlier, whatever is done must not adversely affect the temperature-humidity balance of the property so that the building starts to age prematurely. This is a severe test of environmental controls. How to select a system compatible with building design is the subject of another book. One thing to remember is that operating and maintenance costs go on year after year, so selection of design and equipment should be made with that in mind. And, a wise person

said, "Once the system is installed, if it's not *properly maintained,* you can forget all that life-cycle cost analysis." Considering that advice, the analysis leading to considerations in upgrading includes the following.

PROPER PLANNING [25]

Prior to starting any work, a *capital improvement master plan must* be done to ensure that the upgrading of mechanical, electrical, plumbing, and life-safety systems does not intrude upon the interior's integrity. This master plan should include

1. *Condition survey* of entire building
   a. Condition of interior spaces
   b. Condition of mechanical, electrical, plumbing, and life-safety systems
   c. Effect of codes on the systems relative to the master plan
   d. Owner's wish list
   e. Discover available spaces for new equipment
2. Established *time frame* or schedule of work (i.e., 1 to 5 years, 1 to 10 years)
3. *Documentation of results* of condition survey for historic purposes

[25] Comments of Salvatore Farruggia, Syska & Hennessy, New York.

STEAM WARMING

AND

VENTILATING APPARATUS.

SIMPLIFIED AND ADAPTED TO WARMING RESIDENCES, PUBLIC
AND PRIVATE BUILDINGS, CHURCHES, ETC.

Hay & Prentice Co.

125 and 127 South Clinton Street,

CHICAGO.

PORTABLE AND BRICK-SET.
OVER 5,000 IN USE.

THE DUNNING SELF-FEEDING
MAGAZINE BOILER.

Proposals, Plans and Estimates Furnished for

STEAM AND HOT WATER

WARMING & VENTILATING APPARATUS

FOR ALL CLASSES OF BUILDINGS.

Combined Steam and Hot Water Apparatus

FOR PRIVATE RESIDENCES.

References in all parts of the Country.

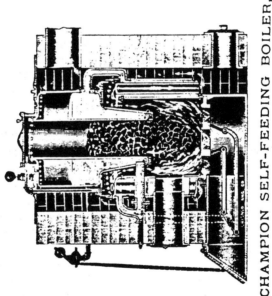

Descriptive Pamphlets on Application.

CHAMPION SELF-FEEDING BOILER,

ALSO

Hot Water Apparatus

FOR WARMING GREENHOUSES, CONSERVATORIES, ETC.

BAKER & SMITH CO.,

CHICAGO, ILL.

81 & 83 Jackson St.

Figure 45a(1). Vintage heating-ventilating advertisements (1888; from *The Inland Architect*).

The "Eclipse" Dining-Room Radiator

Patented August 30, 1887.

Top, showing Tile Decorations.

Can be decorated with porcelain tiles or electro-bronze panels, and the ornamental work of closet and top may be of iron, electro-bronze or nickel-plate.

——— Manufactured by ———

THE ECLIPSE M'F'G CO., 418 Rookery B'ld'g, Chicago.

The Sturtevant

STEAM HOT BLAST APPARATUS

for — HEATING *and* —

VENTILATING

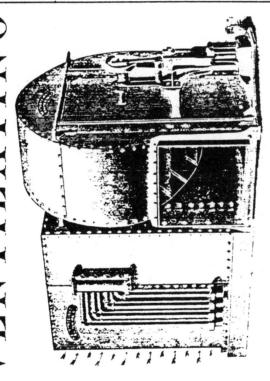

BUILDINGS of ALL KINDS.

A Positive Circulation of warm, fresh air always assured.

——— Send for Illustrated Treatise on Ventilation and Heating. ———

B. F. STURTEVANT, Boston, Mass.

SALESROOM, 115 Purchase St.   OFFICE AND WORKS, Jamaica Plain.

——— BRANCHES: ———

115 Liberty St., NEW YORK.   31 North Canal St., CHICAGO.

Please mention THE INLAND ARCHITECT when corresponding with Advertisers.

Figure 45a(2). Vintage heating-ventilating advertisements (1888; from *The Inland Architect*).

Figure 45a(1). Vintage heating-ventilating advertisements (1888; from *The Inland Architect*).

4. An *action plan*
   a. All items coordinated closely among the owner and a general contractor/construction manager who can help with costs and scheduling of work
   b. Design team consisting of owner, architect, engineers, and contractors, who will control costs and scheduling problems
5. Checklist including
   a. Type of system
   b. Fuel type
   c. Distribution system
   d. Generation system
   e. Codes, regulations, and standards
6. Getting electric power to the systems = the electrical system

   a. Reusing existing spaces
   b. Finding available space to conceal work
   c. Lacking that, creating sympathetic space
   d. Cutting and patching original fabric
7. Ducting and piping
   a. Using existing ducts wherever possible
   b. Finding ways to conceal new ducts and/or piping
   c. Providing adequate access for repair or removal
8. Accessories
   a. Flues and chimneys
   b. Noise and vibration
   c. Fuel storage
9. Protection of the building while under construction
10. Placement of equipment (Fig. 46).
11. Damping of vibration and absorbing noise

Protection of the building during construction (item 9) cannot be overemphasized because of the unique value of the historic building. The placement of exterior equipment (item 10) should be carefully thought out. This is not even a question of time or money, but of simple common-sense planning. The significant roofline of a handsome Beaux Arts railway station was compromised by placing the air-handling units too near the front of the roof (Fig. 46a). There was plenty of space a few feet back, utilization of which would not have created those extraneous lumps.

An infestation of window units indicates *a lack of central planning over time,* and that some other method of cooling should be used. Besides the aesthetics, all those drooling units are eating up the window sills, and moisture is probably filtering through the walls. Also, energy could be saved by using a different method.

In a 1920s hotel, there was enough space above the ballroom ceiling for a person to stand up. It was ignored and the ducts were surface-mounted so that the beautiful arches were obliterated (Fig. 46b).

In a famous hotel built in 1912, there were already perfectly good ventilation ducts. Unfortunately, they were not used during renovation. Instead, the designer unnecessarily wrecked the interior by gouging out marble pillars for new vents (Fig. 46c).

THE BOLTON HEATER IN POSITION.

THE
Detroit Heating and Lighting Co's
HOT WATER HEATER.
(Bolton's Patent.)

"The Most Economical and the Best."

COMBINATION GAS MACHINE FOR LIGHTING
ALL KINDS OF BUILDINGS.

GAS STOVES AND STRAIGHTWAY VALVES.

DETROIT HEATING AND LIGHTING CO.
DETROIT, MICH., and CHICAGO, ILL.

The Jackson Heat-Saving and Ventilating Grate.
COMBINED GRATE AND FURNACE

HEATING ON ONE OR TWO FLOORS.

EDWIN A. JACKSON & BRO.,
50 BEEKMAN ST., NEW YORK.

Figure 45a(2). Vintage heating-ventilating advertisements (1888; from *The Inland Architect*).

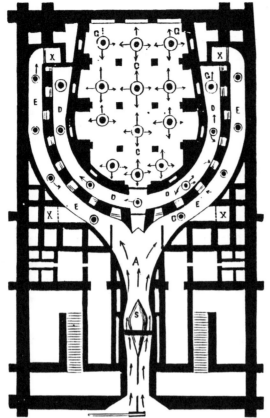

A.—Fresh Air Chamber.
B. C. D. E.—Heating Chambers.
G —Tubes for Fresh Cold Air.
H.—Foul Air Shaft.
S.—Fresh Air Fan.
U.—Foul Air or Aspirating Fan.

Figure 45b(1). Vienna's Grand Opera House, plan (1881).

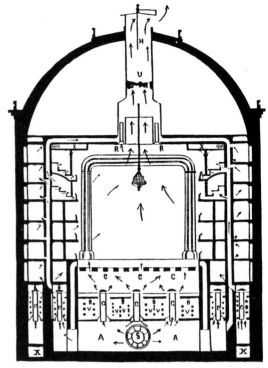

A.—Fresh Air Chamber.
B. C. D. E.—Heating Chambers.
G —Tubes for Fresh Cold Air.
H.—Foul Air Shaft.
S.—Fresh Air Fan.
U.—Foul Air or Aspirating Fan.

Figure 45b(2). Vienna's Grand Opera House, section (1881).

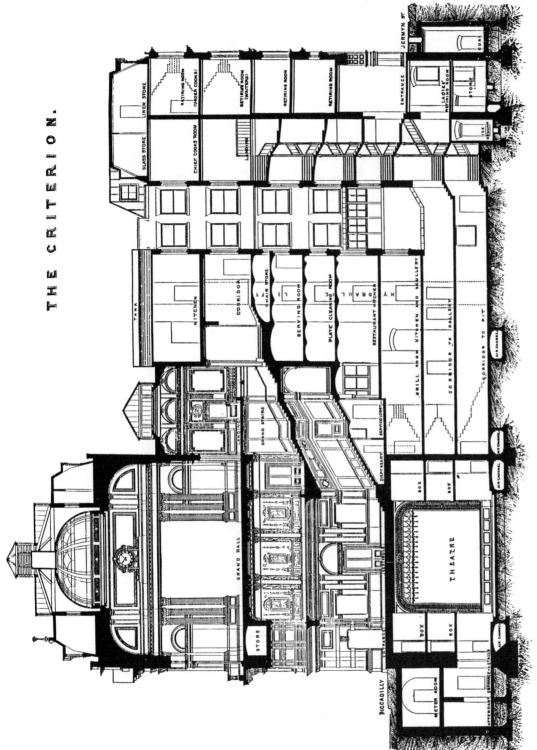

Figure 45b(3). Theater (1882).

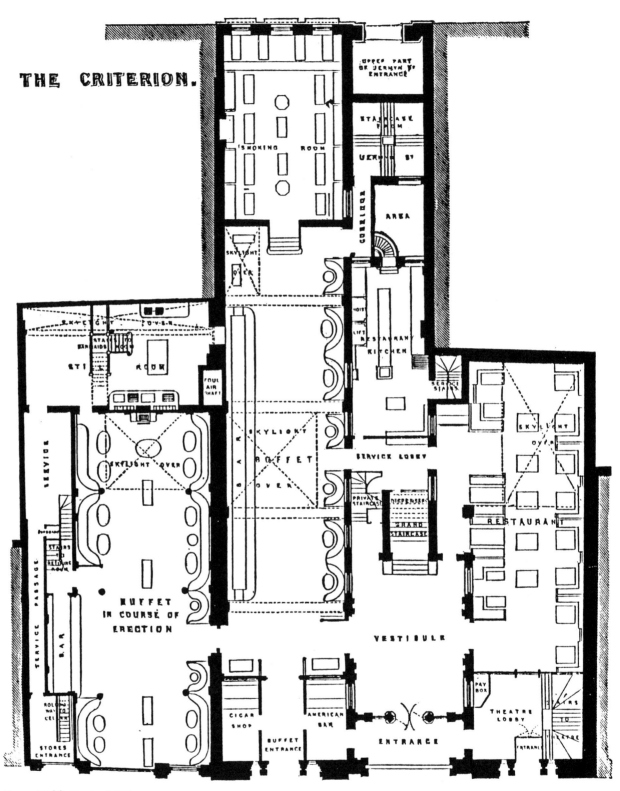

Figure 45b(4). Theater (1882).

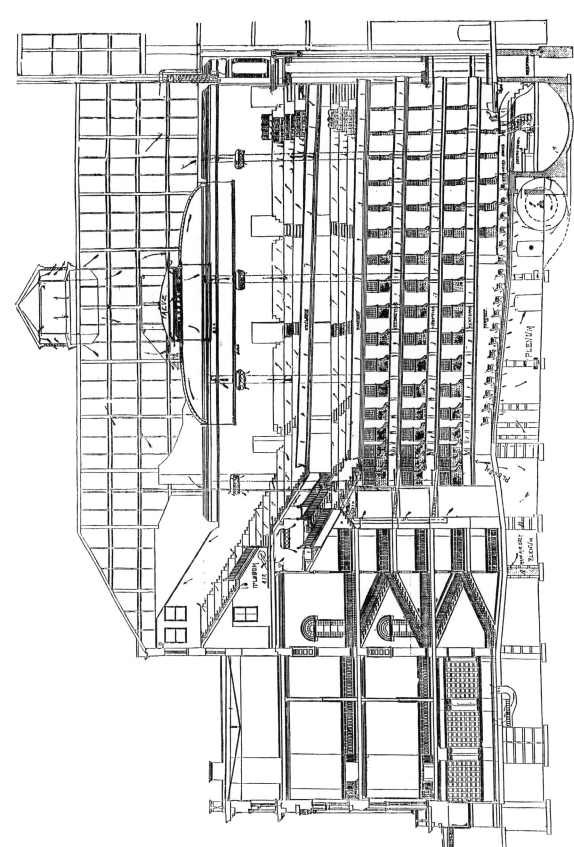

Figure 45b(5). Theater (1883).

METROPOLITAN OPERA HOUSE. NEW YORK CITY.—LONGITUDINAL SECTION.

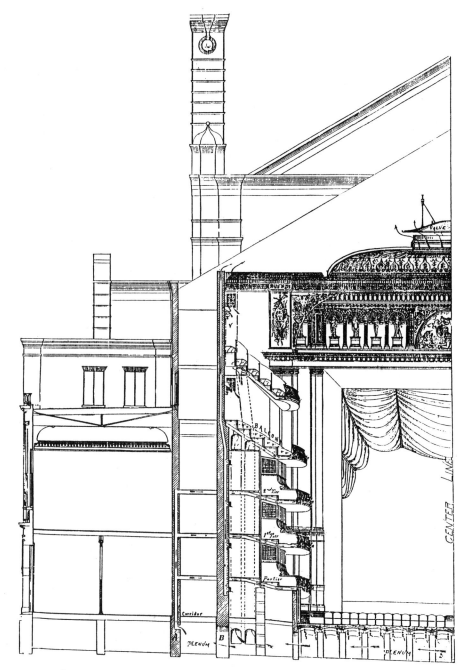

METROPOLITAN OPERA HOUSE, NEW YORK CITY.—TRANSVERSE SECTION

Figure 45b(6). Theater (1883).

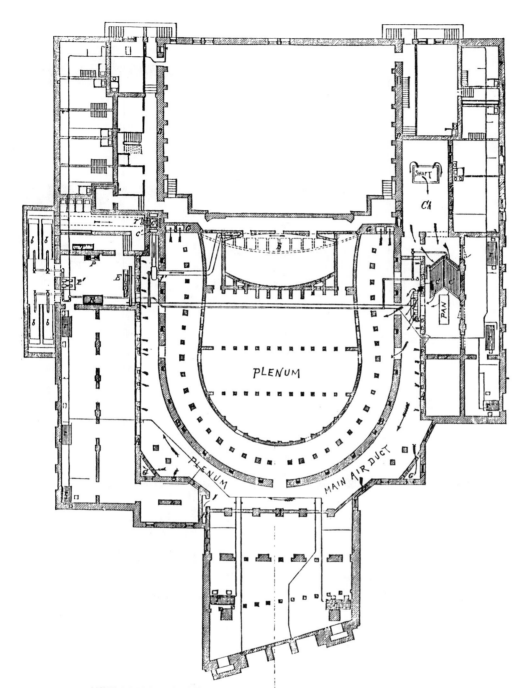

METROPOLITAN OPERA HOUSE, NEW YORK CITY, GROUND PLAN.

Figure 45b(7). Theater (1883).

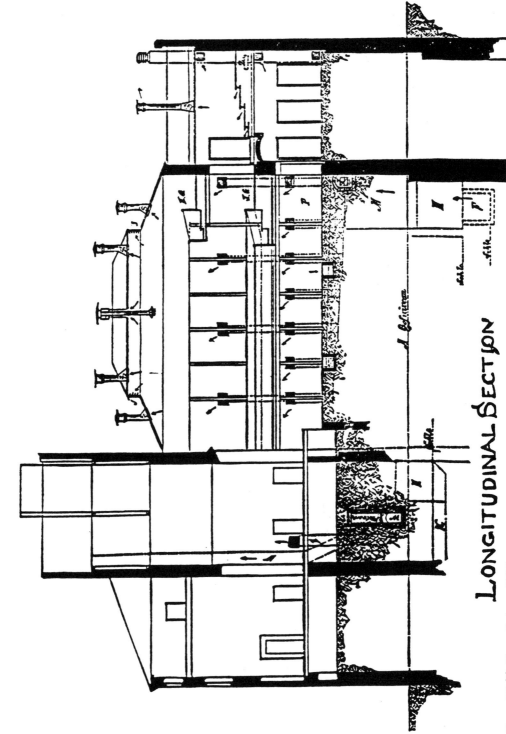

LONGITUDINAL SECTION

Figure 45b(8). Vienna Orpheum (1886).

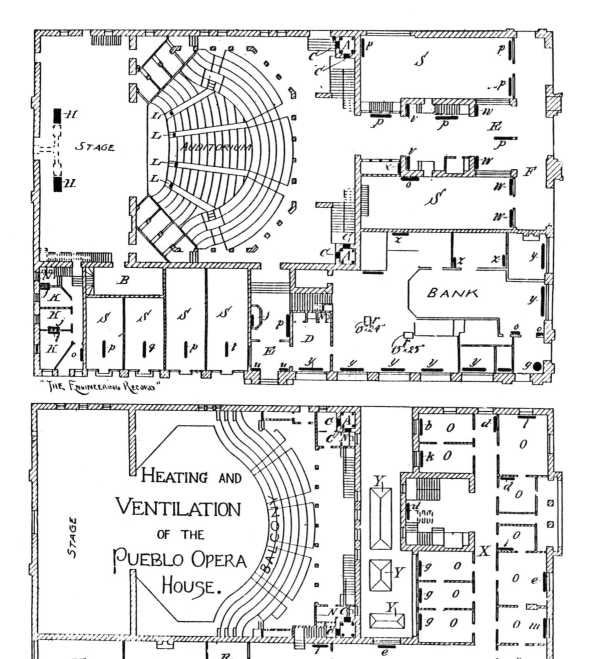

Figure 45b(9). Theater (1891).

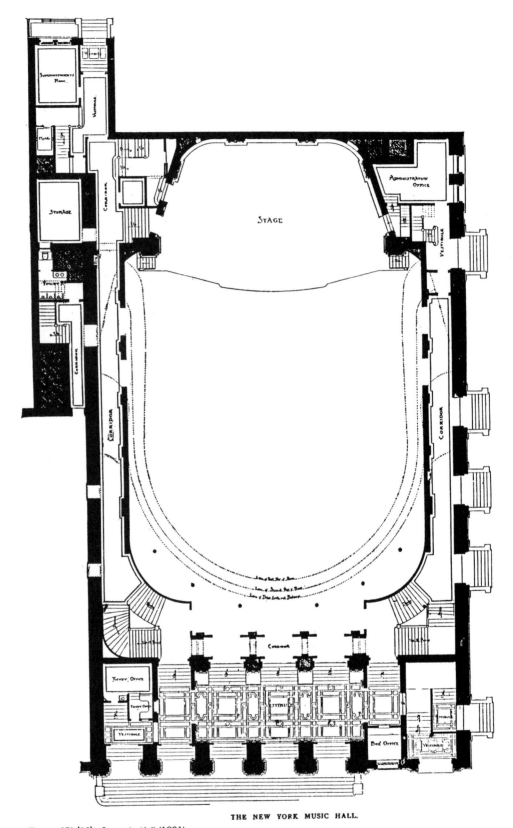

THE NEW YORK MUSIC HALL.

Figure 45b(10). Carnegie Hall (1891).

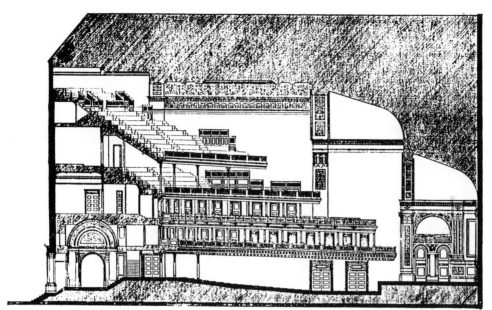

GENERAL SECTION THROUGH MUSIC HALL.

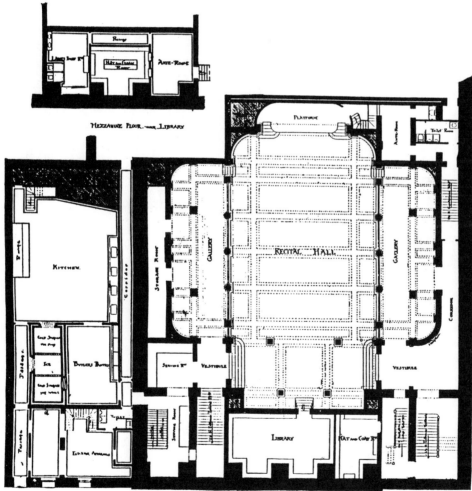

PLAN OF RECITAL HALL.

Figure 45b(11). Carnegie Hall (1891).

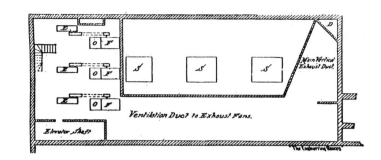

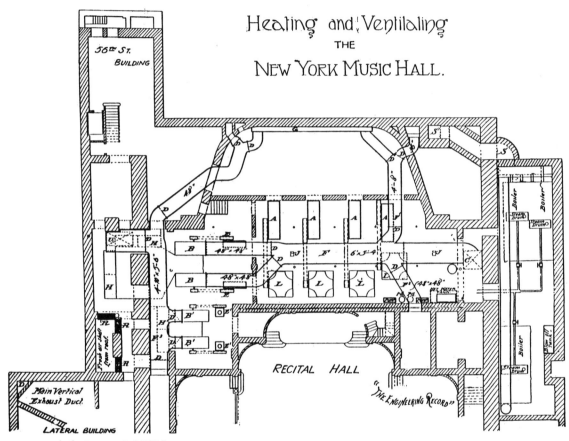

Figure 45b(12). Carnegie Hall (1891).

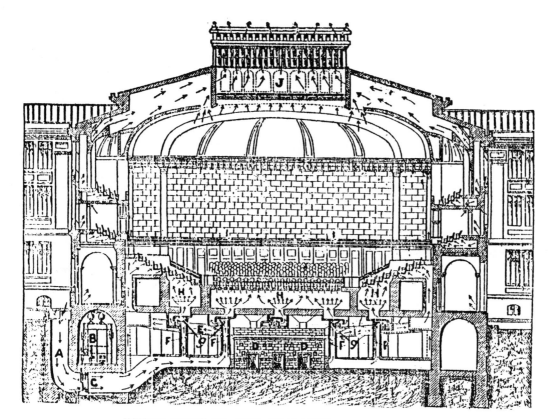

VENTILATION OF THE SORBONNE AMPHITHEATER.

Figure 45b(13). Theater (1892).

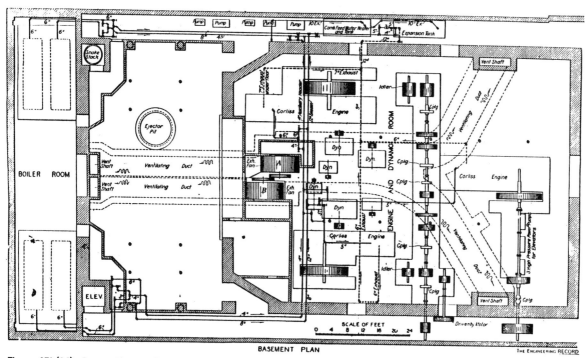

Figure 45b(14). German Theater, Chicago (1895).

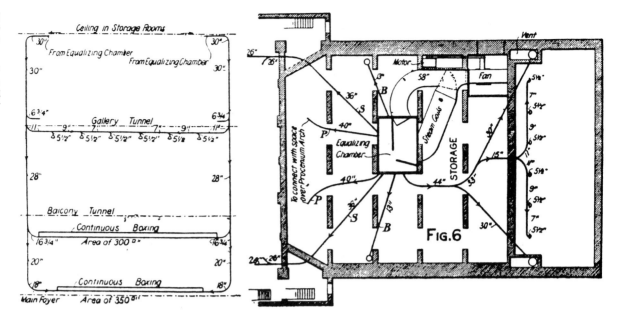

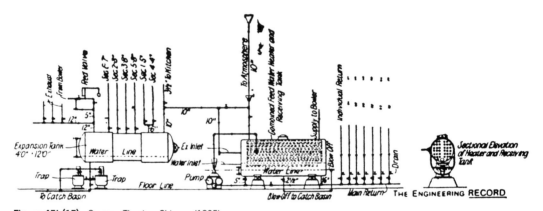

Figure 45b(15). German Theater, Chicago (1895).

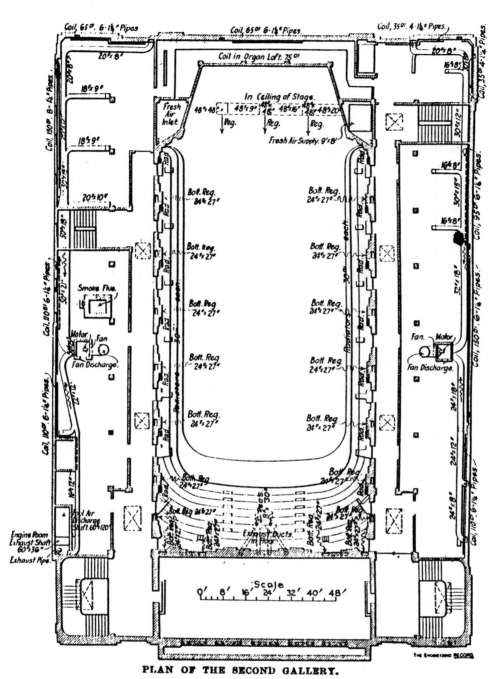

PLAN OF THE SECOND GALLERY.

Figure 45b(16). Symphony Hall, Boston (1901).

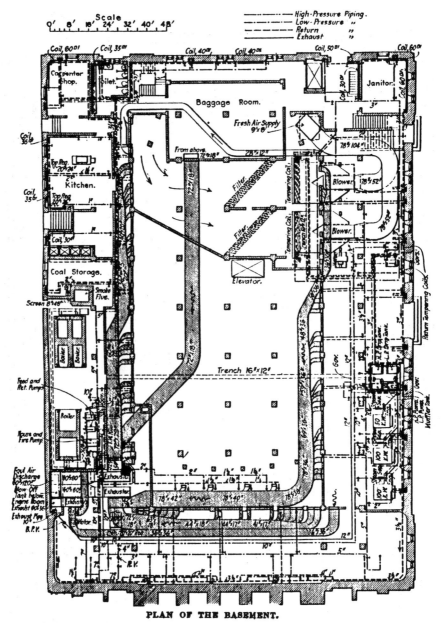

PLAN OF THE BASEMENT.

Figure 45b(17). Symphony Hall, Boston (1901).

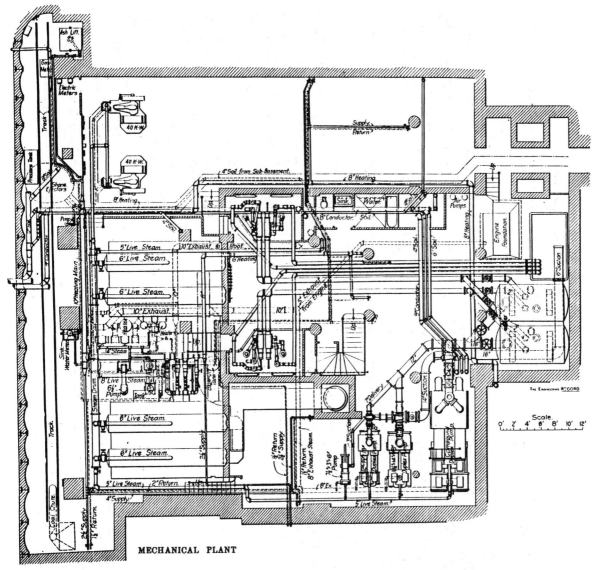

MECHANICAL PLANT

Figure 45b(18). Theater (1901).

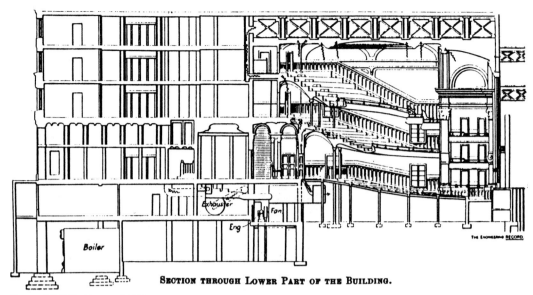

SECTION THROUGH LOWER PART OF THE BUILDING.

Figure 45b(19). Theater (1901).

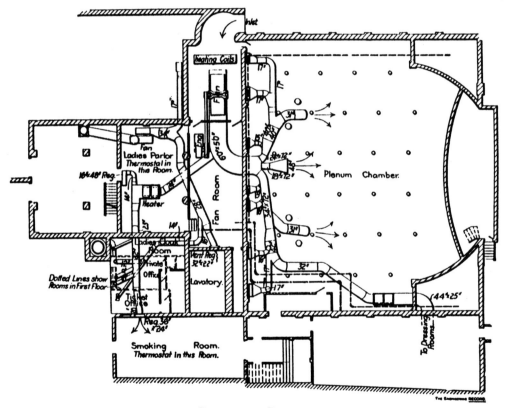

PLAN OF THE BASEMENT.

Figure 45b(20). Theater (1901).

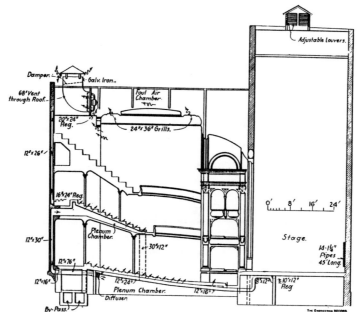

Cross-Section through the Auditorium.

Plan of the Basement of the Franklin Theater, Worcester.

Figure 45b(21). Theater (1904).

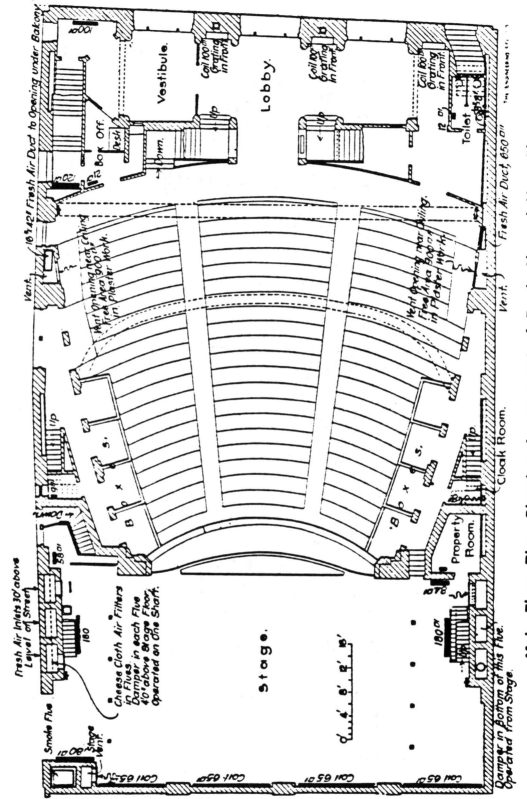

Main Floor Plan, Showing Arrangement of Fresh Air and Vent Flues.

Figure 45b(22). Majestic Theater, Boston (1905).

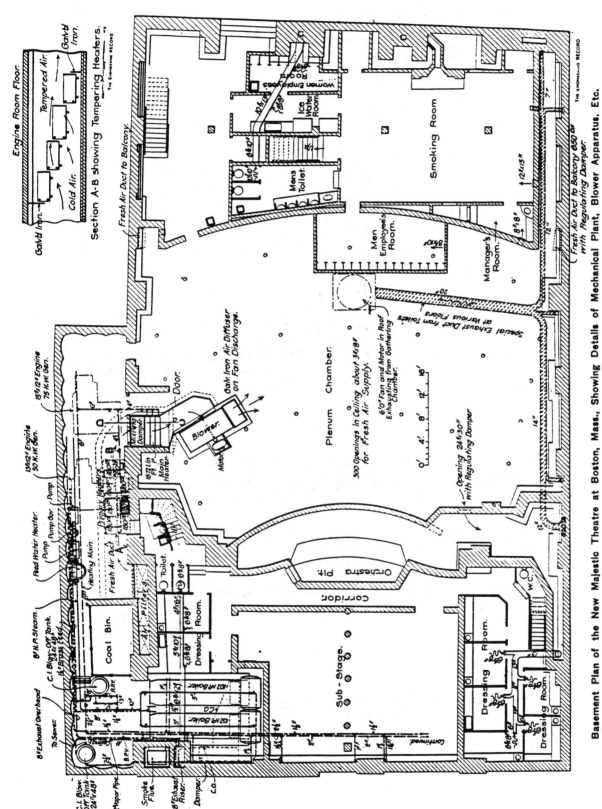

Figure 45b(23). Majestic Theater, Boston (1905).

Basement Plan of the New Majestic Theatre at Boston, Mass., Showing Details of Mechanical Plant, Blower Apparatus, Etc.

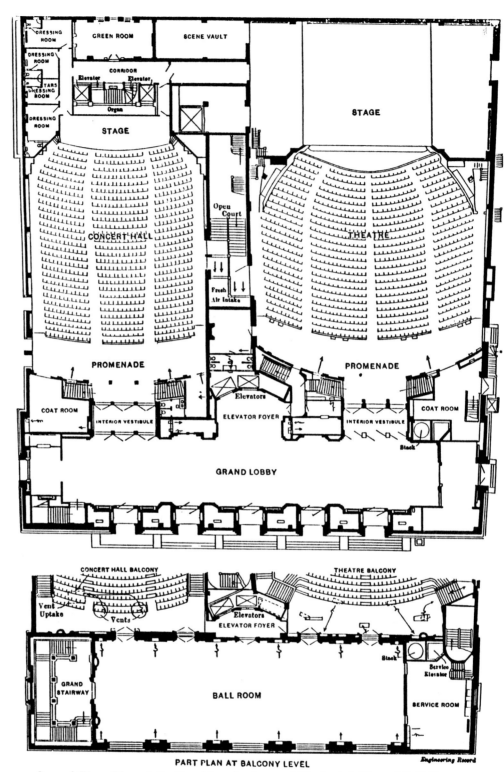

Ground Floor Plan of the Brooklyn Academy of Music and Plan of Ball Room.

Figure 45b(24). Brooklyn Academy of Music (1908).

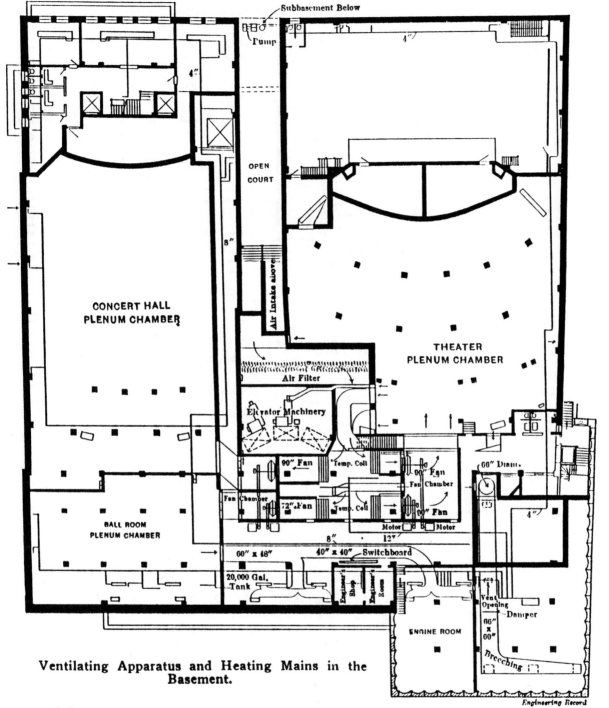

Ventilating Apparatus and Heating Mains in the Basement.

Figure 45b(25). Brooklyn Academy of Music (1908).

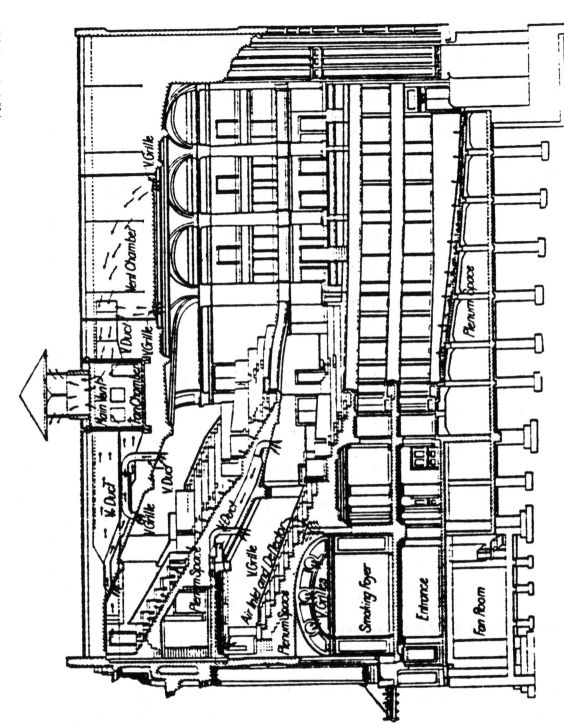

Diagram of General Ventilation Scheme.

Figure 45b(26). Boston Opera House (1911).

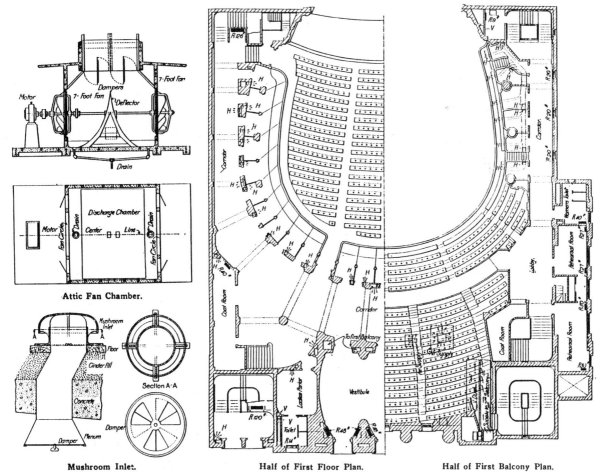

Figure 45b(27). Boston Opera House (1911).

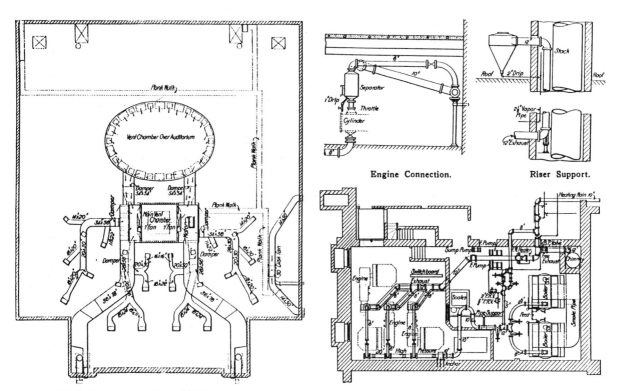

Figure 45b(28). Boston Opera House (1911).

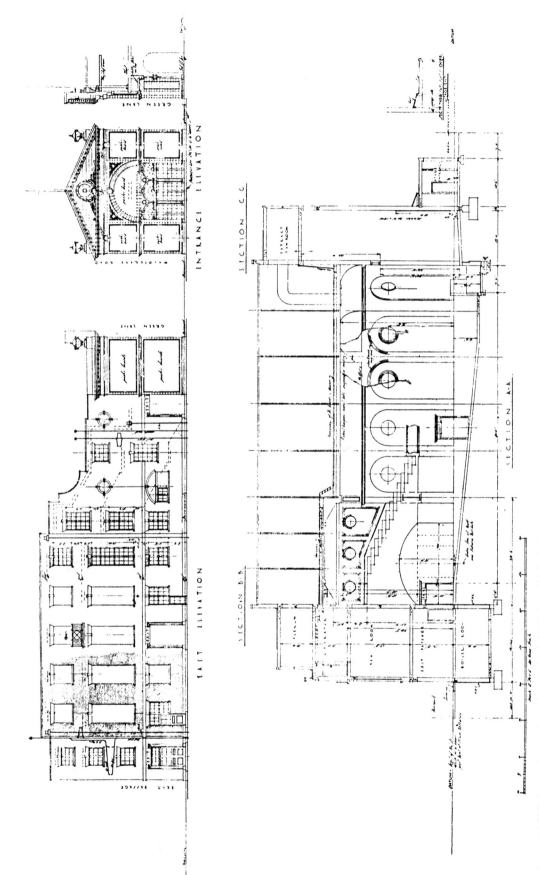

Figure 45b(29). Regent Cinema, Becontree, England (1930; from *The Builder*).

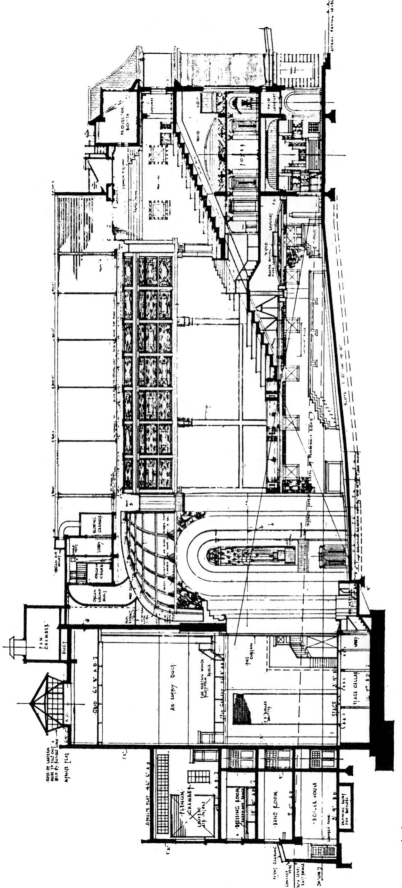

Figure 45b(30). Astoria Cinema, Streatham, England (1930; from *The Builder*).

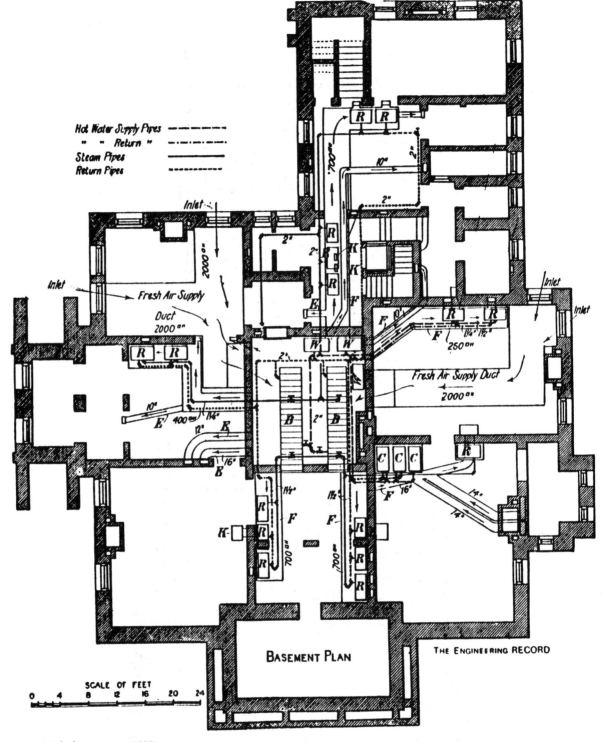

Figure 45b(31). Residence (1895).

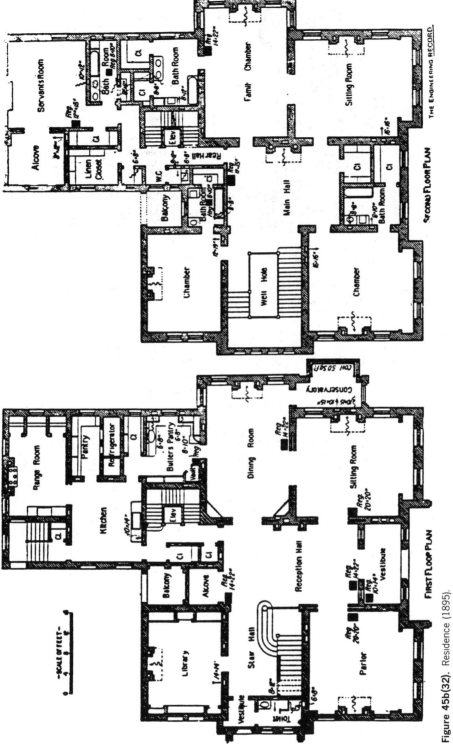

Figure 45b(32). Residence (1895).

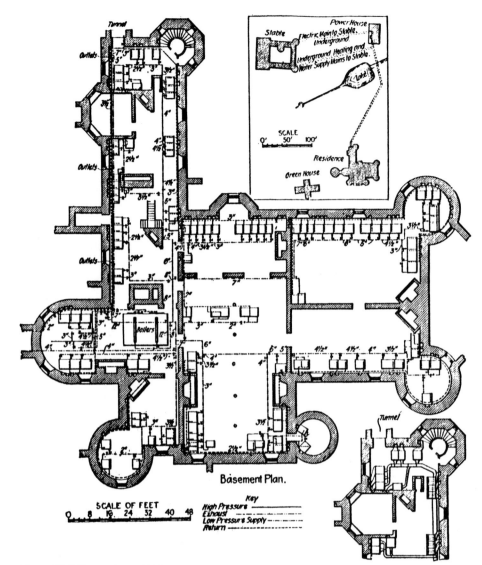

Figure 45b(33). Residence (1896).

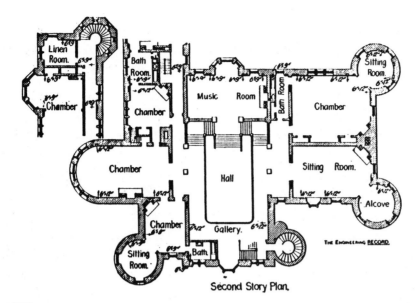

Second Story Plan.

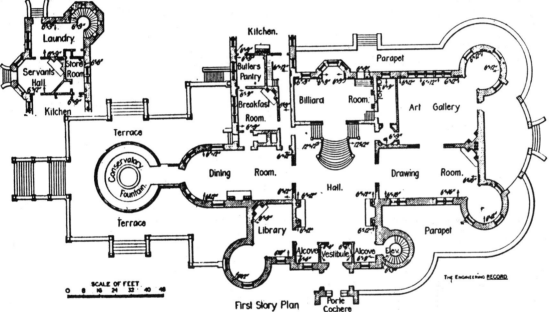

SCALE OF FEET
0   8   16   24   32   40   48

First Story Plan

Porte
Cochere

Figure 45b(34). Residence (1896).

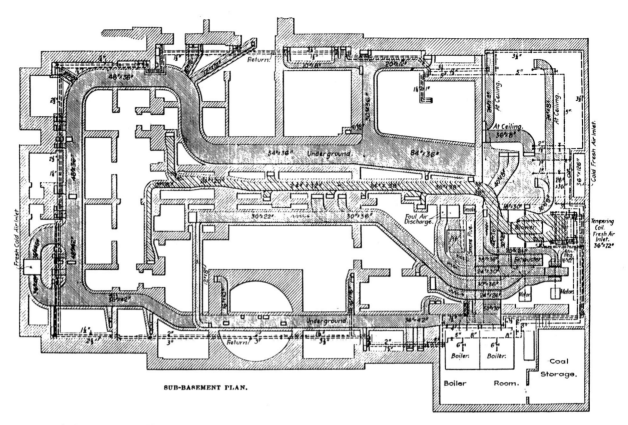

Figure 45b(35). Residence (1899).

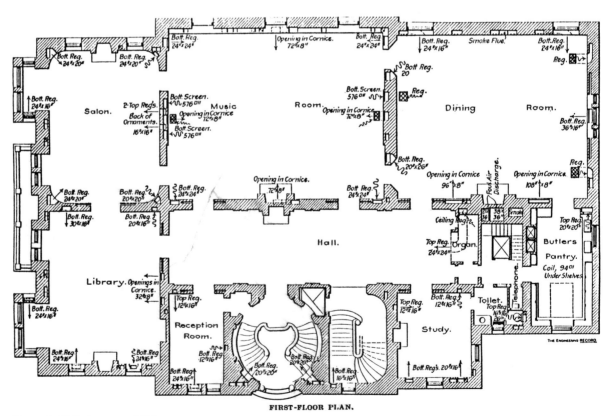

Figure 45b(36). Residence (1899).

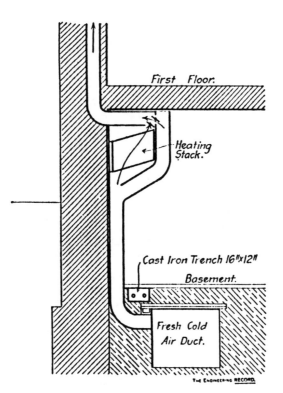

TYPICAL ARRANGEMENT OF THE INDIRECTS.

Figure 45b(37). Residence (1899).

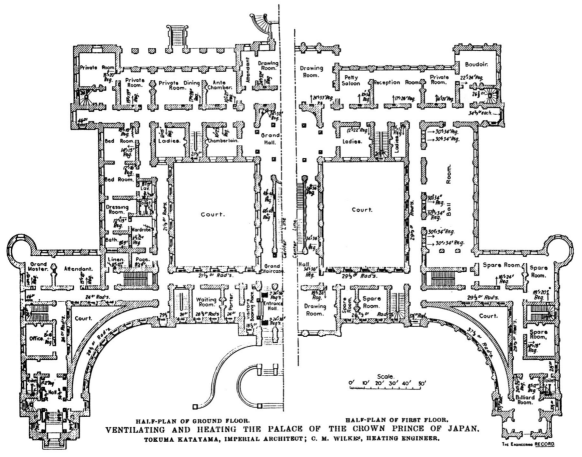

HALF-PLAN OF GROUND FLOOR.   HALF-PLAN OF FIRST FLOOR.
VENTILATING AND HEATING THE PALACE OF THE CROWN PRINCE OF JAPAN.
TOKUMA KATAYAMA, IMPERIAL ARCHITECT; C. M. WILKES, HEATING ENGINEER.

Figure 45b(38). Residence (1901).

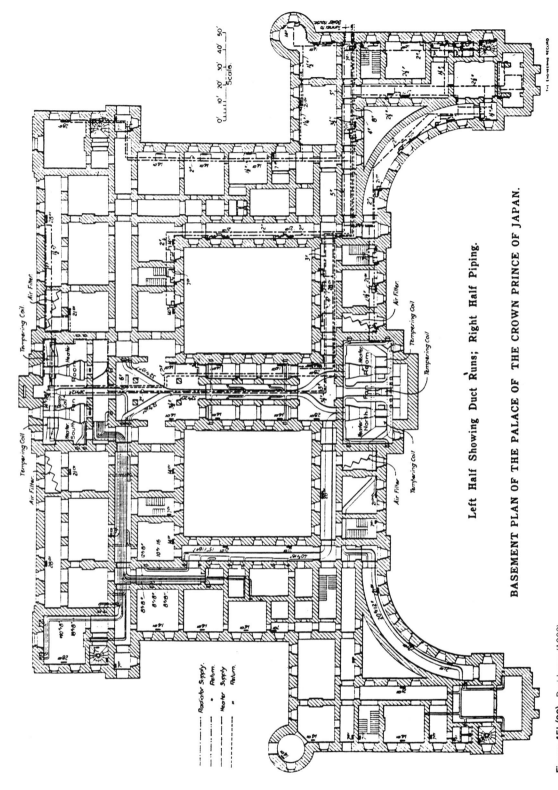

Left Half Showing Duct Runs; Right Half Piping.

BASEMENT PLAN OF THE PALACE OF THE CROWN PRINCE OF JAPAN.

Figure 45b(39). Residence (1903).

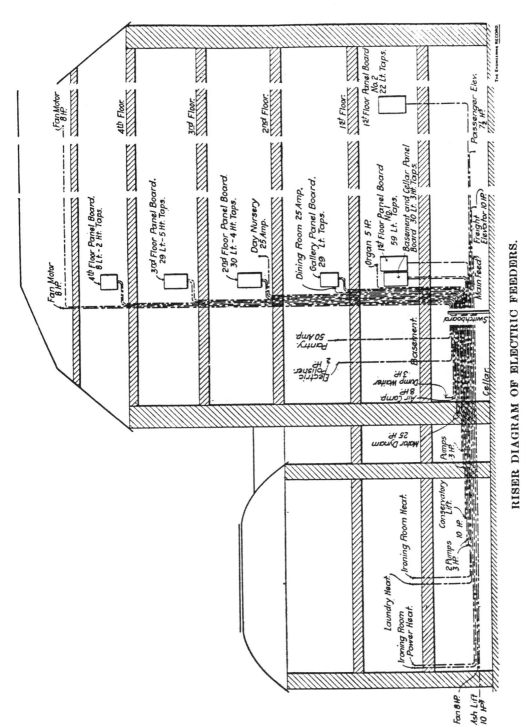

RISER DIAGRAM OF ELECTRIC FEEDERS.

Figure 45b(40). Residence of Andrew Carnegie, New York (1902).

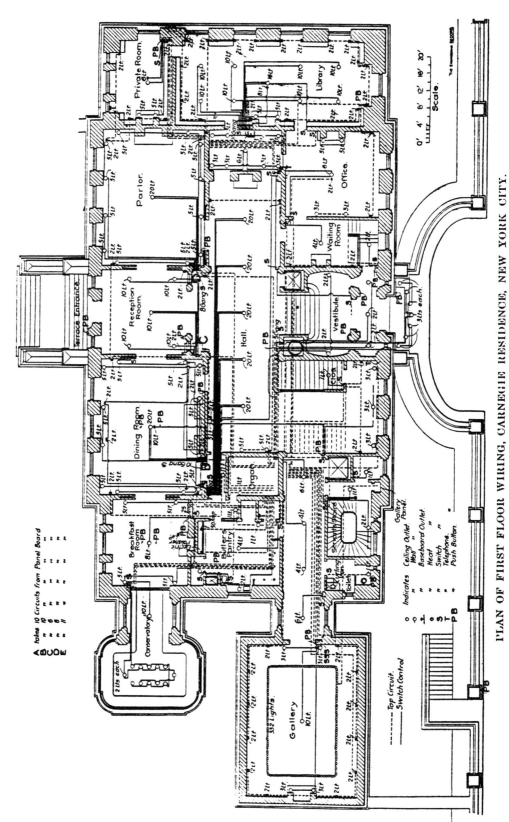

PLAN OF FIRST FLOOR WIRING, CARNEGIE RESIDENCE, NEW YORK CITY.

Figure 45b(41). Residence of Andrew Carnegie, New York (1902).

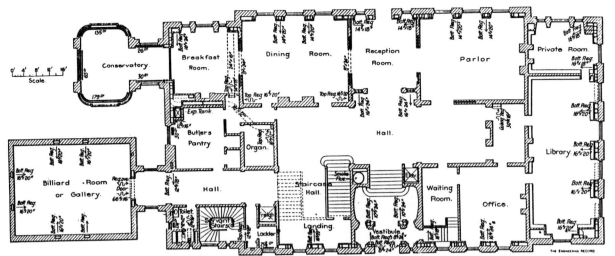

Plan of the First Floor of the Carnegie Residence, New York.

Figure 45b(42). Residence of Andrew Carnegie, New York (1903).

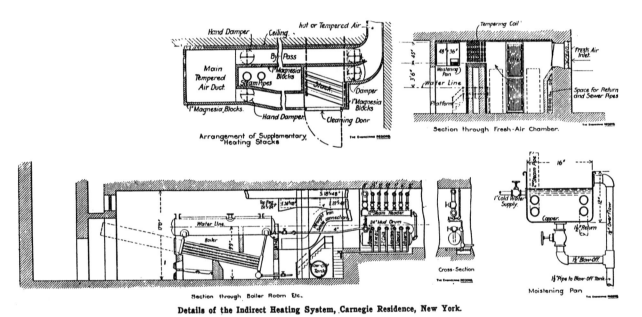

Details of the Indirect Heating System, Carnegie Residence, New York.

Figure 45b(43). Residence of Andrew Carnegie, New York (1903).

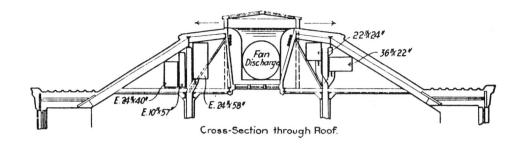

Cross-Section through Roof.

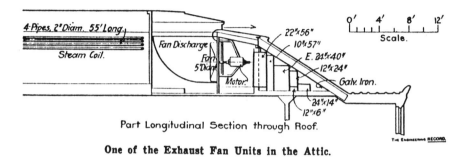

Part Longitudinal Section through Roof.

One of the Exhaust Fan Units in the Attic.

Figure 45b(44). Residence of Andrew Carnegie, New York (1903).

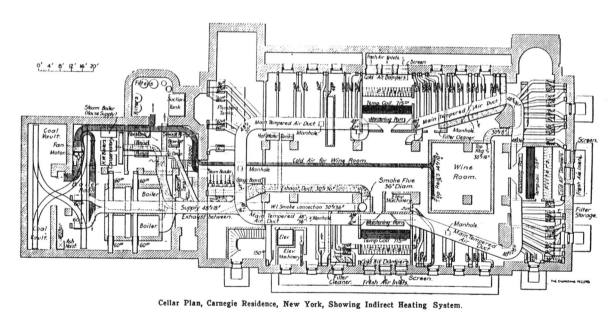

Cellar Plan, Carnegie Residence, New York, Showing Indirect Heating System.

Figure 45b(45). Residence of Andrew Carnegie, New York (1903).

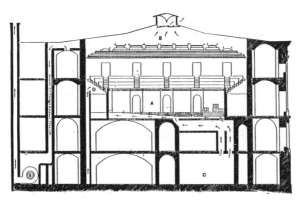

TRANSVERSE SECTION THROUGH SOUTH WING, U. S. CAPITOL.
A—Main Hall; *B*—Space over Hall; *C*—Main Fresh Air Duct; *D*—Fresh Air Supply to Galleries; *E*—Exhaust Fan.

Figure 45b(46). Government building (1881).

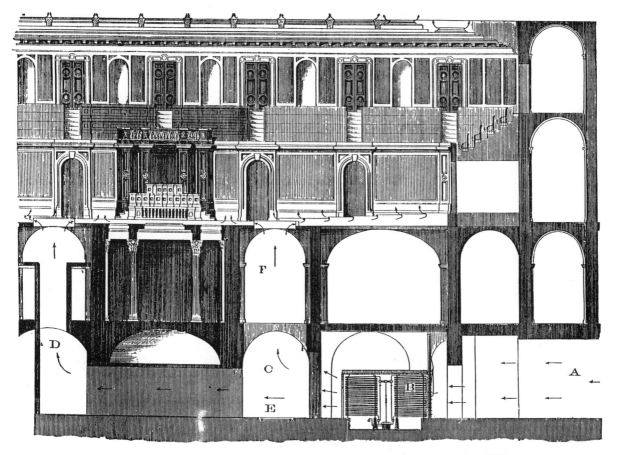

SECTION THROUGH AIR DUCTS AND HEATING APPARATUS OF SOUTH WING, U. S. CAPITOL.
A—Cold Air Duct; *B*—Heating Coil; *C*—Mixing Chamber; *D*—Fresh Air Shaft; *E*—Evaporator; *F*—Fresh Air Shaft.

Figure 45b(47). Government building (1881).

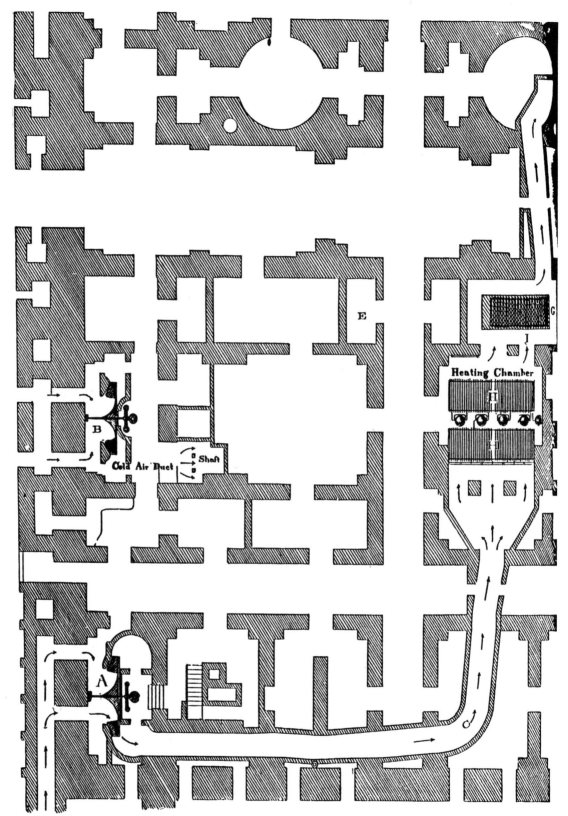

PLAN SHOWING AIR DUCTS, ETC., IN CONNECTION WITH HEATING APPARATUS, SOUTH WING, U. S. CAPITOL.

A—Main Fan for Hall.

B—Small Fan for Committee Rooms.

G—Evaporator and Mixing Chamber.

H—Heating Coils.

Figure 45b(48). Government building (1881).

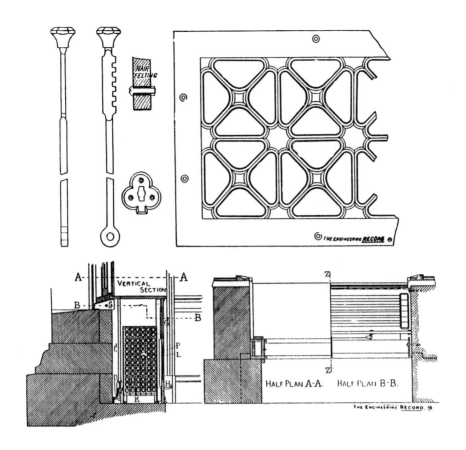

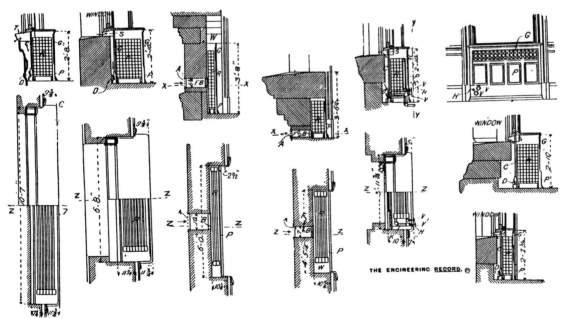

HEATING AND VENTILATION OF THE SUFFOLK COUNTY COURT-HOUSE.

Figure 45b(49). Government building (1893).

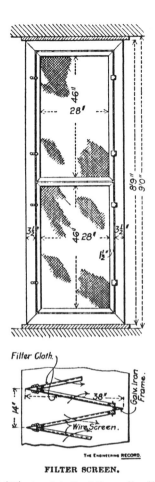

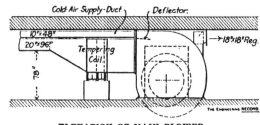

ELEVATION OF MAIN BLOWER.

Figure 45b(51). Appellate Court House, New York (1900).

FILTER SCREEN.

Figure 45b(50). Appellate Court House, New York (1900).

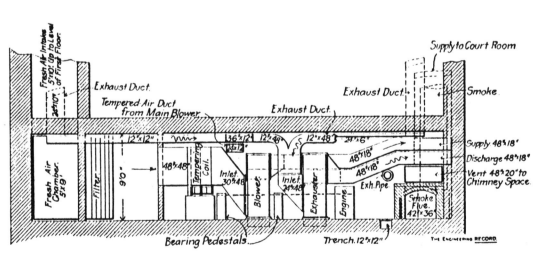

ELEVATION OF COURT-ROOM VENTILATION APPARATUS.

Figure 45b(52). Appellate Court House, New York (1900).

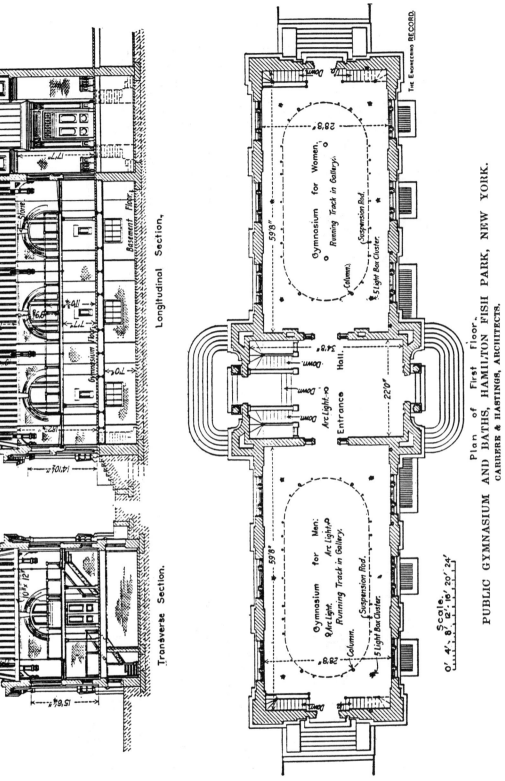

PUBLIC GYMNASIUM AND BATHS, HAMILTON FISH PARK, NEW YORK.

CARRÈRE & HASTINGS, ARCHITECTS.

Figure 45b(53). Government building (1900).

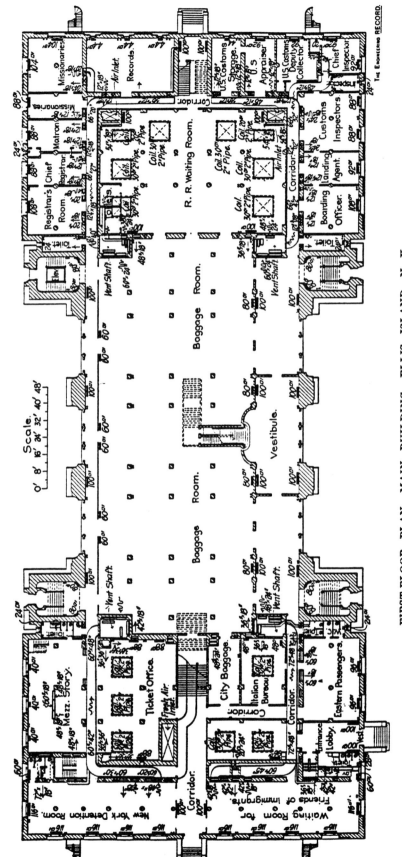

FIRST-FLOOR PLAN, MAIN BUILDING, ELLIS ISLAND, N. Y.

Figure 45b(54). Government building (1901).

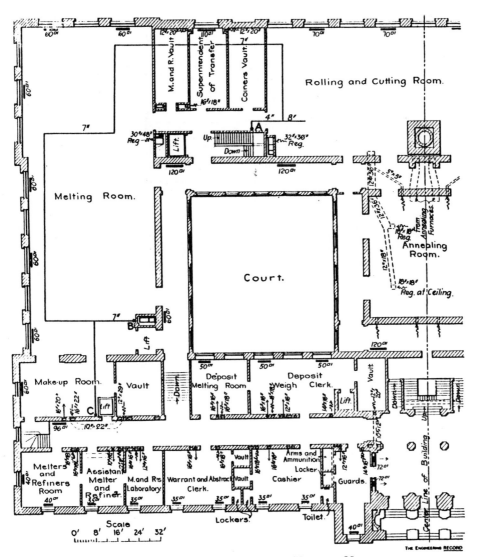

HALF PLAN OF FIRST FLOOR, SHOWING HEATING MAIN.

Figure 45b(55). United States Mint, Philadelphia (1902).

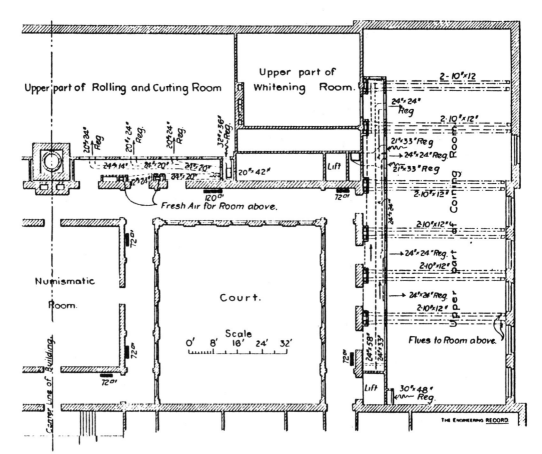

PART PLAN OF THE MEZZANINE STORY.

Figure 45b(56). United States Mint, Philadelphia (1902).

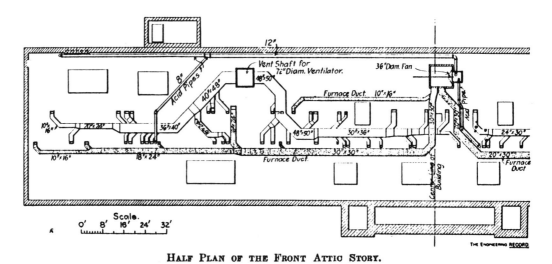

HALF PLAN OF THE FRONT ATTIC STORY.

Figure 45b(57). United States Mint, Philadelphia (1902).

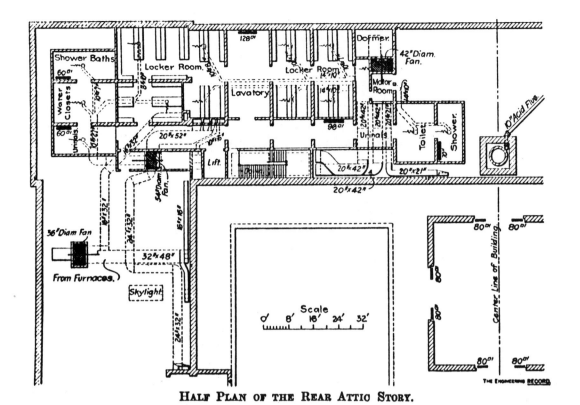

HALF PLAN OF THE REAR ATTIC STORY.

Figure 45b(58). United States Mint, Philadelphia (1902).

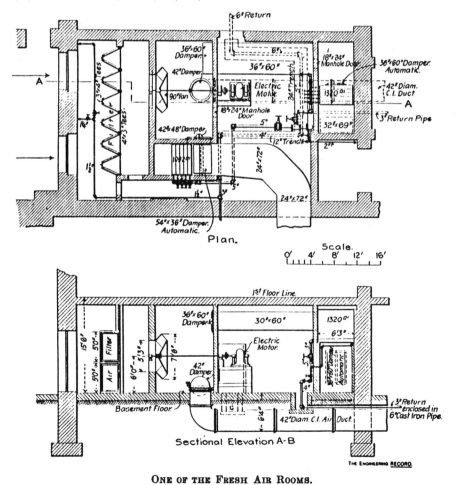

ONE OF THE FRESH AIR ROOMS.

Figure 45b(59). United States Mint, Philadelphia (1902).

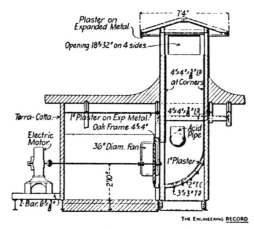

EXHAUST CHAMBER AND FAN.

Figure 45b(60). United States Mint, Philadelphia (1902).

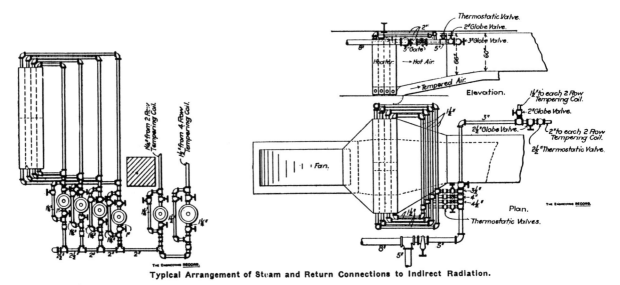

Typical Arrangement of Steam and Return Connections to Indirect Radiation.

Figure 45b(61). Minnesota State Capitol (1904).

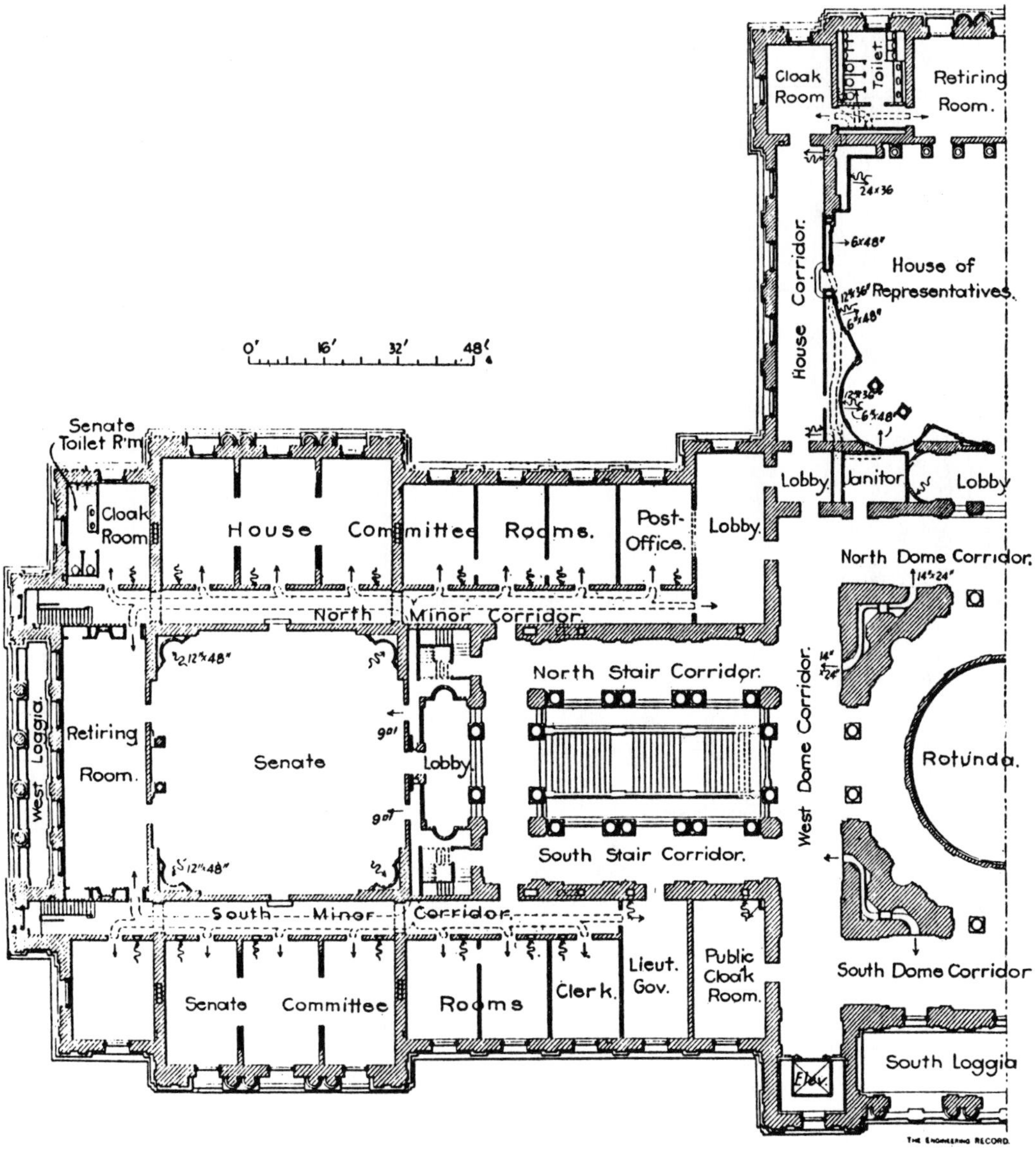

Minnesota State Capitol: Plan of the East Half of the Second Floor.

Figure 45b(62). Minnesota State Capitol (1904).

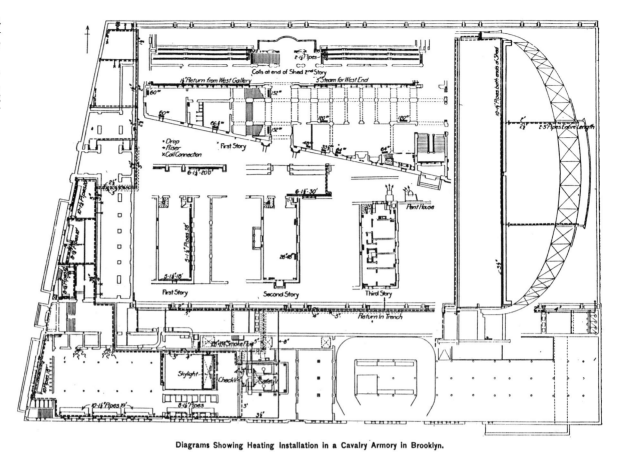

Diagrams Showing Heating Installation in a Cavalry Armory in Brooklyn.

Figure 45b(63). Government building (1905).

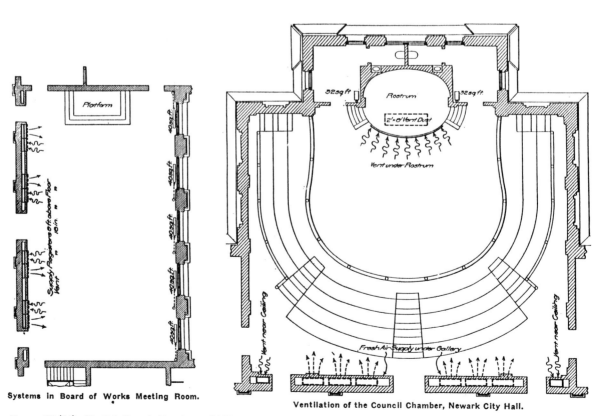

Systems in Board of Works Meeting Room.

Ventilation of the Council Chamber, Newark City Hall.

Figure 45b(64). City Hall, Newark, New Jersey (1907).

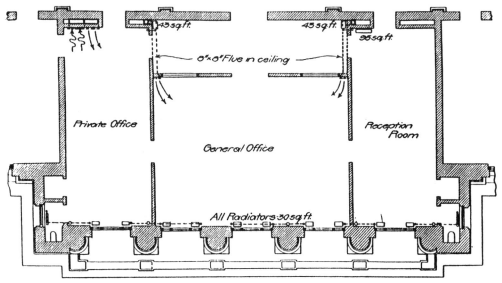

Heating and Ventilation of the Mayor's Office.

Figure 45b(65). City Hall, Newark, New Jersey (1907).

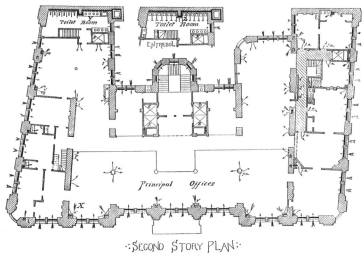

·:SECOND STORY PLAN:·

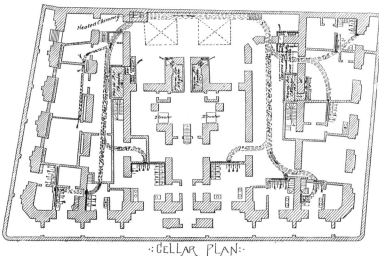

·:CELLAR PLAN:·

MUTUAL LIFE INSURANCE COMPANY'S BUILDING, NEW YORK CITY.—PLANS ILLUSTRATING THE VENTILATION.

Figure 45b(66). Office (1884).

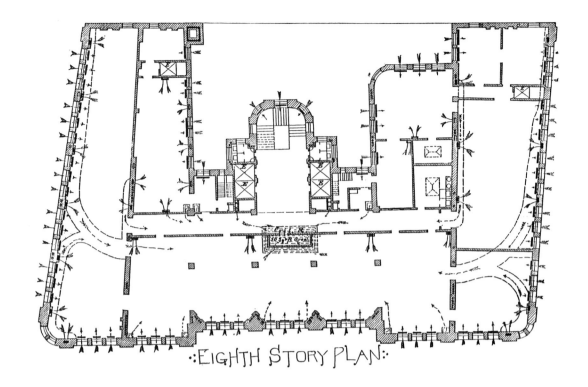

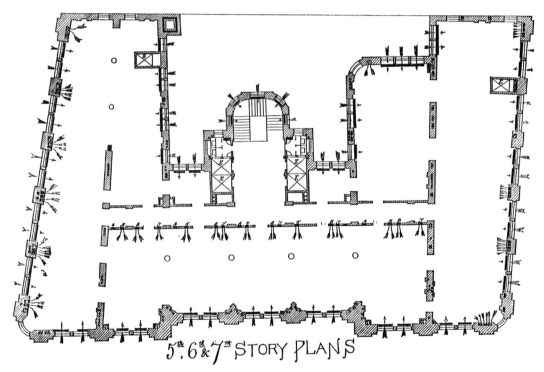

MUTUAL LIFE INSURANCE COMPANY'S BUILDING, NEW YORK CITY.—PLANS ILLUSTRATING THE VENTILATION.

Figure 45b(67). Office (1884).

VENTILATION OF THE PRINCIPAL OFFICE OF THE MUTUAL LIFE INSURANCE BUILDING.

Figure 45b(68). Office (1884).

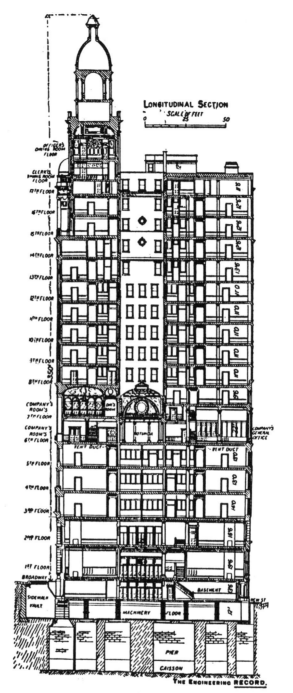

THE MANHATTAN LIFE INSURANCE BUILDING,
NEW YORK CITY.

Figure 45b(69). Office (1884).

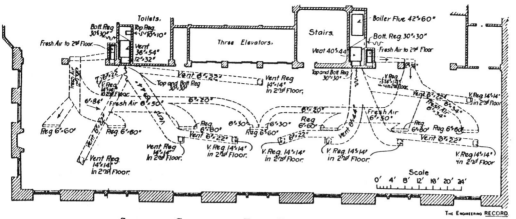

SUSPENDED CEILING OVER FRONT PART OF FIRST STORY.

Figure 45b(70). Office (1901).

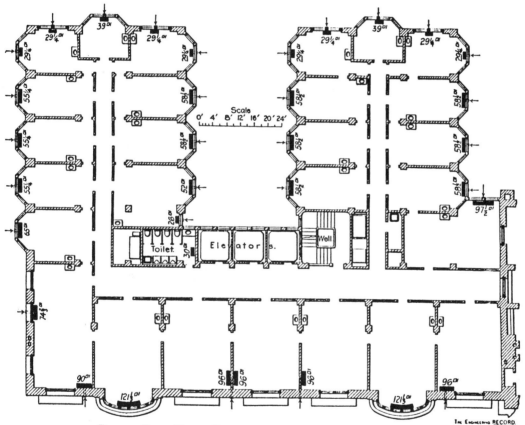

PLAN OF THIRD FLOOR, DUCTS OVER CORRIDOR CEILINGS NOT SHOWN.

Figure 45b(71). Office (1901).

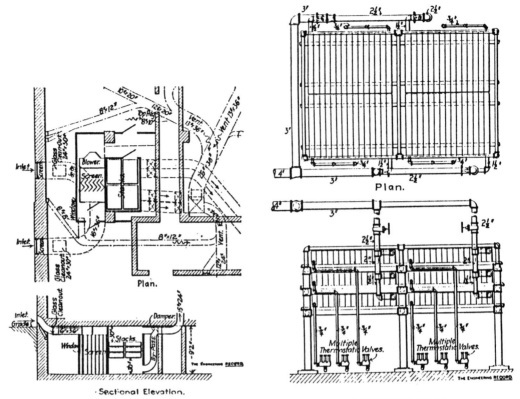

GENERAL ARRANGEMENT.   THE TEMPERING STACKS.

AIR TEMPERING APPARATUS FOR THE MAIN FLOORS FRONT.

Figure 45b(72). Office (1901).

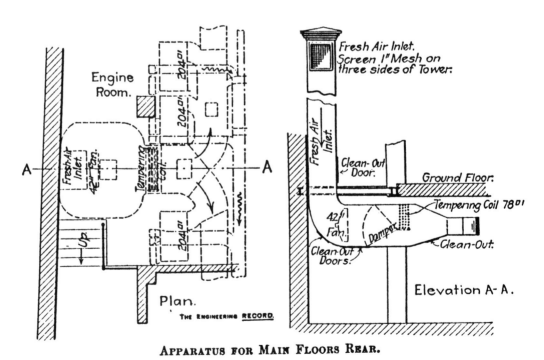

APPARATUS FOR MAIN FLOORS REAR.

Figure 45b(73). Office (1901).

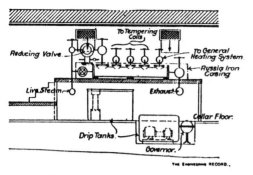

Elevation of Distributing Drum.

Figure 45b(74). New York Stock Exchange (1905).

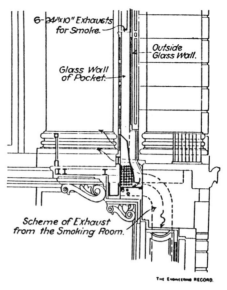

Glass Wall Pocket at Gallery Floor.

Figure 45b(75). New York Stock Exchange (1905).

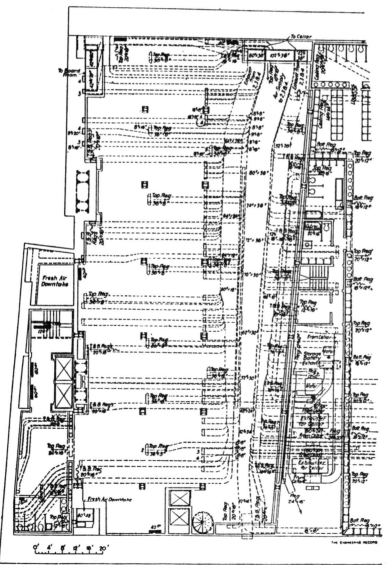

Ducts over Ceiling of Sub-Basement No. 2.

Figure 45b(76). New York Stock Exchange (1905).

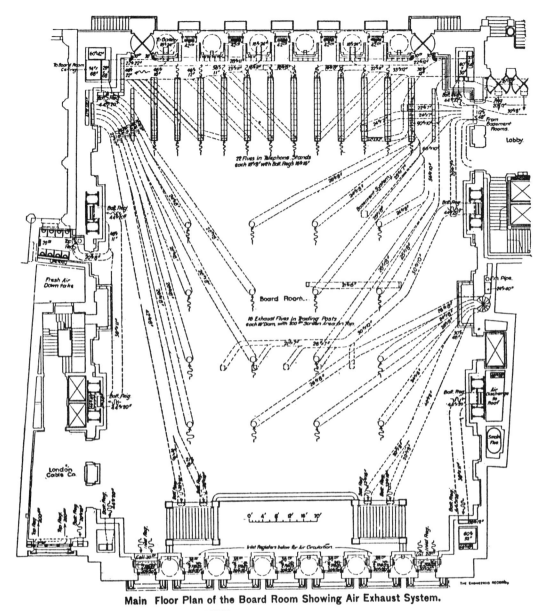

Main Floor Plan of the Board Room Showing Air Exhaust System.

Figure 45b(77). New York Stock Exchange (1905).

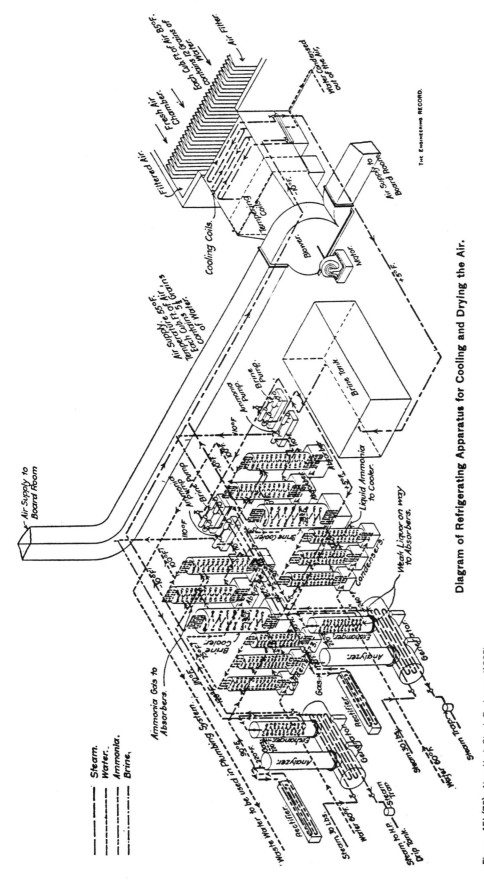

THE ENGINEERING RECORD.

Diagram of Refrigerating Apparatus for Cooling and Drying the Air.

Figure 45b(78). New York Stock Exchange (1905).

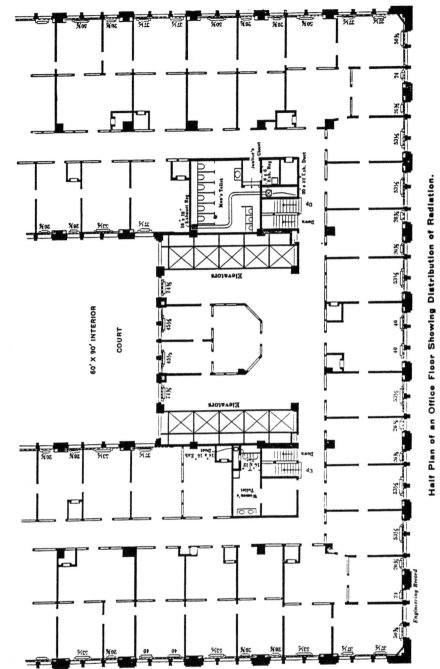

Half Plan of an Office Floor Showing Distribution of Radiation.

Figure 45b(79). Office (1906).

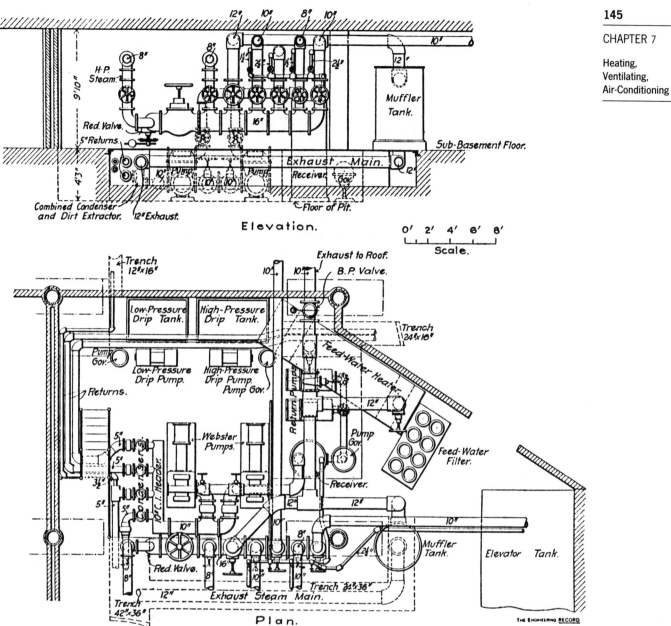

Elevation.

Plan.

DISTRIBUTING CENTER OF THE HEATING SYSTEM.

Figure 45b(80). Department store (1902).

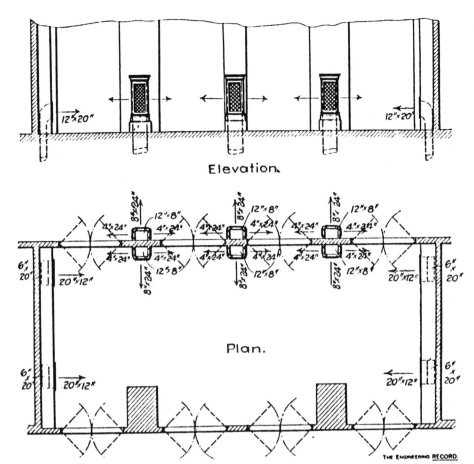

ARRANGEMENT OF REGISTERS IN A TYPICAL ENTRANCE.

Figure 45b(81). Department store (1902).

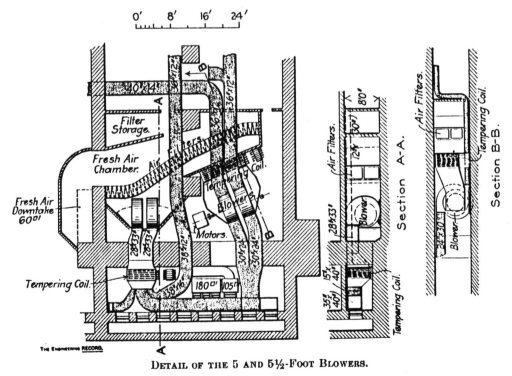

DETAIL OF THE 5 AND 5½-FOOT BLOWERS.

Figure 45b(82). Department store (1902).

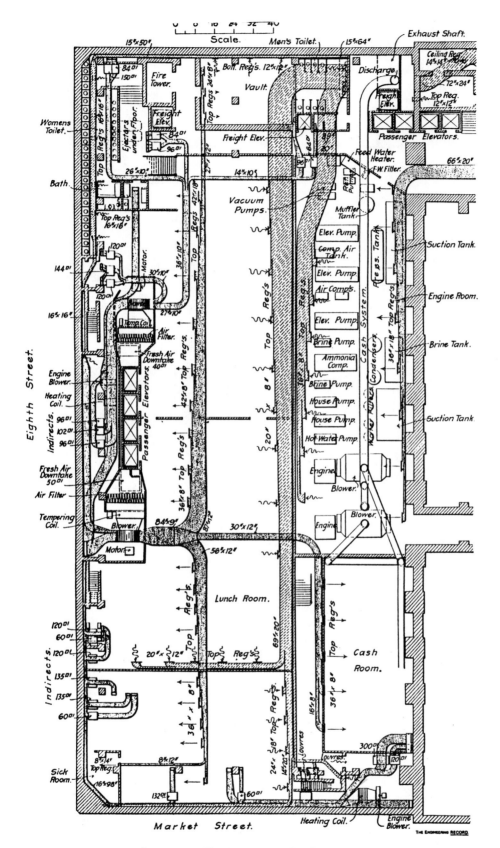

PLAN OF THE NEW PART OF THE SUB-BASEMENT.

Figure 45b(83). Department store (1902).

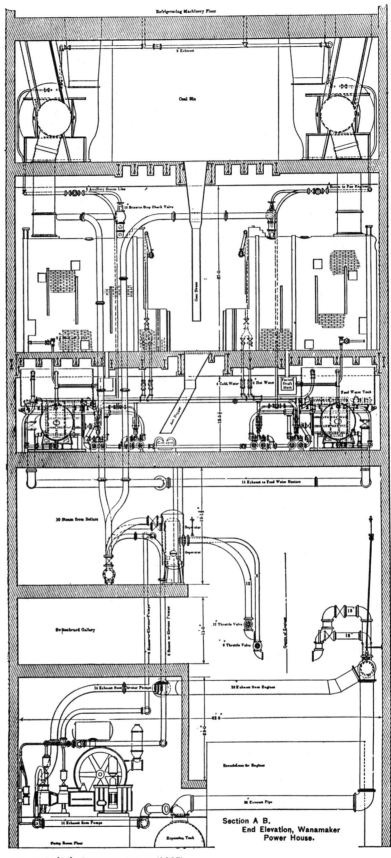

Figure 45b(84). Department store (1905).

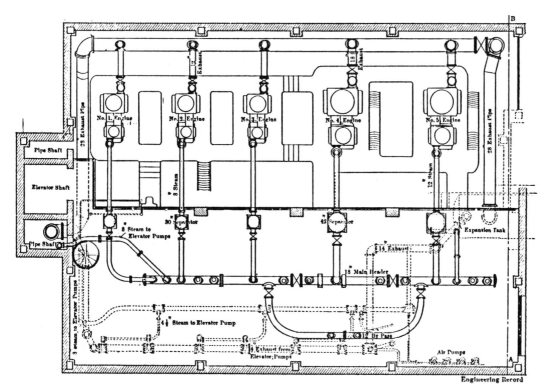

General Plan of Engine Room and Mezzanine Piping, Wanamaker Power House.

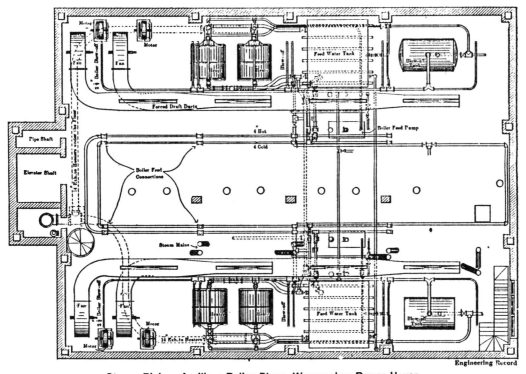

Steam Piping, Auxiliary Boiler Floor, Wanamaker Power House.

Figure 45b(85). Department store (1905).

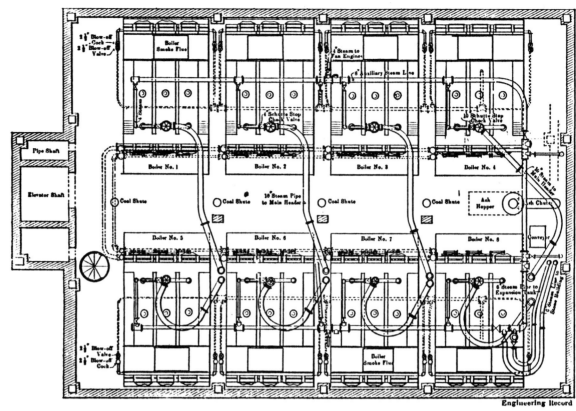

General Plan of Boiler Room and Piping, Wanamaker Power Plant.

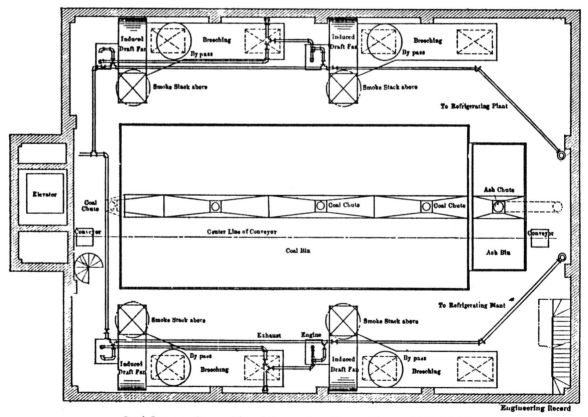

Coal Storage Room Plan, Wanamaker Power House, Philadelphia.

Figure 45b(86). Department store (1905).

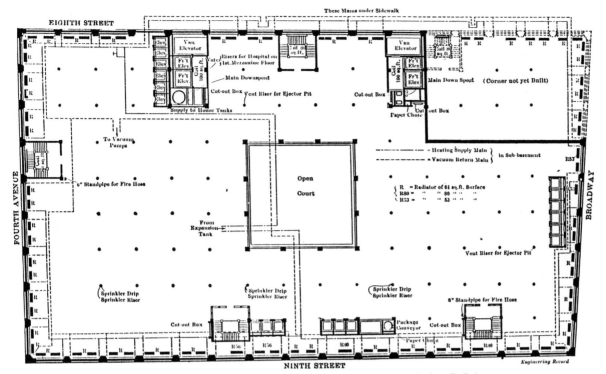

Typical Floor Plan of New Wanamaker Store Building Showing Distribution of Direct Radiation.

Figure 45b(87). Department store (1906).

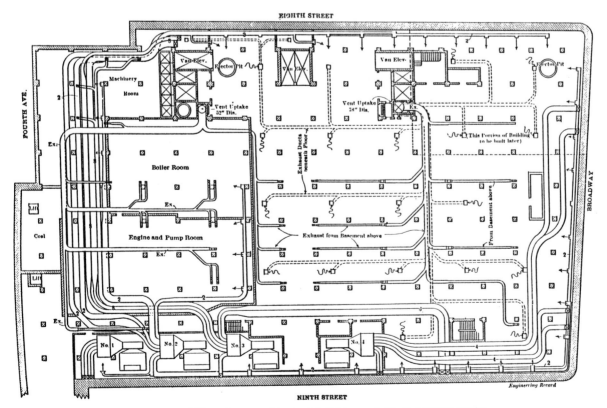

Arrangement of Blower Systems and Ductwork in Sub-basement. Wanamaker Store Building,

Figure 45b(88). Department store (1906).

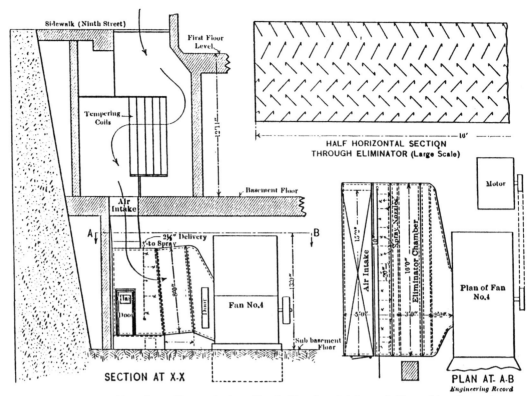

Section Under Sidewalk at Blower System No. 4, Showing Intake and Air-washing Apparatus.

Figure 45b(89). Department store (1906).

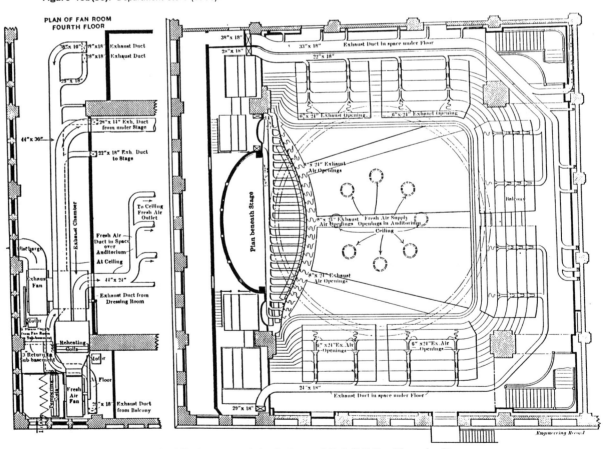

Details of Heating and Ventilating Equipment of Music Hall, New Wanamaker Store.

Figure 45b(90). Department store (1906).

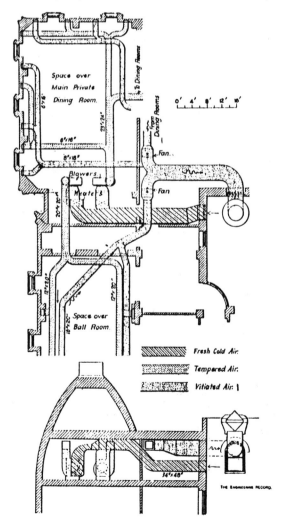

Ventilating Units in the Hotel Astor Cellar.

Figure 45b(91). Hotel Astor, New York (1904).

Ventilating Scheme for the Top Story Rooms.

Figure 45b(92). Hotel Astor, New York (1904).

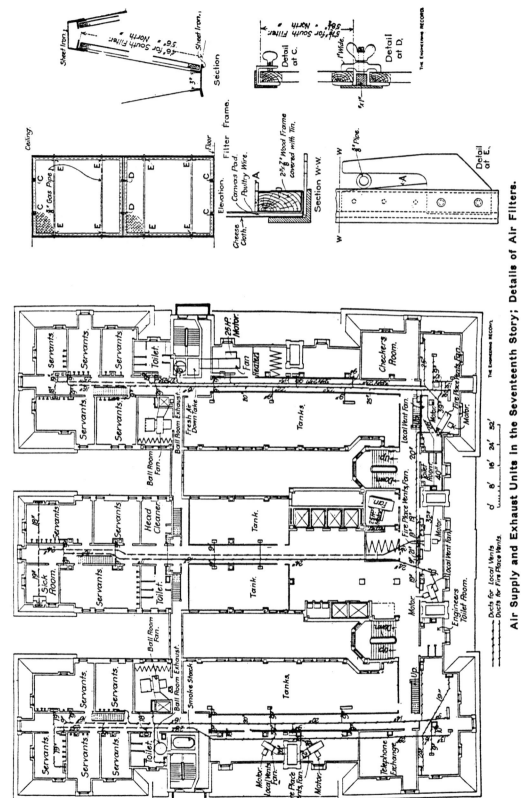

Figure 45b(93). Bellevue-Stratford Hotel, Philadelphia (1905).

Air Supply and Exhaust Units in the Seventeenth Story; Details of Air Filters.

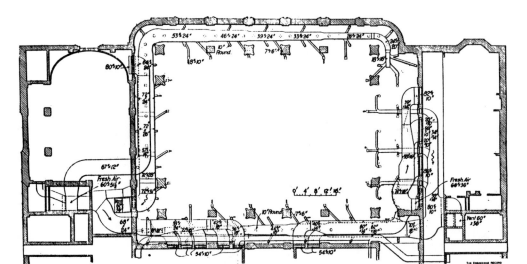

Scheme of Ventilation for the Ball Room.

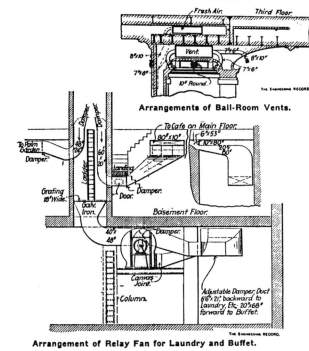

Arrangements of Ball-Room Vents.

Arrangement of Relay Fan for Laundry and Buffet.

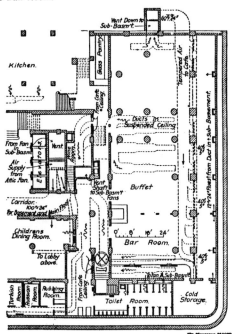

Exhaust Duct System for Buffet and Cafe.

Figure 45b(94). Bellevue-Stratford Hotel, Philadelphia (1905).

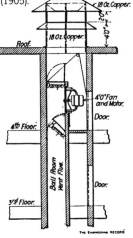

Ball-Room Vent Shaft.

Figure 45b(95). Bellevue-Stratford Hotel, Philadelphia (1905).

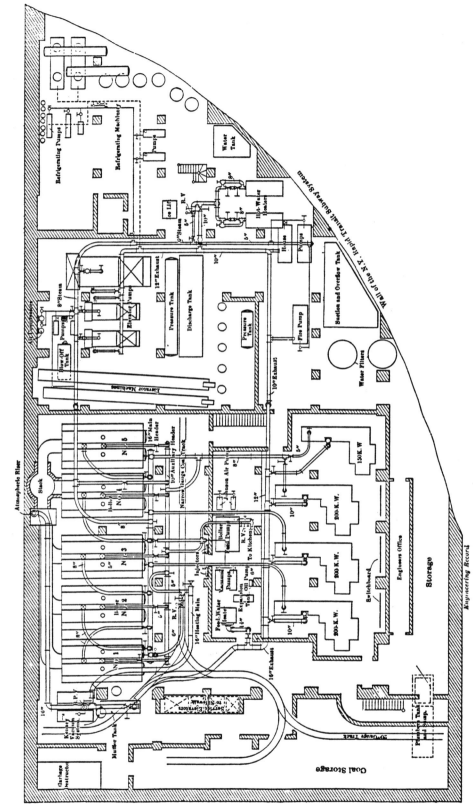

Plans of Fifth Basement, Hotel Belmont, Containing Power Plant, Refrigerating Machinery and Elevator Equipment.

Figure 45b(96). Hotel (1905).

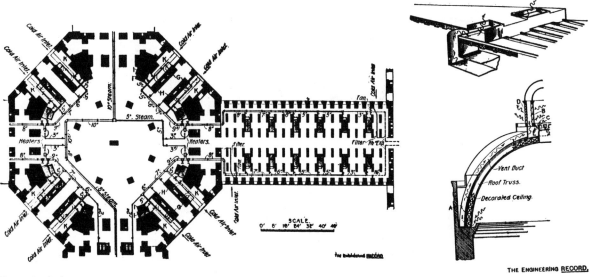

Figure 45b(97). Library of Congress (1897).

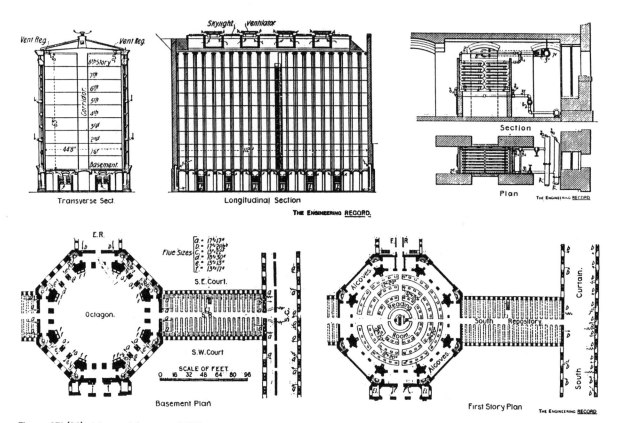

Figure 45b(98). Library of Congress (1897).

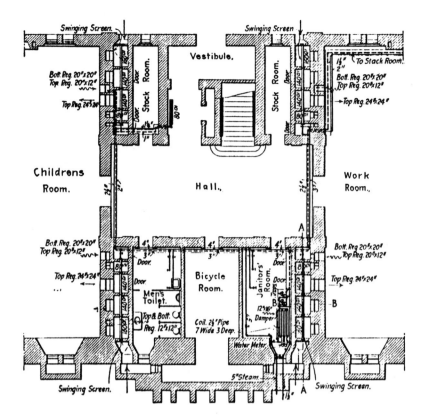

BASEMENT PLAN, SHOWING HEATING SYSTEM.

Figure 45b(99). Atlanta Public Library (1900).

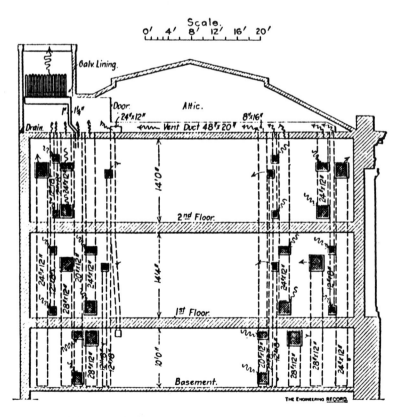

TRANSVERSE SECTION THROUGH THE BUILDING.

Figure 45b(100). Atlanta Public Library (1900).

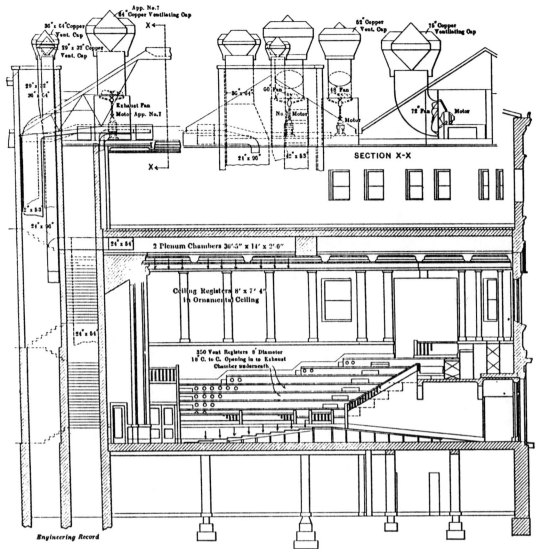

Details of Ventilation of the Lecture Hall and Typical Exhaust Fan Arrangement in Attic.

Figure 45b(101). Carnegie Library Extension, Pittsburgh (1906).

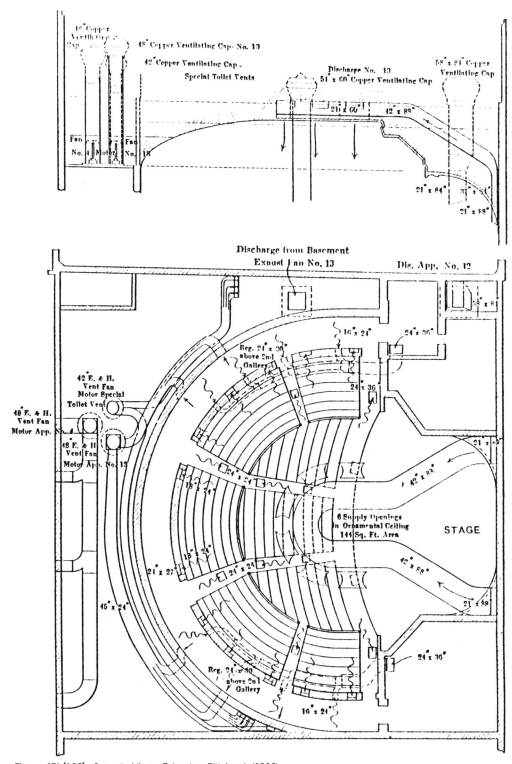

Figure 45b(102). Carnegie Library Extension, Pittsburgh (1906).

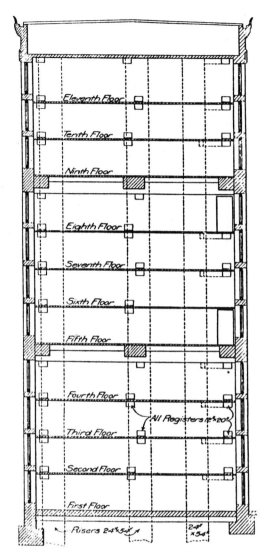

Supply Connections to Book Stack Wing.

Figure 45b(103). Carnegie Library Extension, Pittsburgh (1906).

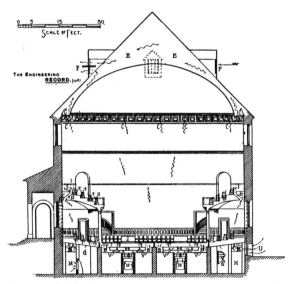

Figure 45b(104). First Methodist Episcopal Church, Baltimore (1894).

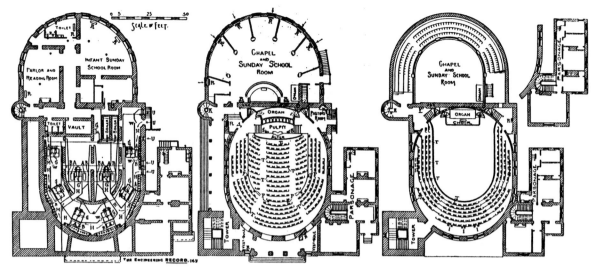

Figure 45b(105). First Methodist Episcopal Church, Baltimore (1894).

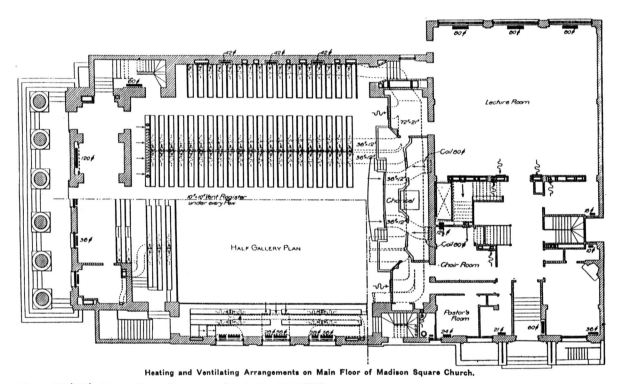

Heating and Ventilating Arrangements on Main Floor of Madison Square Church.

Figure 45b(106). Madison Square Presbyterian Church, New York (1908).

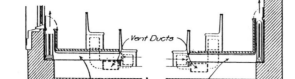

At Rear of Pews   South Gallery   North Gallery

Enclosed Radiation in Auditorium.

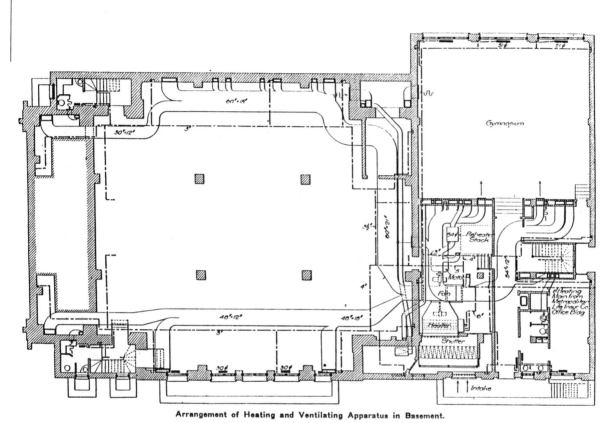

Arrangement of Heating and Ventilating Apparatus in Basement.

Figure 45b(107). Madison Square Presbyterian Church, New York (1908).

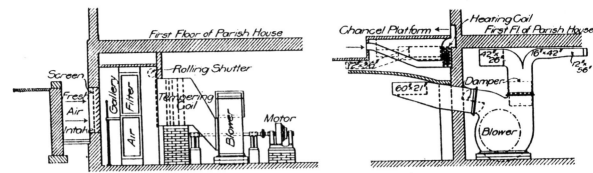

Basement Fan and Discharge Connections.

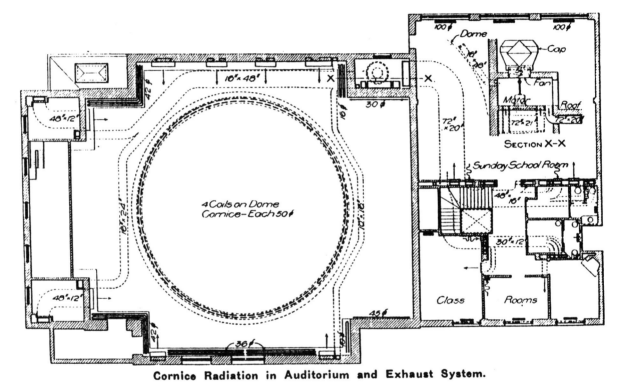

Cornice Radiation in Auditorium and Exhaust System.

Figure 45b(108). Madison Square Presbyterian Church, New York (1908).

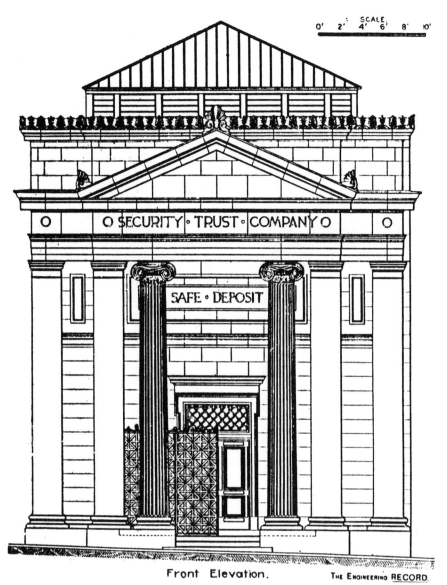

Front Elevation.

THE ENGINEERING RECORD.

Figure 45b(109). Security Trust Company, Rochester, New York (1897).

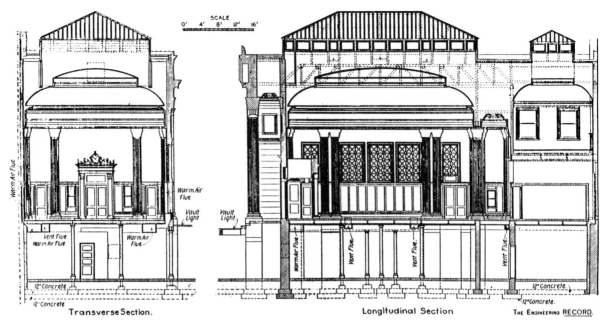

Figure 45b(110). Security Trust Company, Rochester, New York (1897).

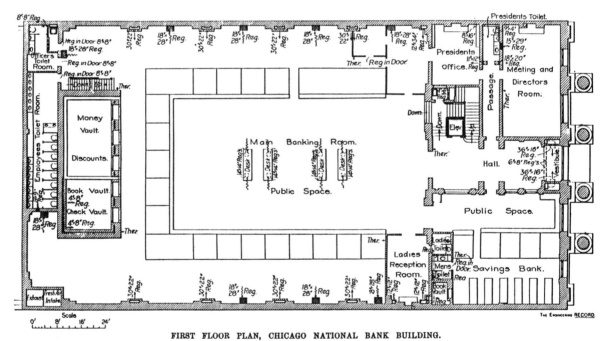

Figure 45b(111). Chicago National Bank (1901).

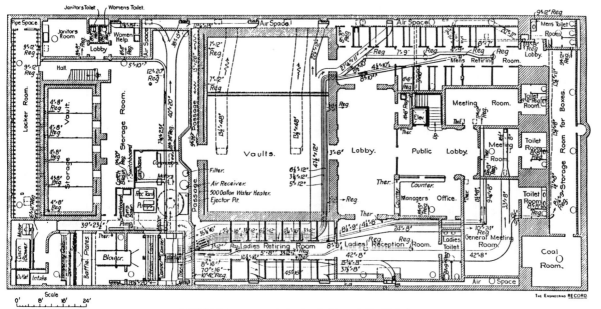

BASEMENT PLAN, CHICAGO NATIONAL BANK BUILDING.

Figure 45b(112). Chicago National Bank (1901).

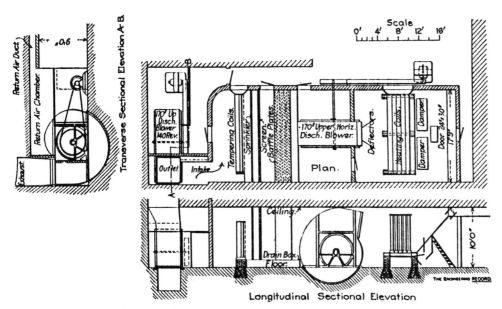

PLAN AND ELEVATIONS OF THE VENTILATING APPARATUS.

Figure 45b(113). Chicago National Bank (1901).

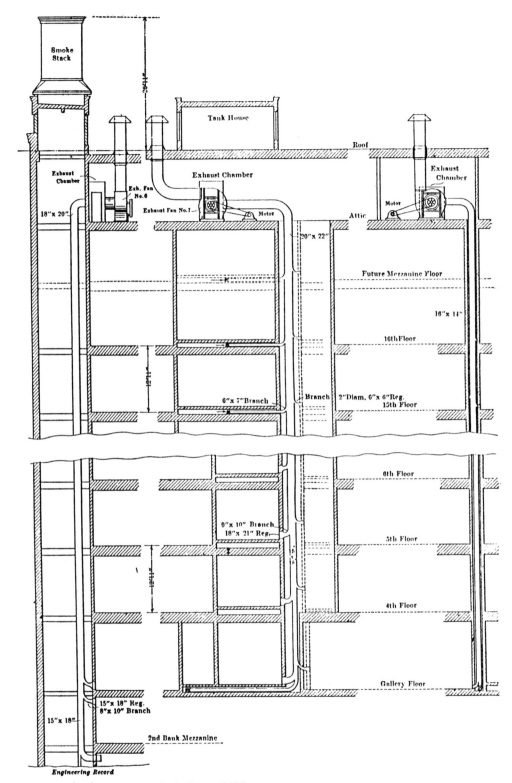

Figure 45b(114). First National Bank, Chicago (1906).

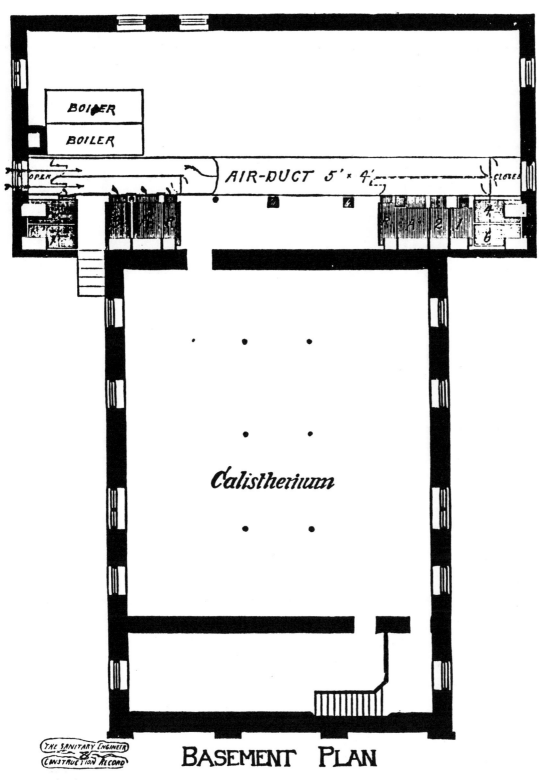

Figure 45b(115). School (1886).

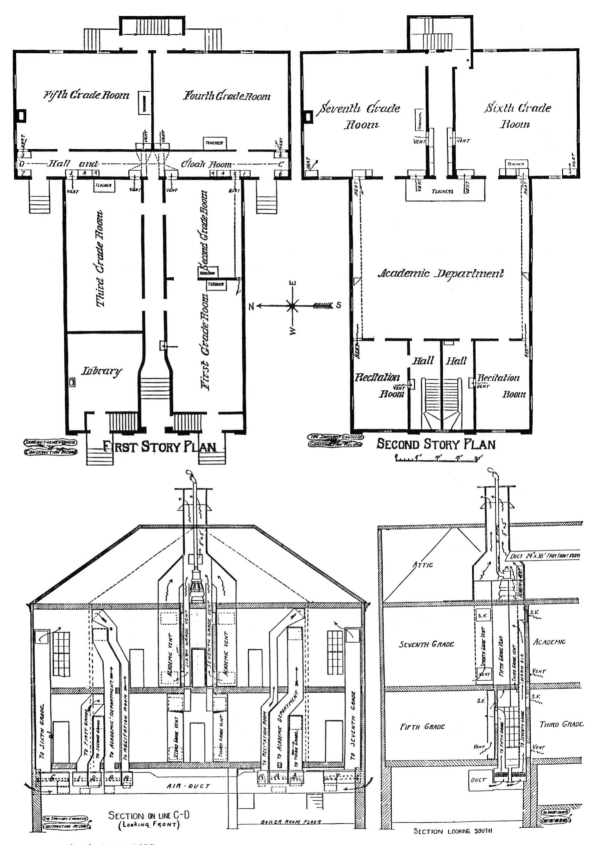

Figure 45b(116). School (1886).

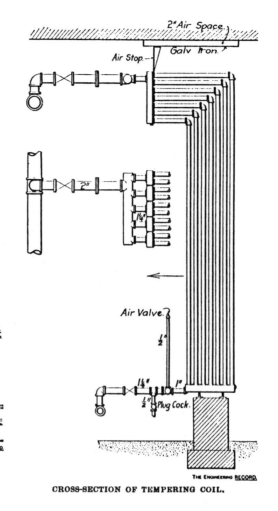

CROSS-SECTION OF TEMPERING COIL.

WINDOW-SILL AIR INLET.

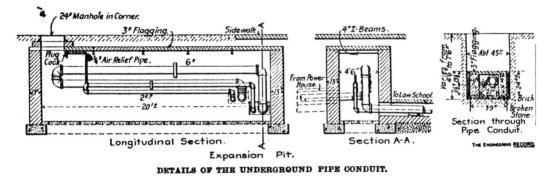

DETAILS OF THE UNDERGROUND PIPE CONDUIT.

Figure 45b(117). School (1900).

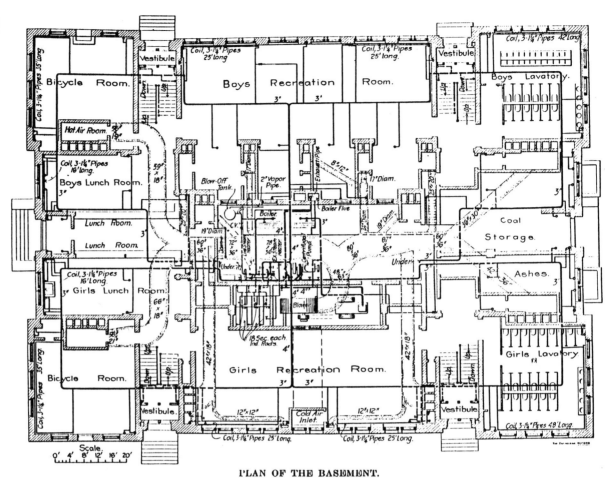

PLAN OF THE BASEMENT.

Figure 45b(118). School (1902).

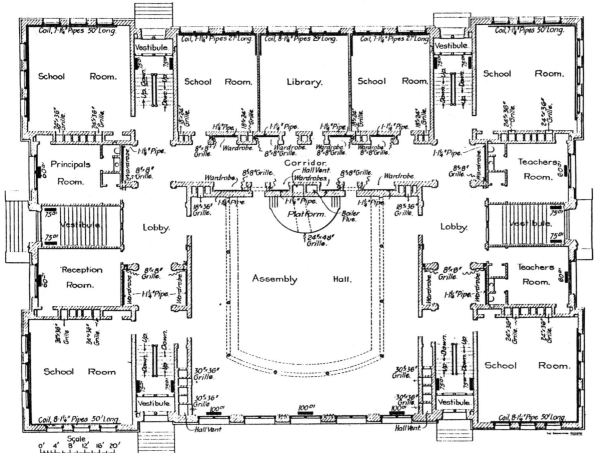

PLAN OF THE FIRST FLOOR.

Figure 45b(119). School (1902).

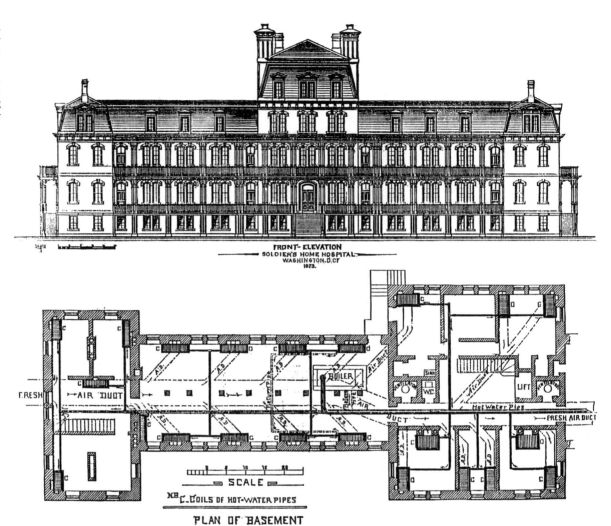

Figure 45b(120). Hospital (1883).

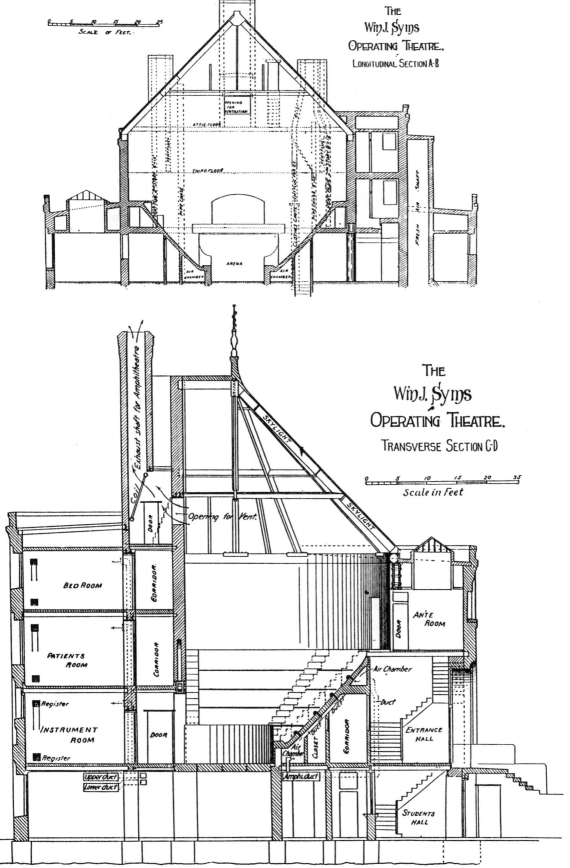

Figure 45b(121). Hospital (1892).

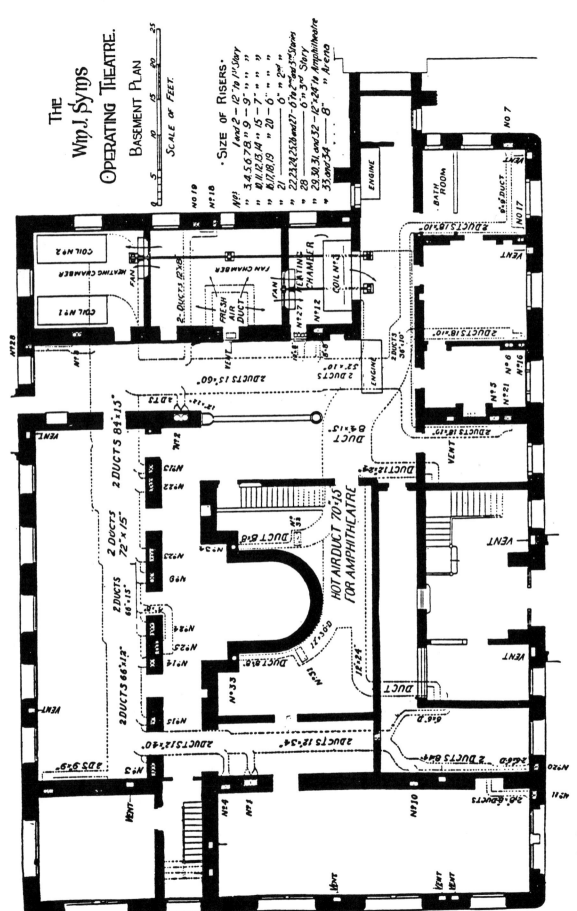

Figure 45b(122). Hospital (1892).

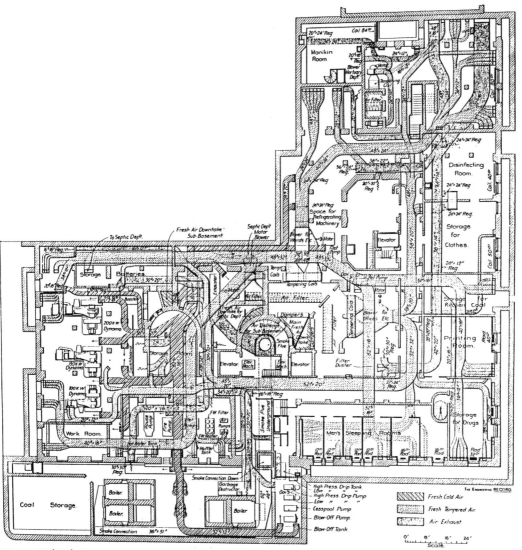

Figure 45b(123). Hospital (1903).

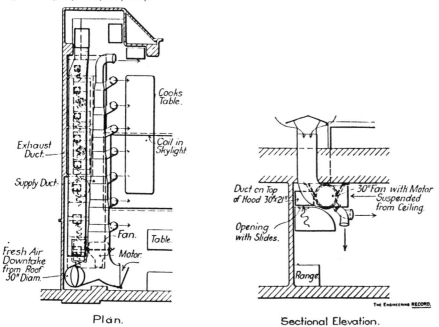

Plan.

Sectional Elevation.

KITCHEN VENTILATION SCHEME.

Figure 45b(124). Hospital (1903).

Figure 45b(125). Dakota Apartment House, New York (1885).

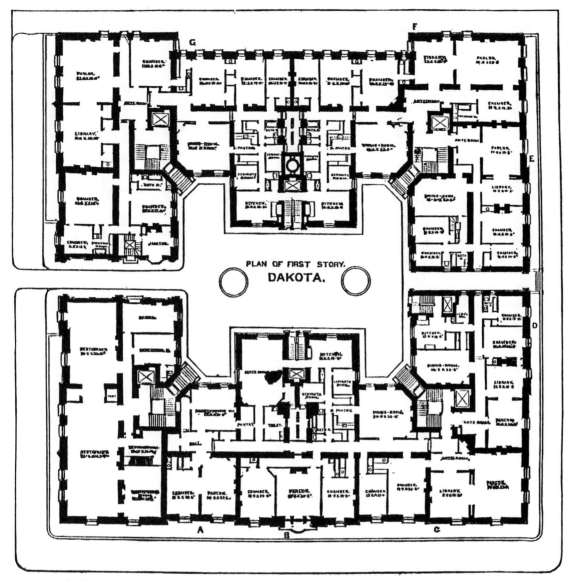

Figure 45b(126). Dakota Apartment House, New York (1885).

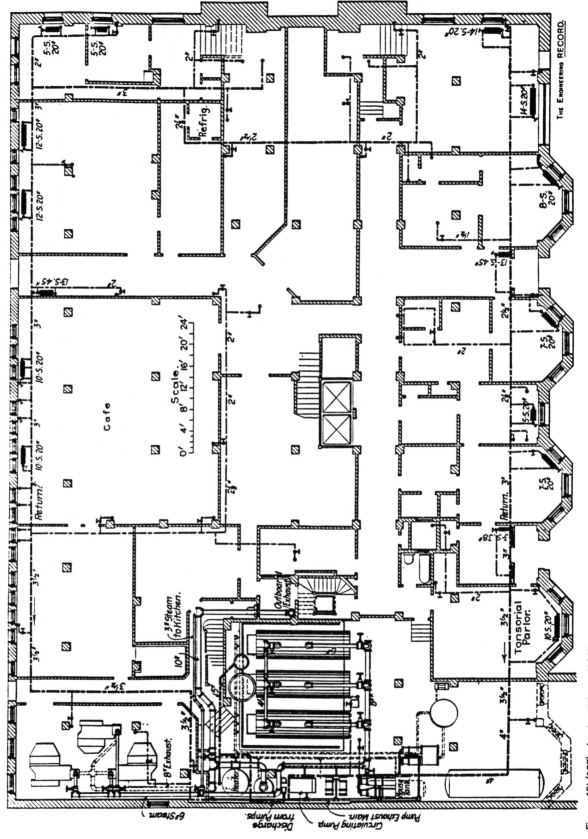

Figure 45b(127). Apartment house (1901).

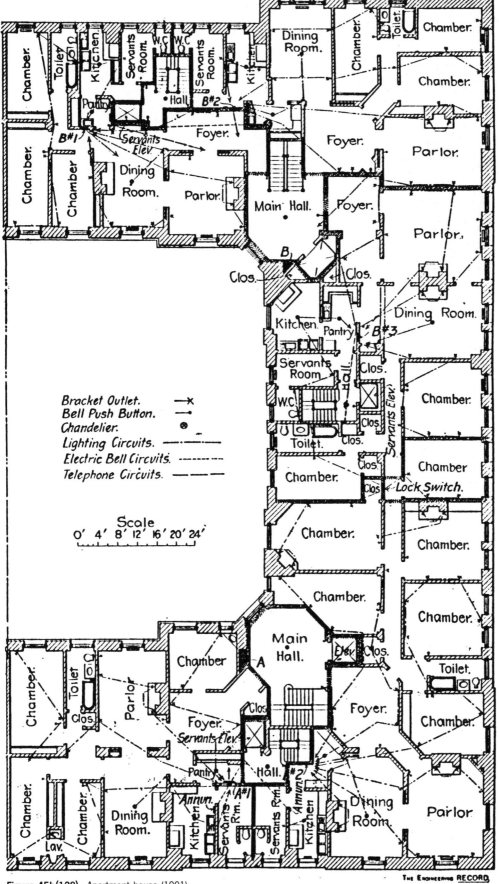

Figure 45b(128). Apartment house (1901).

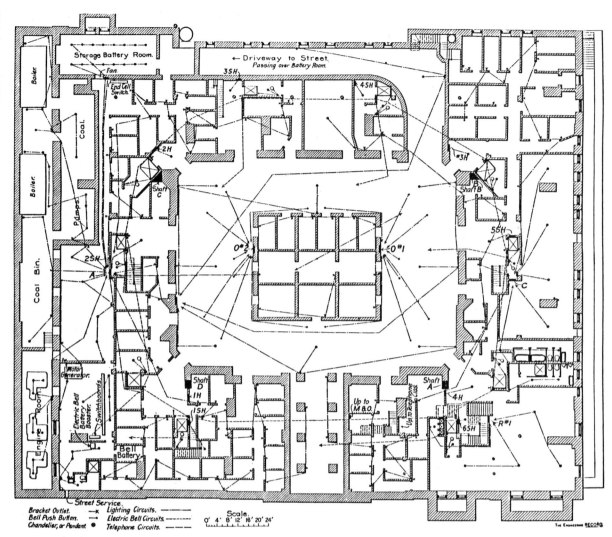

Figure 45b(129). Apartment house (1901).

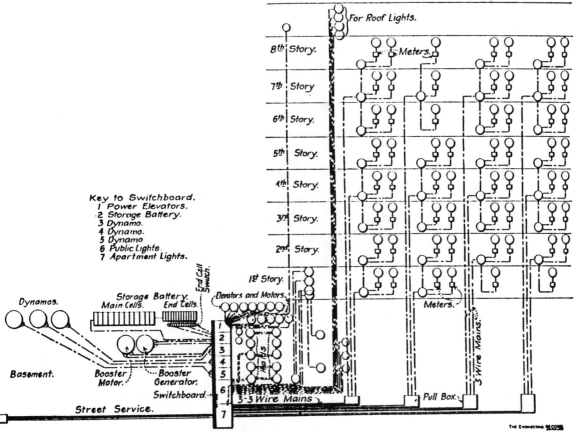

Figure 45b(130). Apartment house (1901).

Figure 45b(131). Ansonia Apartment Hotel, New York (1902).

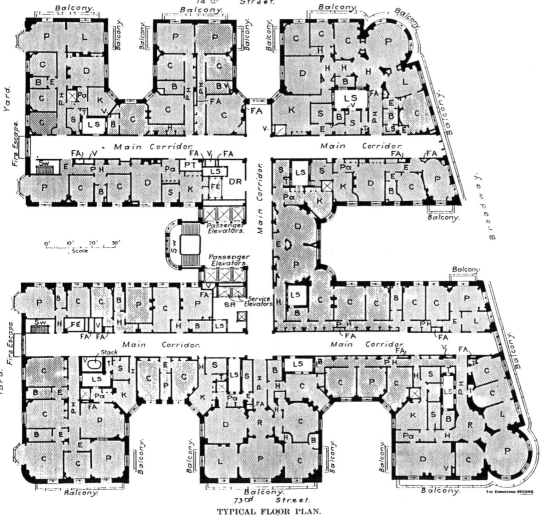

TYPICAL FLOOR PLAN.

Figure 45b(132). Ansonia Apartment Hotel, New York (1902).

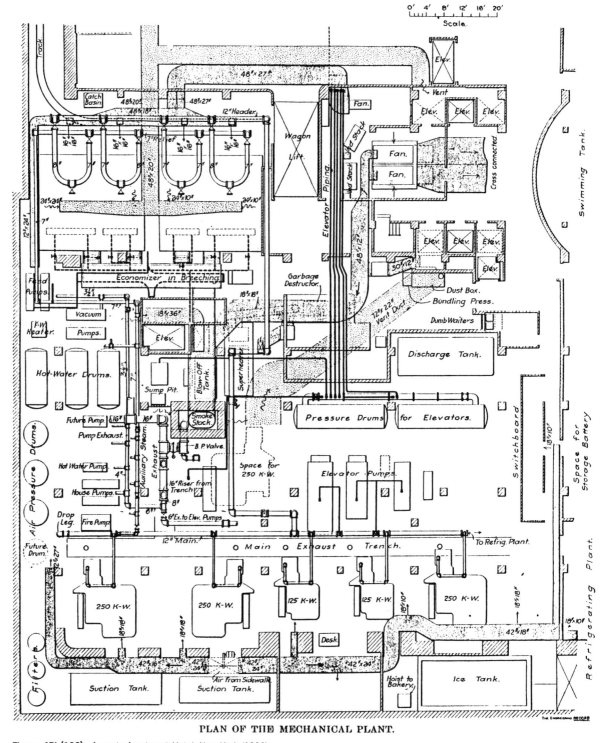

PLAN OF THE MECHANICAL PLANT.

Figure 45b(133). Ansonia Apartment Hotel, New York (1902).

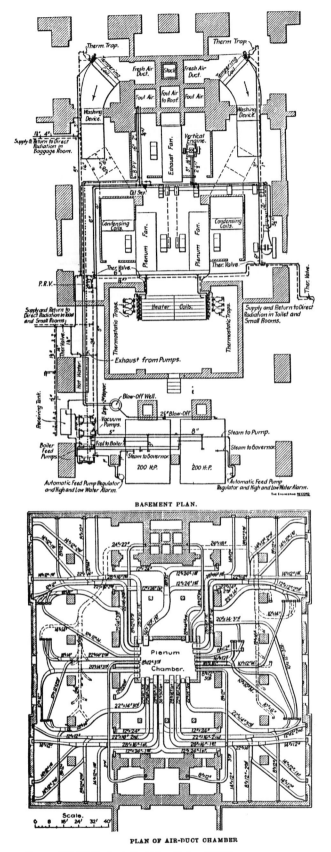

BASEMENT PLAN.

PLAN OF AIR-DUCT CHAMBER

Figure 45b(134). Nashville Union Station (1900).

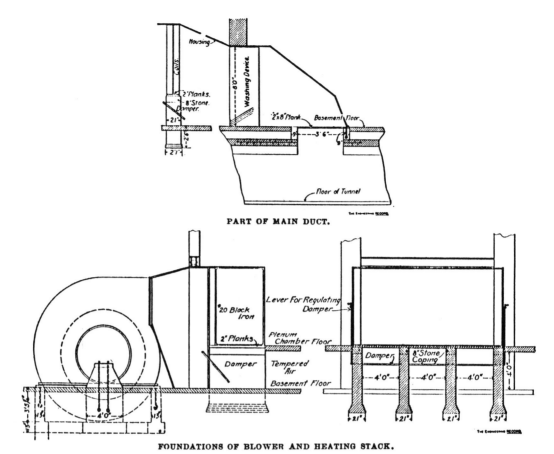

PART OF MAIN DUCT.

FOUNDATIONS OF BLOWER AND HEATING STACK.

Figure 45b(135). Nashville Union Station (1900).

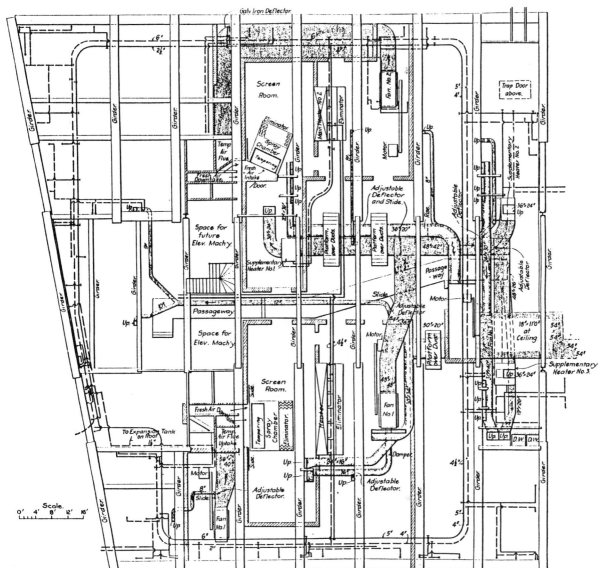

Figure 45b(136). Pittsburgh and Lake Erie Railroad Station (1902).

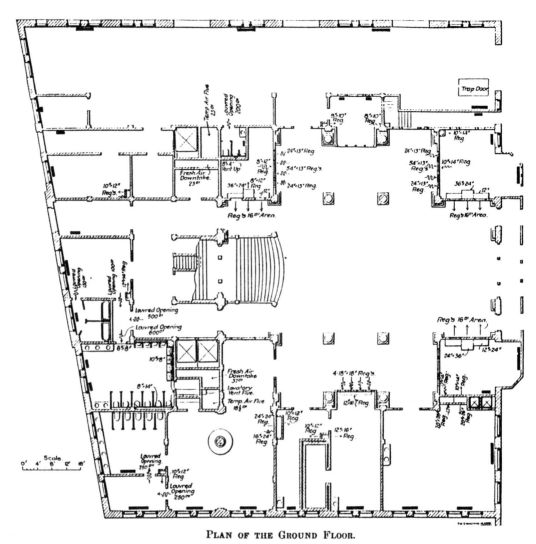

PLAN OF THE GROUND FLOOR.

Figure 45b(137). Pittsburgh and Lake Erie Railroad Station (1902).

Figure 45b(138). Factory (1886).

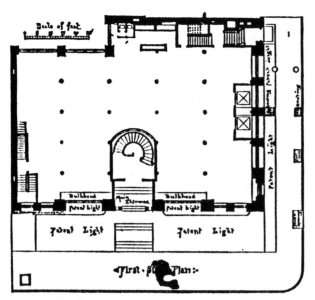

Figure 45b(139). Factory (1886).

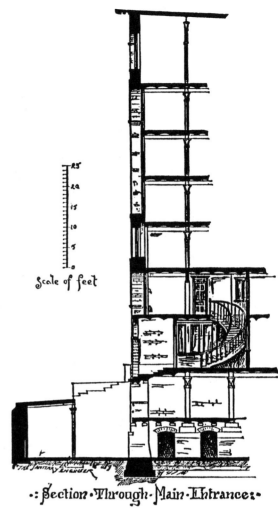

Figure 45b(140). Factory (1886).

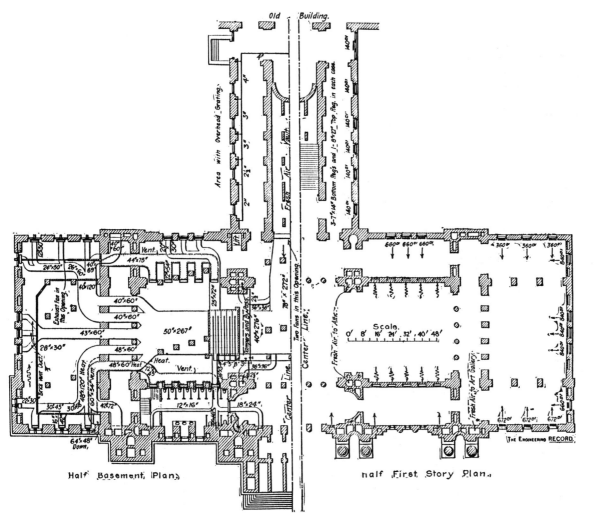

Figure 45b(141). Metropolitan Museum of Art, New York (1900).

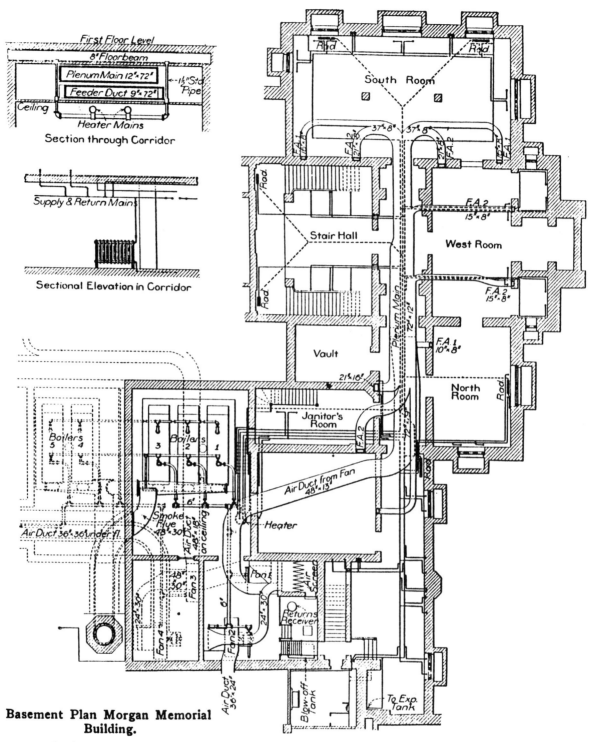

Basement Plan Morgan Memorial Building.

Figure 45b(142). Morgan Memorial Building, Hartford (1910).

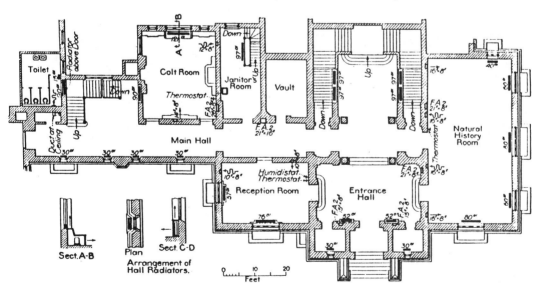

Second-Floor Plan, Morgan Memorial Building.

First-Floor Plan, Morgan Memorial Building.

Figure 45b(143). Morgan Memorial Building, Hartford (1910).

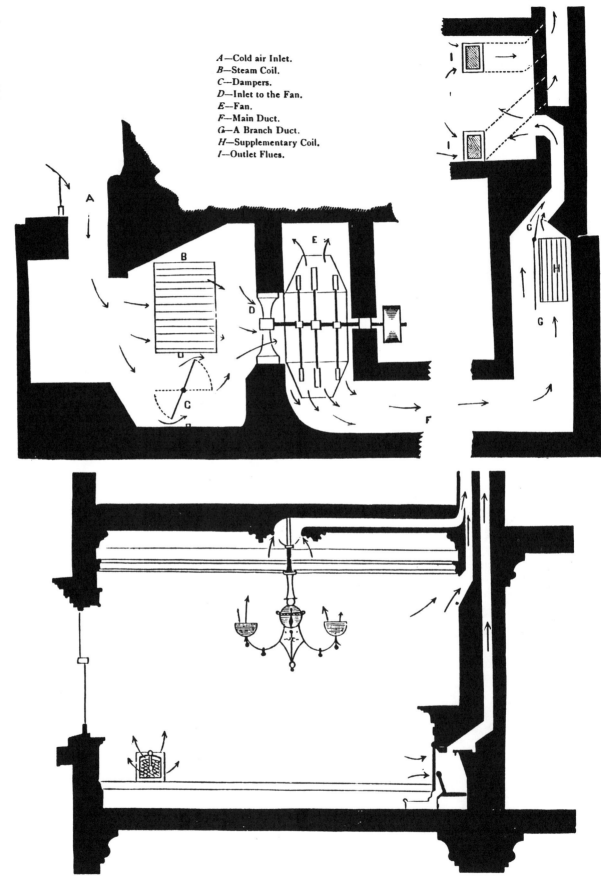

A—Cold air Inlet.
B—Steam Coil.
C—Dampers.
D—Inlet to the Fan.
E—Fan.
F—Main Duct.
G—A Branch Duct.
H—Supplementary Coil.
I—Outlet Flues.

Figure 45b(144). Union League Club, New York (1881).

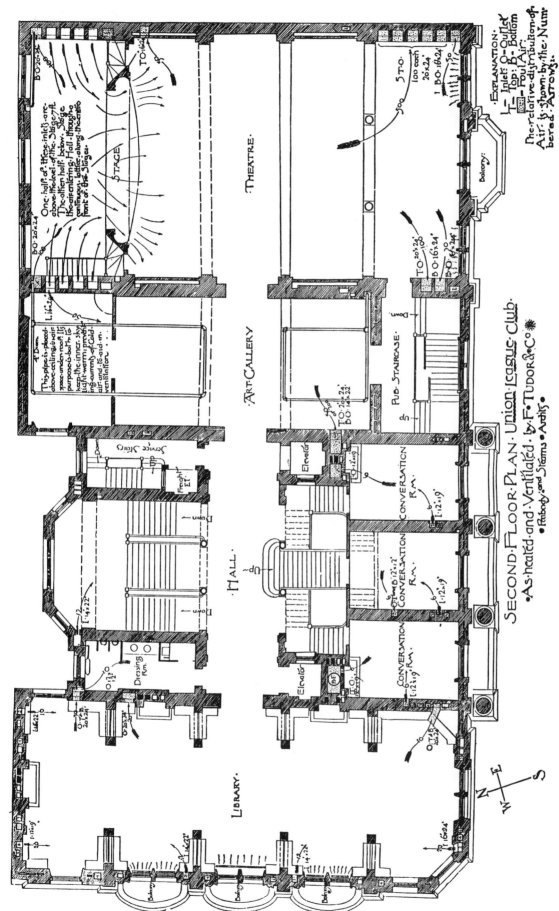

Figure 45b(145). Union League Club, New York (1881).

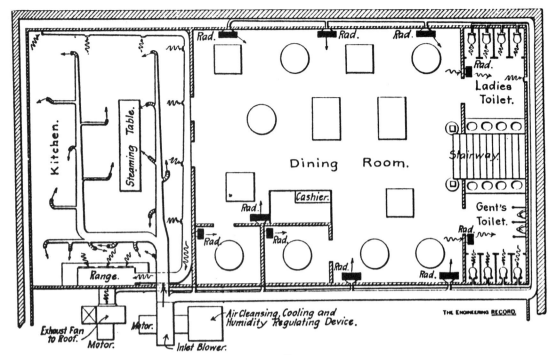

PLAN OF THE RESTAURANT.

Figure 45b(146). Restaurant (1901).

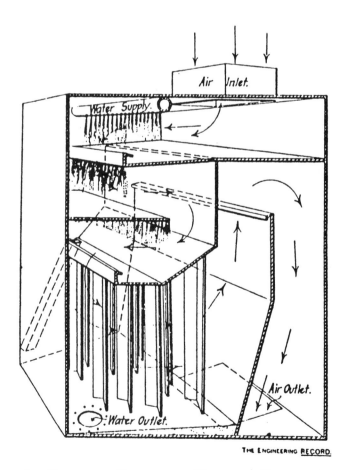

AIR CLEANSER, COOLER AND HUMIDITY REGULATOR.

Figure 45b(147). Restaurant (1901).

Figure 45c(1). Spaces where ducts can be concealed: Under this curved floor in an eighteenth-century landmark is a ventilation duct.

Figure 45c(2). Spaces where ducts can be concealed: Original ventilation opening.

Figure 45c(3). Spaces where ducts can be concealed: Archway containing ducts.

Figure 45c(4). Spaces where ducts can be concealed: Looking up at an exposed plaster ceiling in an early-twentieth-century hotel.

Figure 45d(3). Making space for ducts.

Figure 45d(1). Channeling for ducts: In a Beaux Arts stone entry.

Figure 45d(2). Channeling for ducts: The post–Civil War Pension Fund Building, Washington, D.C.

Figure 45e(1). Reusing existing spaces: A closet.

Figure 45e(2). Reusing existing spaces: A wall vent.

Figure 45e(3). Reusing existing spaces: A ceiling vent.

Figure 45f. Unfortunate positioning of equipment: Ruining archway to install a heat pump behind false wall.

Figure 46a. The air-conditioning units are too close to the visible roofline.

Figure 46b(1). Enough space above the ballroom ceiling for a person to stand up.

Figure 46b(2). There was room to stand up in the space above the ceiling, but the ducts were put below, destroying the arches.

Figure 46c(2). There were already perfectly good ducts, but workers gouged out the marble for new ones.

Figure 46c(1). Perfectly good ducts.

Figure 46d. Poor location for air-conditioning duct—it is even off center.

Figure 46e. Bicycles can hang from the ceiling, but ducts should not.

Figure 47. Space heater in the lobby of a prestigious concert hall.

We are sure no one would purposely do installations that are ugly and useless. An unsightly job indicates very little care and planning went into design and execution (Fig. 46d and e).

Regarding the damping of vibration and absorbing noise, Leonard Swantek advises:[26] "To dampen vibration and absorb noise, a system must be sufficiently *flexible* to accommodate equipment *movement* and thermal *expansion* and contraction without impairing the performance of vibration isolators."

The conundrum of heating has been around a long time. An eighteenth-century wag said "To talk of Architecture is a joke till you build a chimney that won't smoke." It is apparent by the accompanying illustration (Fig. 47) that the positioning of heat sources was not considered very important in this venerable building.

Ventilation perhaps started with a hole in the roof of the tent, igloo, or cave. Some form of air-conditioning has been in use as soon as a cake of ice, a fan, and a slave were available.

However, now that both buildings and contents are of such great value both historically and financially, thought must be given to the following factors.

ENVIRONMENTAL CONTROLS FOR INTERIORS

Temperature and lighting Light is a factor in controlling temperature, so consider the amount and type of lighting fixtures installed. Additional air-conditioning may have to be used to counteract the heat factor.

[26] From Leonard S. Swantek, "Flexible Pipe Couplings Dampen Vibration, Noise," *Heating/Piping/Air Conditioning,* July 1990.

Humidity and heat Materials less affected by light or heat include metals, ceramics, enamel, stone, and glass. Anything containing water (e.g., wood or plaster) contracts and expands with changing humidity. It may not return to its original shape and may crack under severe movement.

For most materials, ideal humidity is between *50 and 60 percent*. Humidity above 70 percent promotes mold growth, and below 40 percent, organic substances such as paper and absorbent materials become brittle and wood shrinks, causing it to warp and crack. Marquetry and veneers, leather, and natural adhesives (animal glues), especially in church organs, suffer. These figures are now subject to change, with increased research being done. The physical law is that hot air holds more water than does cold air.

Heating Central heating causes dehydration of materials, lowering the relative humidity to 20 percent. It can severely affect ornamental plaster. This means that during the cold season, humidity must be introduced into the building, just as it should be removed during the summer months. A person gives off as much heat as a 100-W bulb, so a theater or indoor congregation of people can heat up considerably, even in winter.

Avoid wide swings in temperature. This means not turning off the heat entirely if the building is unoccupied in winter, or the air-conditioning in a hot, humid climate.

Condensation This occurs when temperature of a solid surface is lower than that of ambient air. When air cools in contact with a cold surface, it cannot absorb the water and precipitates it on the surface.

Extra care should be taken to eliminate condensation on window sills because the water will go through the building, destroying it.

Ventilation Buildings, as well as people, need to breathe. Sufficient circulation of fresh air prevents mold and stale atmosphere. Sal Farruggia (of Syska & Hennessy) notes that a central heating system with large ductwork extending throughout a building is in many cases out of the question. In that case, you must consider bringing hot water for heat and chilled water for cooling from the central boilers and chillers through distribution pipes throughout the structure to local heating and cooling units. Using existing spaces is the challenge. To conserve space, there are *combination heater-chiller units* producing hot water for heat and chilled water for cooling. This type of unit may fit into the location of an obsolete boiler very well. *Fan-coil units* are also useful for spot heating or cooling.

Ever since the oil shortage in the 1970s, the use of an *economizer cycle* has been developed for air-conditioning. A damper regulates the cooling operation according to the temperature of the outside air drawn into the building. If it is 80°F outside and the final room temperature desired is 70°F, the air exiting the register would be 58°F. On mixing with the existing air in the room, it would reach the 70°F point. However, if the outside temperature were only 58°F, the damper would control the action so as to achieve *free cooling*.

THE SICK-BUILDING SYNDROME[27]

Sealing up a structure at every opening, with added insulation, and closing up air dampers on mechanical systems results in a suffocating building.

[*Author's comment:* It is wise to repair and even double-glaze windows. Interior storm windows with sufficient space between them and exterior windows are fine, *if* provision is made for proper ventilation.

However, to close up originally operable windows actually requires *more* energy use instead of less, because in spring and fall when neither heating nor cooling is needed, artificial means must be employed if fresh air cannot be brought in simply by opening a window.

Cross ventilation, as the Victorians knew, was a very cost-effective way of cooling. Older buildings were designed to make use of this factor, and should not be altered to eliminate it.]

An improper outside-air/exhaust ratio cannot curb the amount of contaminants within the space. Certainly, increasing outside-air intake uses more energy and costs more money, but compared to what? It is less expensive than possible illness for occupants or insidious damage to a building's structural components.

The American Society of Heating, Refrigerating and Air-Conditioning Engineers' (ASHRAE) Standard 62–1989, "Ventilation for Acceptable Indoor Air Quality," calls for specific minimums for achieving acceptable conditions.

This standard in itself will not improve air quality. What is needed besides the recommendation for an increase in the level of outside air per occupant is *qualified adjustment* of the outside-air damper minimum position in winter and summer. The owner's pocketbook will benefit, too.

Testing and adjusting by qualified specialists are integral to an effective HVAC system and energy conservation. A system of filters, particulates, charcoal, and chloride must be employed to maintain air quality.

BUILDING PRESSURIZATION

Whether a building is under positive or negative pressure is a function of the relationship between the amount of outside air brought in and the quantity of air exhausted.

If the intake exceeds exhaust, the building is under *positive pressure*. If exhaust exceeds intake, there is *negative pressure*. Aside from ensuring that interior environment is safe, there are additional benefits from positive pressure:

1. Increased gas- or oil-fire equipment efficiency

2. Increased building structural component life

3. [*Author's comment:* Increased protection from fire-generated smoke]

Unfortunately, most buildings today operate under negative-pressure conditions, simply because it costs money to hold a position. What is not realized is that when the maintenance technician manually closes the outside-air dampers, reducing intake, ostensibly to reduce the energy bill, savings are minimal unless the exhaust is also reduced equally. What has actually

---

[27] Adapted from Fred C. Schulz, P.E., President, EnerVation Inc., Milwaukee, "Testing and Balancing: Energy Versus Performance," *Consulting/Specifying Engineer Magazine*, June 1990.

happened is the negative pressure has increased, and merely "relocated" the outside-air intake to every door and window.

The simple fact is that for every cubic foot of air exhausted, a cubic foot of outside air enters the building. Thus, if every effort is made to seal the structure so it switches to a negative-pressure mode, outside air enters at every available leakage point, *even a masonry wall.* With the current use of weatherstripping, caulking, and sealing, chimneys and vents have become the new outside-air intakes in negatively pressurized buildings. Moreover, the temperature of each component within a wall, roof, window frame, etc., is reduced considerably in negative-pressure instances.

Consider the effect on

1. Burner combustion efficiency when the chimney has a strong downdraft.

2. Domestic hot-water heaters and standing pilot lights when a strong downdraft exists.

3. Indoor-air quality when stack downdraft forces combustion products into the occupied space instead of allowing fumes to be vented.

INADEQUATE HEATING[28]

There can be *heat loss* through windows and walls, which, if not corrected, can cause drafts and lowered heat levels. Inadequate heating may be caused not by the heating system itself, but by a *failed insulation system* (the insulation, its attachment and the air-vapor barrier). Air moves through the building insulation envelope as a result of the *stack effect, wind* and *building negative or positive pressure* from the mechanical ventilation design. When air moves out through a wall, there is air moving in somewhere else. If the vapor barrier facing joints are not sealed, condensation results on the cold steel building's exterior. Rusting of the structural steel is a result.

If taping of vapor barrier does not stick, it is the wrong tape or the application is faulty. Pressure-sensitive tape must be pressed onto a *clean* surface.

Other factors to correct heating include installation of air filters to eliminate blocked heat pipes and proper connection of control wiring.

VARIABLE-AIR-VOLUME (VAV) HVAC SYSTEMS[29]

Most systems are sized larger than usually needed. These recognize the fact that HVAC systems generally are designed to handle extreme weather conditions that may occur only a few days out of the year. However, most of the time, the fan or pump will not require the motor to operate at full capacity. Variable-frequency drives are so efficient because they change voltage and frequency to give a lower speed (in revolutions

per minute), so they can operate at the maximum efficiency of the motor at partial load.

TOURIST POLLUTION

Because the topic is historic buildings, something should be said about the effects of tourism on these venerable structures:[30] "The figures are dizzying: tourism is already, as predicted thirty years ago, the largest single industry in the world, providing something like [112 million jobs, according to Wharton Economic Forecasting Associates]. The World Tourist Organization predicts a rise from 300 to 600 million people shuffling in slow, pavement-grinding queues around the world.

"Notre Dame Cathedral in Paris gets more visitors than the Louvre or the Beaubourg. They peak at the rate of 108 a minute. Each day they breath out 650 lbs. of vapour, 50,000 gallons of carbon dioxide, 1.5 million kilocalories of heat, and they burn 250 lbs of paraffin candles. They spill their Coca-Cola on the black and white pavement, and the softer white marble tiles are literally dissolving."

SCHEDULED MAINTENANCE

The job is not done unless *scheduled maintenance is designed in* from the inception of the job. All the efforts of the team could be for nought if subsequent attention is not paid to retain the intentions of the owner. This would be a case where a "smart" building is "dumb." Leaving the care of expensive equipment to sometimes illiterate or ill-trained personnel is simply not good business, and could lead to personal injury in addition to property damage.

CASE HISTORY: THE RIGGS NATIONAL BANK, FARMERS AND MECHANICS OFFICE, WASHINGTON, D.C.[31] (Fig. 48)

The Farmers and Mechanics National Bank Building was erected in 1922 by Marsh & Peter, Architects, at the corner of Wisconsin Avenue M Street in Georgetown. The building was built to house the bank established in 1814 and originally located at 31st and M Streets. In 1928, the Farmers and Mechanics Bank merged with the Riggs National Bank. The building was renovated by Mills, Petticord & Mills in 1961 and dictated by the taste of that time, much of the original interior ornamental features were either altered or removed. Beginning in 1988, the branch was restored to its original neoclassical design by John Blatteau Associates. Using the original architectural drawings, the original interior design was recon-

---

[28] Adapted from William A. Lotz, P.E., "Inadequate Heating or Failed Insulation?" *Heating/Piping/Air Conditioning,* September 1990.

[29] Adapted from Paul E. Beck, Managing Editor, "Variable-Frequency Drives Take Hold in HVAC Market," *Consulting/Specifying Engineer Magazine,* September 1990.

[30] From an article by Maev Kennedy in *Apollo Magazine,* August 1990.

[31] Courtesy of John Blatteau Associates, Philadelphia.

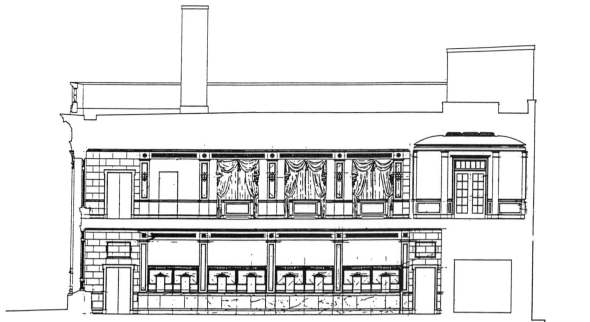

Figure 48a. The Riggs National Bank, Washington, D.C.: North view.

Figure 48b. The Riggs National Bank, Washington, D.C.: West view.

structed, and many decorative details were rebuilt, while bringing the building up to modern banking, environmental and life-safety requirements.

The *exterior* of this bank building, with its dignified, neoclassical façade and distinctive dome, is perhaps the most prominent landmark in the Georgetown business district. The dome has been cleaned and regilded to bring back its original glitter. The large two-story windows have been totally restored. The ornamental bronze entrance gates, bronze doors, and wood pocket doors that were removed and lost during the 1961 renovation have been rebuilt to recreate the original design. The north and east façades, which were originally brick

party walls, have been refaced with limestone-colored brick. These new façades are designed to compliment the rhythm of the columns' cornice lines of the limestone façades on M Street and Wisconsin Avenue.

The *Banking Hall* is a high, octagonal-shaped space with two-story columns and a beautiful coffered ceiling. The columns have been repainted in a faux marble finish, as they originally were. [*Author's comment: Faux* (French for false) finishes imitate natural stone or wood materials with paint, sometimes giving a three-dimensional effect.] Partitions added in 1961 have been removed from between the columns at the mezzanine level, bringing light from the large windows into the

Banking Hall. The original ornamental plaster panels at the fascia of the mezzanine floor were uncovered as part of this work. New ornamental metal handrails have been supplied. Dropped ceilings have been removed on both floors, and original wood and plaster moldings and radiator covers have been restored or rebuilt. The teller screen has been relocated and rebuilt as closely as possible to the original design. The teller screen is constructed of white oak with decorative ornament, and bullet-resistant glass with an etched border. The marble front of the teller counter is "fior di pesco carnico," a lilac-gray-colored marble similar to that used in the original bank. At the safe deposit area, the original marble entrance archway with its ornamental bronze gate and bronze clock has been re-created exactly. The new wood and marble check desk is a reconstruction of the original design, once located in the Banking Hall.

In addition to restoring the Banking Hall to its original splendor, the building has also been brought up to date with a new heating and air-conditioning system, and sprinkler system. An elevator has been added for the convenience of customers visiting the officer's area located on the newly restored mezzanine level. The *Conference Room* on the mezzanine has been completely restored. This beautiful room, with its original marble fireplace and wood wainscot, has been stripped of old paint and refinished. The skylight and the original herringbone-patterned wooden floor have been uncovered and restored.

The interiors have been designed to compliment the neo-classical character of the bank. The walls have been painted with a stone texture and joint lines similar to the original "caen stone" finish. The faux marble columns and the painted and gilded coffered ceiling are in keeping with the style of the bank and emphasize the ornamental plasterwork. New light fixtures have been carefully chosen or custom-designed to continue the style. The traditional furnishings, carpeting, and drapery treatments complete the ensemble. These renovations and reconstructions of the bank interior make the Farmers and Mechanics Branch of the Riggs National Bank a landmark inside as well as outside.

Examples of typical problems in M/E system design in an historic structure are

1. Downlights inserted in ornamental coffered ceiling

2. Added walls and dropped ceilings blocking out natural lighting that most historic buildings were designed to maximize

3. Choice of lighting out of character with original style of building

4. Supply and return-air diffusers incorporated in an insensitive manner

5. Dropped ceilings for ductwork hiding ornamental plaster

6. Downlights an anachronism

Corrections and additions made on this project included the following:

1. Supply and return-air diffusers were set behind plaster or punched-metal grilles that were designed as part of the architecture.

2. Ductwork was located in service areas to allow higher ceilings in public areas.

3. Recessed sprinkler heads were carefully placed to minimize visibility.

4. Historically accurate lighting fixtures were used for general illumination, while concealed high-efficiency fixtures providing task lighting where required.

5. Original radiator cover design was reconstructed but now hides modern four-pipe convectors that both heat and cool the space.

6. The former lightwell had been filled in to provide additional office space and room for the cooling tower and air-handling units. A new screen wall covers this mechanical space from view and is designed to match the column rhythm and cornice height of the front neoclassical limestone façades.

7. The skylight in the Conference Room was uncovered and reilluminated.

8. Electrical and telephone wiring were carefully integrated into wood bases.

9. A former closet and radiator cabinet were reused as a return-air plenum behind an ornamental grille.

10. The teller screen was designed with task lighting built in.

11. A new elevator was designed as part of the architectural space.

CASE HISTORY: 30TH STREET RAILROAD STATION, PHILADELPHIA[32] (Fig. 49)

The main concourse of 30th Street Station is a grand space, 315 ft long, 156 ft wide and 96 ft high, with tall banks of windows on all sides. The goal of the air-conditioning design is to supply cool air at a low level, below the windows and just above the storefronts; provide return-air openings in the lower ceilings of the South Concourse and Ticket Arcade areas; and allow the upper portion of hot air to stratify.

The challenge was to provide ductwork and air-supply elements in a way that minimized its visual impact on the historic character of the main concourse. This is accomplished by using the sign boxes between the north and south piers.

A new painted-wood air-handling box is built behind the existing sign box, and new linear supply diffusers are installed at the top and bottom of the sign face. The ductwork exposed in the space is nearly arranged at each sign box and painted to match adjacent metal panels.

[32] Courtesy of Sherman Aronson, AIA, of DPK&A, Philadelphia.

Figure 49a. 30th Street Railroad Station, Philadelphia: Exterior view. (*Photograph courtesy of DPK & Associates.*)

Figure 49b. 30th Street Railroad Station, Philadelphia: Interior view of waiting room. (*Photograph courtesy of DPK & Associates.*)

Figure 49c. 30th Street Railroad Station, Philadelphia: Note combination signs, air-conditioning, and custom scaffolding for ceiling work. (*Photograph courtesy of DPK & Associates.*)

CHAPTER EIGHT
PLUMBING

Early on, the proud owners of buildings with indoor plumbing let the pipes run wherever needed, so that onlookers would know that they were "up to date." In Europe, where it seldom is cold long enough in winter for pipes to freeze, the properties were plumbed on the outside for convenience of installation. Never mind that the structures were encased in pipes, completely hiding the sometimes elaborate façades (Fig. 50a to c).

One of the pleasures of staying in an older London hotel was the luxurious marble bathroom, with its towel warming pipes, telephone, huge pedestal sink, and swimming-pool-sized bathtub. Granted, it was only a telephone shower, but these late-nineteenth-century and early-twentieth-century buildings still managed to anticipate all the conveniences now considered *de rigueur.*

At the turn of the century, even the wealthiest citizens had very few bathrooms in their grand estates (Fig. 50d). A look at the real estate ads in *Country Life Magazine* (U.K.) still shows a 14-bedroom mansion with possibly two loos (toilets).

The question always arises as to whether to use the existing piping and/or radiators, especially if they are ornamental. Ideally, a *four-pipe system* is the most flexible, delivering heat or cooling at the same time. For example, hotels and office spaces may need cooling even during spring or fall, if the assembled people are not near windows. The *two-pipe system* allows either chilling or heating and must be changed seasonally. The *single-pipe system* (steam) is very uneven. It takes a long time to cool down if heat is not wanted.

The original radiators were successfully reused by Salvatore Farruggia of Syska & Hennessy at Ellis Island. First the units were put to a *pressure test* to determine their continued

integrity. Then they were *boiled out* for cleaning. It may not be possible to reuse all the radiators in a building, but if enough of them are salvageable, those still usable should remain.

Mr. Farruggia says that upgrading can be a lot of fun as well as a rewarding challenge to expertise. Of course, the owner must hire a competent, experienced professional team to do adequate planning and coordination, otherwise there will be little amusement for anyone.

Figure 51 presents vintage illustrations from 1878 to 1898 on plumbing.

From a plumbing standpoint,[33] the term "high-rise building" does not necessarily mean a towering skyscraper. A structure becomes a high-rise to plumbing engineers when water pressure provided by city lines is no longer sufficient to deliver water to the top of the building. At that point—usually four to six stories, depending on local conditions—some type of system is required to provide adequate pressure to fixtures on the upper floors.

[*Author's comment:* The age of the piping can be determined by the type. The Romans used lead; wood was used from medieval times to the eighteenth century. From then, it was iron, galvanized mild steel, copper, stainless steel, and polyvinylcloride (PVC). From advertisements of the period, it can be seen that fixtures could be very elaborate. If they still function, they should be retained (Fig. 50a and b).]

At one time, that system involved, almost invariably, a *storage tank* on top of the building, if it were commercial or industrial. [*Author's comment:* In fact, in some very large private homes erected from the mid-nineteenth century, there often was a huge ($\geq$ 10,000-gal) storage tank concealed within the structure, providing running water which was gravity-fed. This

---

[33] Adapted from Paul E. Beck, Managing Editor, "Choosing the Right Plumbing Systems," *Consulting/Specifying Engineer Magazine,* June 1990.

THE "MARNA"—DESIGN H.

Figure 50a(1). Late-nineteenth-century plumbing advertisement. (From *The Inland Architect.*)

facility could not be seen from the outside. If the property were near a natural source, such as a river or a lake, a system of various-sized pipes working on the ram principle, delivered the water.

In addition, as early as the 1850s, washerless faucets (which still work) were in use, proving that there is really nothing new under the sun.]

In commercial sites, later technology used *demand-based booster-pump systems* in order to

1. Maximize leasable space
2. Provide early building occupancy, if constructed anew
3. Minimize structural requirements

SOME SYSTEM COMPONENTS

BOOSTER PUMPS

This system generally consists of several pumps located at the building's base. The pumps' combined capacity is often somewhat higher than the peak-demand requirements, providing a degree of redundancy.

A small *lead pump* handles the average flow, with duty larger lumps cycling on as demand increases.

One of the main concerns in a high-rise is getting water to the top floor where you need it. Gerry M. Richey, plumbing designer, The Everett I. Brown Company, Indianapolis, says "Analyze what pressures are available and then calculate water-pressure and water-flow requirements at the end of the longest lineal run of pipe, which is generally the top floor. Then work backward from there."

Sizing the lead pump is critical in ensuring energy efficiency. The key is to make the pump sufficiently large that the larger pumps do not have to constantly cycle on and off.

Because pumps are selected to maintain minimum pressure requirements at the end of the longest lineal run of pipe, system pressure on lower floors may be significantly higher than that at upper levels. As building height increases, this difference becomes more significant.

To compensate for these pressure differences, the building is divided into zones, approximately 7 to 10 floors each in most cases. Interestingly, the same division can be used for heating. Since heat rises, the number of heat sources can be reduced, using zone areas.

Within each zone, a pressure-reducing valve lowers water pressure to utilization levels. Often, the valve is located at the top of the zone, allowing distribution within the zone to take advantage of gravity.

Mr. Farruggia suggests "Try to maintain 30 pounds per square foot at the top of the zone, and at the bottom. You don't want to go much beyond 80 to 85 pounds per square foot." He contends that if the pressure becomes excessive it limits the height a zone can be, and creates excessive wear on faucets and seats, water hammer, and shock on the system. He further states that "at the bottom of the building, where pressure on the main riser may exceed 200 pounds per square foot, an automatic emergency shutoff system should be included in case the pressure-reducing valve for that zone fails. Otherwise, valve failure could create a safety hazard on the lower floors."

Obviously in historic buildings, the original fabric of the structure as well as the contents and occupants would be at risk in this situation, so that special measures have to be taken to protect life and property.

L. WOLFF M'F'G CO

MANUFACTURERS OF A FINE GRADE OF

PLUMBERS' GOODS and SANITARY SPECIALTIES.

Wolff's "MONITOR" Porcelain Lined RECESS Bath Tub.

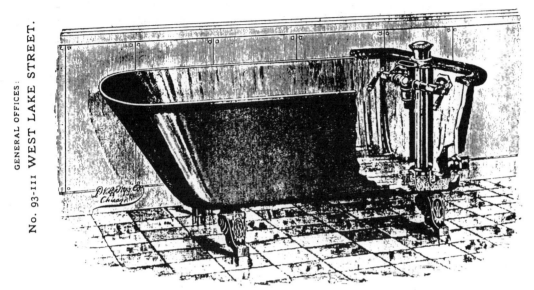

Figure 50a(2). Late-nineteenth-century plumbing advertisement. (From *The Inland Architect.*)

THE CELEBRATED

"SANITAS"

PLUMBING

APPLIANCES.

These appliances are admitted by all authorities to be the best in the market. Used together they form the simplest, cheapest, and only perfectly safe sanitary system now known.

THE

"SANITAS"

MFG. CO.

THE "SANITAS" WASH BASIN AND TRAPS,
SET IN TILE-WORK.

"SANITAS" TRAP
OPENED.

The Sanitas Trap, whether vented or unvented, has shown itself when properly set to be capable of resisting indefinitely siphonage, back-pressure and all other adverse influences met with in plumbing.

The "Sanitas" Basin flushes out the pipes and keeps them clean.

THE

"SANITAS"

MFG. CO.

Described and illustrated as the inventions of Mr. Putnam in

"*The Popular Science Monthly*,"

for July, 1888, in Figures 2, 6, 7, 12 and 13, of Mr. Hoyt's article on

"SAFETY IN HOUSE DRAINAGE."

THE "SANITAS" WATER CLOSET.

THE "SANITAS" WASH-BASIN.

("SANITAS" BATH TUB and PANTRY-SINK on same principle as Basin.)

Figure 50a(3). Late-nineteenth-century plumbing advertisement. (From *The Inland Architect*.)

Figure 50b. Early outside pipes for plumbing in Europe.

Figure 50c. An antique sink that is still usable.

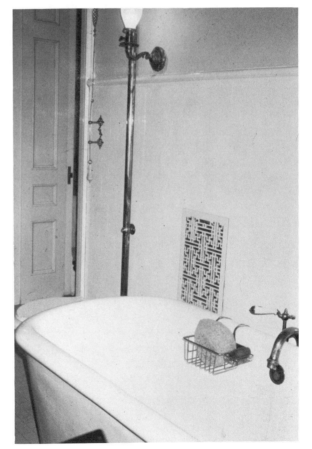

Figure 50d. The bathroom in a Vanderbilt mansion.

Figure 51a. Logo heading of *The Sanitary Engineer* (later *Engineering News Record*), the periodical in which most of the vintage plumbing drawings in this book were found.

Gus Zinuga, vice president and chief plumbing engineer, Hellmuth, Obata & Kassabaum, Inc., St. Louis, often incorporates a *dual boosting system*. One set of pumps handles the lower floors and a second set pumps water to the building's upper levels. This second set can be located in the building's basement, with an express line carrying water to the first level of service, or it can be located on the first floor of the building section it serves. Mr. Zinuga states: "By splitting the system, you are able to reduce the high end of the pressure to something that is not quite as dangerous. It also affects cost. The higher the pressure, the higher the cost for fittings and piping systems. And you have to employ additional safety factors."

He recommends designing the system to maintain a maximum water velocity of eight feet per second, although 10 feet per second generally is accepted. The slower speed allows for flexibility in sizing and quiet operation, which is particularly important in residential buildings. Mr. Zuniga continues: "Some people would say you are adding cost to the project by not taking it to the limit. In a large system, you could be adding a few dollars because of that. But to minimize problems associated with velocity, try to stay around the range of eight feet per second."

STORAGE TANKS

Water tanks still offer a number of advantages, *especially for older buildings:*

1. *Energy conservation.* A properly designed tank can be filled during off-peak hours, significantly reducing pumping energy costs.

2. *The tank's storage capacity* provides a buffer during high-use periods. As a result, rather than specifying pumps to handle varying loads, an engineer can specify a larger, more efficient pump designed for a relatively constant load.

Try to look at whether a tank will be feasible, and that is contingent on architectural considerations such as

1. *Whether there is space* to provide water storage.

2. *Structural impact on the building.* Storage tanks are gravity-fed, although a small booster pump is required to provide adequate pressure on upper floors. As water drops through the system, it picks up pressure.

As with the booster pump system, pressure-reducing valves are added at various zones to compensate for the pressure

difference. However, with a storage tank system, the range of pressure difference generally is smaller.

A major drawback of a storage tank system is the space that the tank itself occupies. It can also have a significant structural impact.

Occasionally, the structural engineer argues for a tank on a tall building. Sometimes they need a lot of mass at the top to damp out the period of the building. They want the 250,000-lb weight up there as a stabilizing factor.

HOT WATER

Hot-water systems, in order to maintain temperature, require some sort of recirculation system (Farruggia). Pressure-reducing valves are not good devices for recirculation, however, because when you recirculate, you do it at low flows.

All you really want to do is overcome friction in the line and get some movement in the water to maintain temperature. The pressure-reducing valve doesn't recognize those small flows.

As a result, systems generally are designed either with one or two large heaters per zone or with small instant heaters or point-of-use heaters located near restrooms, kitchens, and other areas where hot water is required.

POINT-OF-USE HEATERS

These work well because you don't have to worry about recirculation; you just use the heater where you need it. Minimizing the amount of hot-water piping also reduces energy loss.

A disadvantage appears when a great many individual heaters could create added costs and a potential maintenance headache.

Mr. Farruggia states: "One solution is to use one heater for every three floors. Try to use the principle of *convection* by putting the heater in the middle and allowing the natural convection of the heated water to create circulation. When tied back into the hot water line to create a loop, it works very well. It also cuts the number of heaters needed by two thirds."

With central zone heaters, a recirculation system generally is required, depending on client requirements. HOK's Zuniga says dead-end runs should be kept as short as possible to eliminate temperature drop.

A recirculation system reduces the time from when you turn on the faucet to when you get hot water. You design the

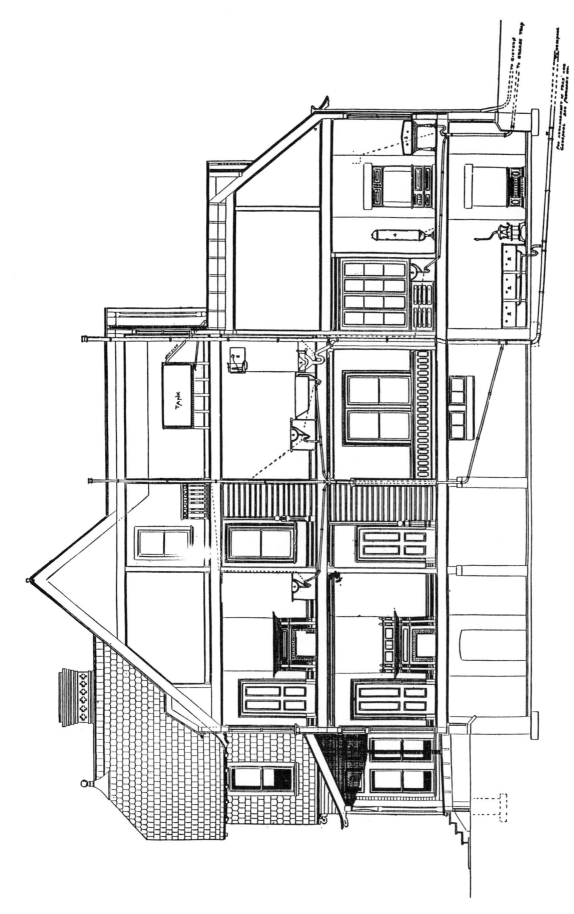

Figure 51b. Vintage plumbing drawing (1878).

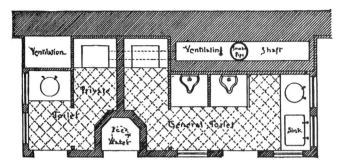

Figure 51c. Vintage plumbing drawing (1882).

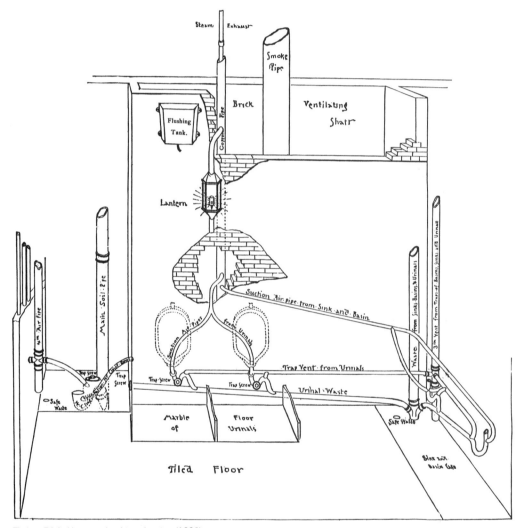

Figure 51d. Vintage plumbing drawing (1882).

system to meet the client's requirements. Generally, if you have to wait too long for hot water, you end up wasting water.

HEAT TAPE

This is an alternative to recirculation systems. A self-regulating electric resistance heater is wrapped around hot-water supply pipes and provides heat as required to compensate for temperature loss. Mr. Farruggia says because heat tape eliminates the need for a recirculation system, it opens new alternatives for system design.

"The real innovation in the heat tapes is that, if you don't

need to do recirculation anymore, you can, theoretically, have one heater for the entire building. This could have an impact in places with significant hot water use, such as hotels and apartments, but may not be appropriate for a typical office application. Careful economic study and a review of local codes and regulations is needed."

MIXING VALVE SELECTION

Selection of the proper mixing valve can be an important part of energy- and water-conservation efforts. *As water use de-*

Figure 51e. Plumbing fixtures in New York's Mutual Life Insurance Company building (1884).

Figure 51f. Plumbing fixtures in New York's Mutual Life Insurance Company building (1884).

creases, so do pumping and heating requirements. The effect on energy is obvious.

Mr. Farruggia is working with the U.S. Wildlife Federation to obtain grants and tax incentives for systems that use "gray water," such as the water that comes off air-conditioning coils, bathroom lavatories, and kitchen and slop sinks, for flushing water closets and similar applications. It is basically clean water and could be recycled easily, instead of going to waste.

State and local governments are putting increasingly tight restrictions on water use. Some localities are mandating 1.5 gal per flush where 5 to 7 gal were formerly used.

The amount of noise produced by a mixing valve can also be a selection factor. Familiarity with various products, in the absence of manufacturers giving noise characteristics, is needed.

SANITARY AND STORM DRAINS

Several factors influence this design. As water falls approximately 10 floors, it reaches its terminal velocity of 32.2 feet per second. As a result, the piping system must be designed with adequate support at horizontal elbows and offsets to maintain its structural integrity.

According to Mr. Farruggia, the main concern is:

1. The type of piping material. You certainly would not want to use a compression-type fitting that is good for only 30 to 40 ft of head. If you did get a backup and the line experienced the full height of the building, it would not hold up.

2. Another major concern with sanitary drain systems is providing adequate relief venting to prevent the system from becoming air-bound. As the water swirls to the bottom of the stack, it converges on itself and closes off the bottom of the pipe. As that happens, if there is a lot of flow, the water begins to back up because there is air in front of it to constrict it. A relief vent is put right at that point so that any air in there will exhaust itself up the relief vent, resulting in a nice, even flow of water down the offset.

DESIGNING FOR FLEXIBILITY

Flexibility to meet future tenant requirements is accommodated using a *wet-stack* design concept. In addition to the main stack, wet stacks are located throughout the building, each with a complete cold-water, waste, and ventilation system and valved outlets on each floor.

The important feature is the space in the ceiling to run for long distances. It really becomes an issue with the drain line because you are *pitching an eighth of an inch every foot*. You

Figure 51g. Hemenway Building, Boston (1885). Figure 51h is the diagram of the building's plumbing and water supply.

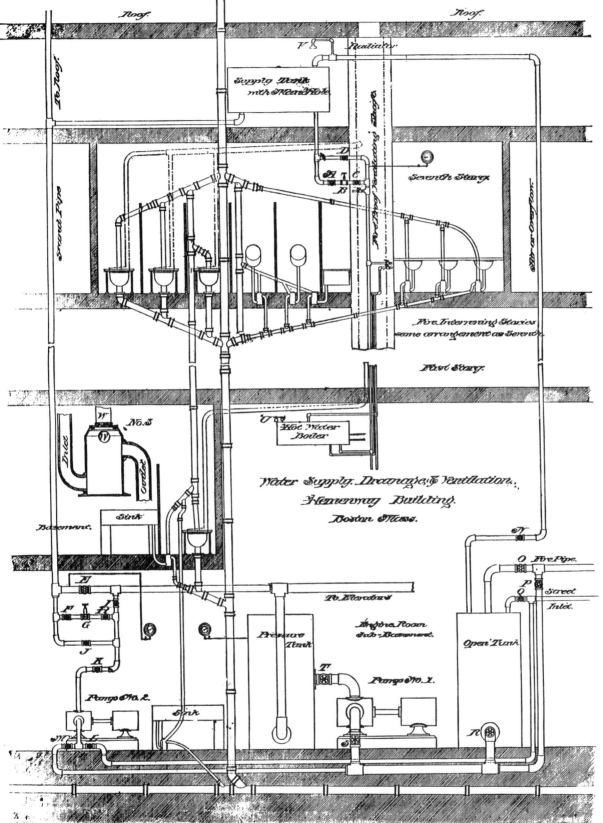

Figure 51h. Diagram of the plumbing and water supply in the Hemenway Building, Boston (1885).

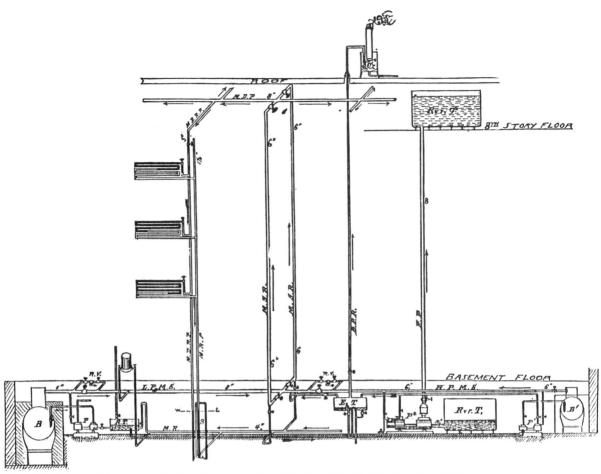

Figure 51i. Scheme of the piping in the Manhattan Company's and Merchants' Bank Building, New York (1885).

can't go too far without banging into something below the ceiling. Careful investigation has to be made in the beginning of the design procedure.

Where the owner is unwilling to spend extra money for wet stacks, other options are available. For instance, Mr. Zuniga says, "For a small floor plate, flexibility can be built in from the toilet room cores. You can take off from the major stacks and stub out from the ceiling of each floor and provide for future connections if they want it.

"A building's location may determine certain special plumbing requirements. For example, in an area with particularly hard water, a systemwide water softener may be necessary to prevent pipe corrosion and fixture staining.

"In hotels and apartments, extreme peak use periods in the early morning can make it difficult to design a cost-effective system that meets the building's needs.

"With historic buildings, the type of construction and usage, and not blindly used tables, must determine the system." (End of section adapted from Beck.)

Having read the engineering aspects, comments by a master plumber[34] can augment the picture:

"In many ways, installation of plumbing in older buildings is easier to install than in the modern ones. Many historic properties have a basement and a sub-basement to handle

the mechanical equipment for the plumbing, HVAC, and sprinkler systems. The main drains for the sanitary, storm drainage, and water mains are exposed to a point where they leave the building above the floor, thereby making it easier to repair in case of leaks. A typical old office building normally has what is called 'central toilet rooms,' namely, centered in the middle of the building for use from all directions.

"There is the advantage of having pipe spaces behind all plumbing fixtures, so that if a leak occurs, a plumber can get into the pipe space and make repairs. Vertical pipe chases are common in historic property.

"In some cases, access doors are only located at every other floor for the pipe chases. Still these are accessible. Soil pipe, steel pipe, and copper tubing should be cut in 10-ft lengths for installation in these structures. Welding can be difficult in some cases, but the use of *victaulic* couplings (mechanical joints) is great for installing wet or dry standpipe systems. They are also useful for chilled water and condenser water feeding and returning from chilled water systems installed on the roof, regardless of the height of the building.

"The weight of all plumbing pipes should be supported at each floor by using riser clamps so as to take the weight off of the total load proportionately.

"The average older office building has a minimum of two

---

[34] Comments by Joseph C. Rudolph, master plumber, W. Kramer Associates, Philadelphia.

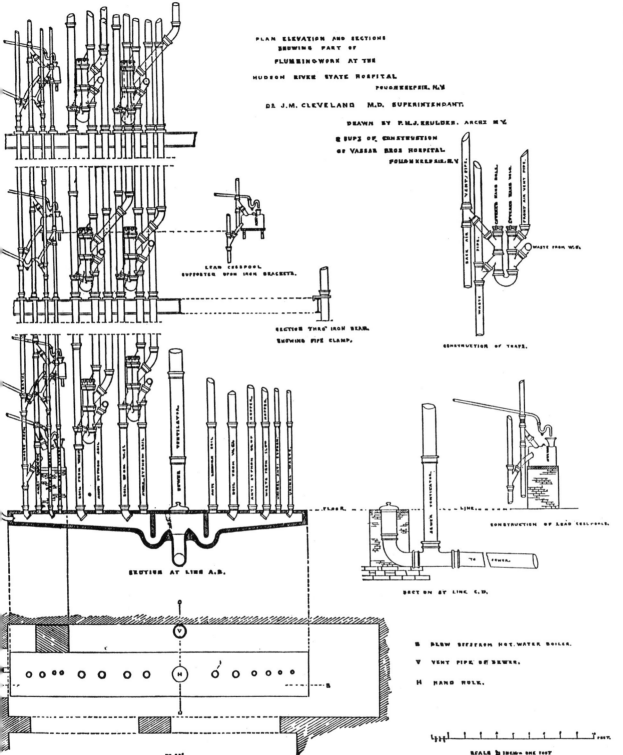

Figure 51j. Part of the plumbing of Hudson River State Hospital, Poughkeepsie, New York (1886).

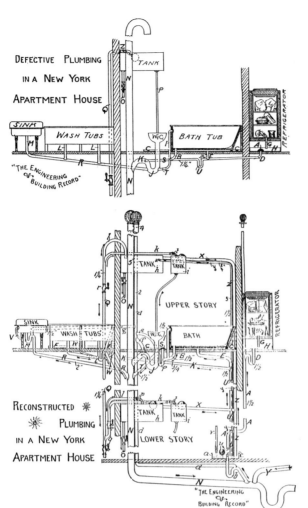

Figure 51k. Vintage plumbing drawing (1888).

stairwells. New piping can be installed at each floor by coring new holes at each stair landing."

For installation of new plumbing when no original drawings are available, Mr. Rudolph recommends the following:

1. Go outside the building and look for *fresh-air inlets* (FAI). These pipes relieve the sewer or storm system of excessive air blockage. They allow the system to drain without being slowed down by an air lock when there are drains being discharged from more than one toilet room.

2. Look for *water shutoff valves* or *water meter pits* on the outside of the building. The same goes for the gas service.

By doing the above, you will know where the starting point is for the various utilities.

3. Next, go into the basement or sub-basement and look for the continuation of the various systems. Check the vertical risers in the walls, and then go to the top floor. Usually there is access to the ceiling space, normally a minimum of 5 ft. Look for the vertical pipes that come from the floors below.

Quite often the sanitary vent pipes, which are the extension of the sanitary stacks tied together, go up through the roof

at one or several points, depending on the complexity of the system.

4. Where there are plaster walls with decorative trim on the ceilings, it is easy enough to cut walls and repair them. Stay away from the ornamental trim if you can! [*Author's comment:* Work on the flat.]

5. Many older office buildings with banks on the first floor have a two-story ceiling on the ground floor, with a mezzanine level. Most of these have 100 percent marble walls. However, in many cases there are back stairwells and halls which are accessible to the upper floors and it is not necessary to penetrate the marble.

6. Assembly rooms on upper floors with domed ceilings may present a problem repairing drain lines on the floor above. Look for an *access* ladder and door.

7. *Local vents* (air spaces) for the gang toilet rooms are generally no longer used. Mechanical exhaust fans have replaced them in most locations.

8. [*Author's comment:* One of the most annoying things is repairing or replacing old plumbing faucets that were made prior to World War II. Many companies have gone out of business and the existing ones have discontinued the lines. Cultivating a specialty company who can make the parts is a necessity. They do exist.] It is wise to use widely distributed name brands for replacements. You will have a better chance to find fittings when they wear out.

9. Plumbing fixtures (lavatories, etc.) have changed quite a bit over the last 90 years. The wall-hung sink placed in a battery in older offices and hotels may still be existence. So is the pedestal free-standing type. In the past, the water closets (toilets) were always floor-mounted. Today there are wall-hung units which need chair carriers to hold them off the floor.

10. The water seal in the traps of older floor drains may have dried up. Floor drains are still a very useful feature for public bathrooms.

11. Take advantage of modern materials for repairs to existing systems:
    a. Galvanized piping and galvanized drainage fittings have been replaced by cast-iron soil pipe (either bell or spigot or no-hub) or DWV copper tubing.
    b. Galvanized steel or brass pipe for water piping has been replaced by L-type copper tubing.
    c. Because of improved equipment, work on existing buildings has been made considerably easier. Diamond-coring machines for concrete, and electric Sawzalls, Bandsaws, and power demolition hammers are some of the items currently in use.

[*Author's comment:* Owners of historic buildings should seriously consider repiping the entire property, if the original pipes are disintegrating. This move is much more cost-effective than replacing one length at a time, and can eliminate a disastrous flood, damaging irreplaceable collections, furnishings, and materials. It also eliminates calling in contractors in the middle of the night on double time.]

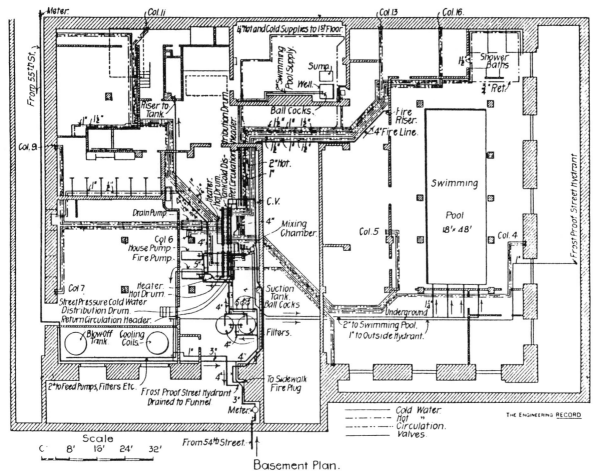

Figure 511. Plumbing in the University Club, New York (1898).

Mr. Rudolph further states, "The main thing to be taken into consideration is the coordination of the architect's design and that of the mechanical/electrical engineers. All systems which are to be installed in the same area have to be overlaid so that each gets necessary space. [*Author's comment:* Quite often this is overlooked and water pipes end up in the same location as the electrical system.] The actual size and location of the ductwork, piping, and drainage must be noted *before* construction. Never forget that drainage only goes one way—*downhill!*"

Appendix C contains a checklist for engineered plumbing and fire-protection systems.

CHAPTER NINE
LIGHTING

A selection of original diagrams from 1889 to 1905 on lighting and wiring is presented in Fig. 52 for an appreciation of these vintage installations in historic buildings.

The purpose of this chapter is simply to enhance *awareness* in accomplishing the desires of the client cost-effectively, while being careful of the building's architectural integrity. It is not intended as a treatise on lighting since there is wealth of technical information on the subject.

INTERIOR LIGHTING

It should be remembered that upscale clients have been using electric lights since the 1870s, even if, early on, in combination with the more dependable gas (combination fixtures with the electric bulb facing down, and gas jet burning up).

USES OF LIGHT

There are five basic uses of light: ambient light, task lighting, emergency lighting, security, and decoration.

Ambient light (the general illumination of the space) must be tailored to the date and use of the building. When historic properties are recycled for modern offices or other uses, *task lighting* (over the desk or work space) is needed to see properly. The light levels must be sufficiently high for the purpose. To date, much task lighting built into office furniture still leaves much to be desired, because most of the time it reaches only the back edge of the desk. More research in design would be helpful to deliver the light to the front of the desk, where it is required. Until such time, floor and table lamps in suitable types may augment what is lacking. If separate *emergency lights* do not fit into the historic design, it is always possible to hard-wire (place wire in protective metal conduit) existing period fixtures for emergency use. A well-lighted area is an

effective means of *security.*

LIGHT LEVELS

If an authentic period look is desired, lower light levels should be used than what the modern eye expects. It was only after World War II that the blinding brilliance of illumination, prior to the 1970s oil shortage, was in vogue. Before that, people used natural light, if available, or, in the beginning, crude sources such as rushes, candles, whale oil, kerosene, argon,

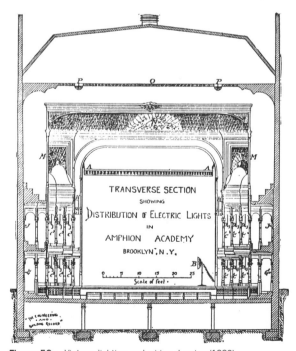

Figure 52a. Vintage lighting and wiring drawing (1889).

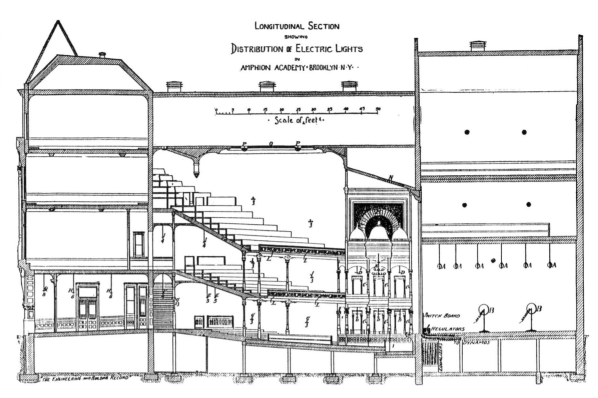

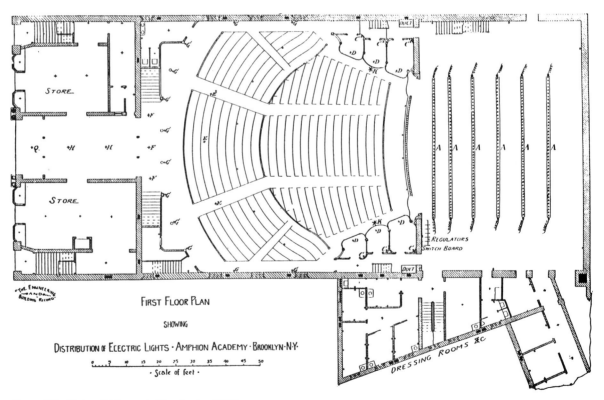

Figure 52b. Vintage lighting and wiring drawing (1889).

Figure 52c. Illuminated fountains at the Paris Exposition (1889).

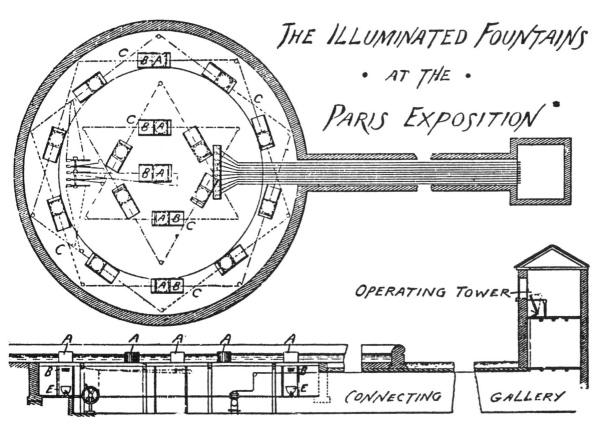

Figure 52d. Illuminated fountains at the Paris Exposition (1889).

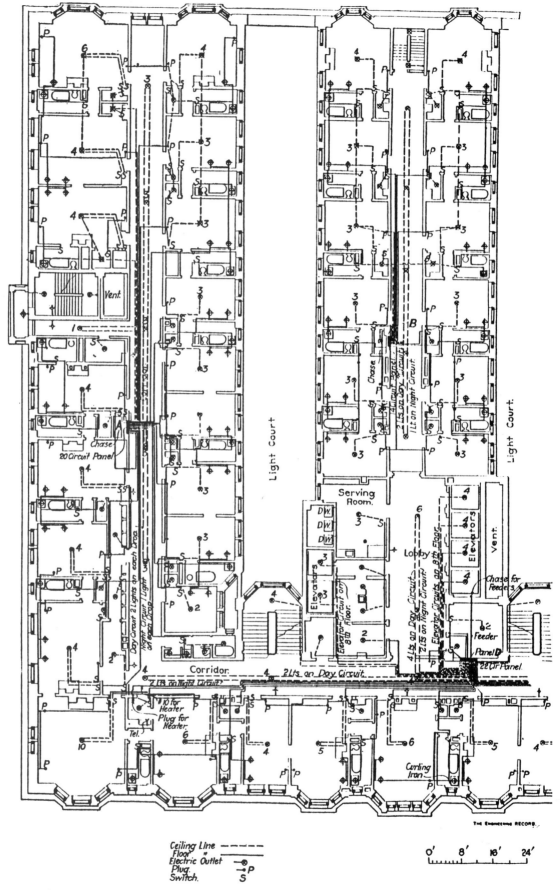

Figure 52e. Wiring of a typical floor of the Bellevue-Stratford Hotel, Philadelphia (1905).

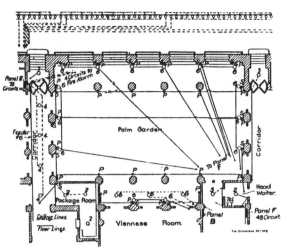

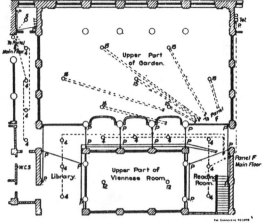

Figure 52f. Wiring of the Palm Garden of the Bellevue-Stratford Hotel, Philadelphia (1905).

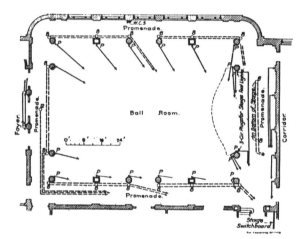

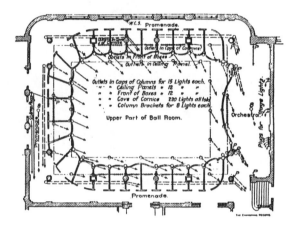

Figure 52g. Wiring of the ballroom of the Bellevue-Stratford Hotel, Philadelphia (1905).

and, after the 1830s, piped gas. The colors and fabrics of earlier times were selected for this dimmer light, and would appear strident and disappointing under modern illumination (Fig. 53). With the expanded use of computers, light levels have become lower, to avoid glare on the screen.

Light levels for museum-quality protection The *lux* is a unit of illumination of one lumen (uniform source of one candela) per square meter. For traditional (i.e., not the new fiber-optics) lighting, higher light levels (200 lux) are recommended for *oil*-based paintings; and lower levels (50 lux), for *water*-based paintings, drawings, documents, and similar. The lower (50-lux) intensity is recommended for the majority of materials—polymers such as textiles, photographic materials, plant-derived materials such as wallpaper, marquetry and veneer furniture (especially that secured by organic or animal-based glues), and animal-derived materials (feathers, fur, ivory, leather, etc.).

The effects of light that is too strong are irreversible. Thus light levels and time of exposure have to be controlled. Chemical changes caused by light energy include

1. *Fading* from ultraviolet (UV) rays invisible to the human eye.
2. *Drying* out from the infrared end of the spectrum from
   a. Visible daylight
   b. Artificial light

(1) Avoid uneven patches of light from tungsten incandescent.
(2) Shield fluorescent tubes from UV radiation.

The reason for attending to environmental controls for the *whole* museum building, instead of just having instruments in cases, is apparent from this equation:

$$UV \text{ rays } + \text{ moisture } = \text{ peroxide } = \text{ bleaching}$$

While the rays themselves may not be that dangerous, the water contained in humidity, people's breath, and condensation can combine with light to hasten disintegration of organic materials.

SPECIALTY LIGHTING

Period lighting (Fig. 54a to d) When specifying *period lighting,* there are varied sources:

1. Original pieces can be rewired, refinished, and cleaned.

2. Antique fixtures of the same period are available through dealers.

3. Custom shops can duplicate existing pieces.

Figure 53. Fifteenth-century lighting—only the very rich could afford to burn more than one candle at a time, except for special occasions.

4. If there is a sufficient market, major manufacturers can be convinced to reproduce needed styles for stock.

Although the American National Park Service goes out of its way not to confuse the onlooker into thinking that reproduction units are the real thing, a compromise selection suiting the period better than starkly modern fittings would be less jarring to the viewer.

Incorrect versions of period fixtures should not be used. Gas fixtures should have gas cocks and be suspended by gas pipe, not chain link (how can you get gas down a loop?); argon lamps should not have modern turn-off switches.

Examples of good and bad fixture design for period interiors are compared in Fig. 55.

Example

A recent "restoration" succeeded in turning a historic landmark into an antiseptic space more suitable for an operating room than to evoke previous events which occurred there. Modern lighting fixtures were selected which simply did not relate to the early-twentieth-century design. Together with the seemingly less-than-truthful "interpretation" of what had taken place in this building, the total glaring lighting scheme (sometimes downright theatrical) and wholesale removal of original fabric managed to lose the feel of the place completely. The ghosts were eliminated. Just walking through the modern glass doors after approaching under a 1970-type glass and metal canopy

was enough to eliminate the spell of antiquity.

Theatrical lighting in historic theaters   Again, this is a topic well-documented elsewhere, but inexperienced non-profit or new entrepreneurs should be aware of the extreme weight of modern stage lighting. Often, the roof structure has to be reinforced to accept the latest designs. Obviously, this may increase the total cost of recycling beyond the ability of the client to pay.

Something should also be said about backstage life and fire safety as a result of altered spaces.

Example

A repertory company took over an elaborate turn-of-the-century theater. They retained the ornate entrance lobby with its marble and stained glass, but elected to gut the entire interior auditorium to construct several levels of performing areas. Taste aside (this group was extremely avant garde, which in their case, translates as filthy), the condition of the wiring, the structural condition, and the general mess made it easy to see why directors kept leaving. If the audiences could see backstage, it is doubtful that they would have stayed, either, because the entire building was an approaching disaster.

Apparently the stage designer thought up the whole concept, without benefit of any design professionals. One look at a set he had mounted indicated the extent of his expertise.

It must not be forgotten that when an assemblage of people is part of the building's use, *life safety must be paramount.*

Television lighting   A great deal of heat is generated by lighting for television (e.g., 800 kW in the case of St. Paul's Cathedral in London). It requires additional cooling to avoid damaging interiors.

Seasonal provisions for lighting   Since Christmas comes around every year, permanent provisions should be made for interior and exterior special lighting. This would avoid the spaghetti festoons of wiring in otherwise acceptable spaces.

European fiber-optics lighting   In 1990, this system was just introduced for use in the United States. Here, all new inventions must await the approval of the American Underwriters' Laboratories before they can be used.

However, installations have been operating in other parts of the world for some years. There is still experimentation to expand the length of the effective wiring, but the possibilities are endless. This concept is what the museum world has been seeking for a long time—light that does not produce heat or ultraviolet rays to injure delicate organic materials.

Conceivably, the light levels where books, fabrics, paintings, and other items prey to disintegration can now be raised to ones that make it possible to see detail more clearly.

Any antique fixture, wall sconce, or even candlestick can be wired with fiber-optics. The light source ranges from incandescent to HID and most importantly, is remote from the point of emergence. This means that display cases need not be disturbed when the light source burns out. It also means that the inconvenience of reaching highly placed fixtures is eliminated. Care must be taken to avoid light falloff. Especially in historic spaces, where modern lighting would be inappropriate, the tiny fittings are ideal. The benefits of this type of system include

Figure 54a. How to furnish period lighting: Refurbishing original units.

Figure 54c. How to furnish period lighting: Purchased antique ceiling fixtures of the same period. Note small emergency lights over door to stairway, and concealed piping to fire alarm pull.

Figure 54b. How to furnish period lighting: Custom reproductions.

Figure 54d. How to furnish period lighting: Right out of stock.

1. Miniaturization of fixtures (some no larger than a fingernail)

2. No destructive heat or ultraviolet rays produced

3. Remote relamping, so that display cases do not have to be disturbed

4. Energy savings from lighting and room air-conditioning

TIPS ON INSTALLATION

Heat dissipation   No matter what the fixture, adequate provisions must be made for *heat dissipation*. Energy that creates light also creates heat. This heat must be dispersed so that surroundings do not blacken, bulb life is decreased, or a fire starts (Fig. 56).

This means leaving space for enough ventilation to eliminate the heat, or providing mechanical means to dispel it. Ceiling fixtures must have sufficient space above the ceiling to accomplish this. Lighting fixtures themselves can have ventilating holes. For dimmers, small exhaust fans may have to be employed. Timers, dimmers, and occupancy sensors can all be used for energy conservation and protection of contents.

Example

A world-famous historic property was illuminated by newly designed outdoor floodlighting which reached such high temperatures that it was actually cooking the tourists who approached. Back to the drawing board!

Figure 55b. An example of a bad choice of fixtures for a period interior: Unacceptable downlights in ornate space.

Figure 55c. An example of a bad choice of fixtures for a period interior: Wrong color and insensitively mounted.

Figure 55d. An example of a bad choice of fixtures for a period interior: No Victorian fixture was ever like this! (Compare to Fig. 55f.)

Insulation   Lighting fixtures attached to an interior of an exterior wall should have *insulation* (as simple as a cork) to allow air to circulate between the wall and the back of the fitting.

Location and baffling   Practical methods of installation do not need an engineer to decide that wall mounted sconces should not be at eye level of a 6-ft man. Nor should the stems of those fixtures be cut off so that the heat from the lamp is dangerously close to the wall covering, causing blackening or worse. No matter whether the fixtures are ceiling, wall, or

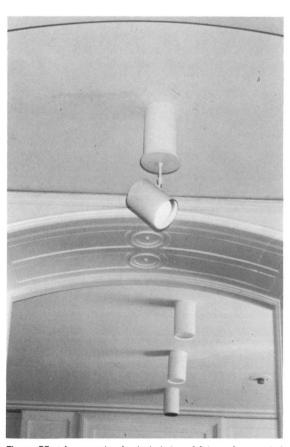

Figure 55a. An example of a bad choice of fixtures for a period interior: Unnecessary numbers of unsuitable surface-mounted units.

otherwise mounted, the source of light must be shielded from the viewer's eye.

Rewiring crystal fixtures The following measures are recommended:

Photograph all details before dismantling.

Put pieces in *labeled* cardboard boxes as soon as dismantled.

Check metal hooks and connections for weakness or corrosion.

Dry every piece carefully—a portable hair dryer set at cold is useful.

Ordinary fishing line can hold up sagging arms invisibly (Fig. 57).

If there is a winch in the ceiling, try to repair it so the fixture can be lowered for easier service.

Example

A 1930s ornate bank retrofit some mezzanine chandeliers from incandescent to high-intensity-discharge (HID) usage. It was possible to install the ballast within the fixture itself, instead of in a remote location. Selected fixtures were hard-wired (in conduit) for emergency use, thus eliminating the necessity for intrusive emergency lights on the marble walls (Fig. 58).

The difference in light, once changed, was so marked that the rest of the units on the banking floor below looked pale by comparison. There are energy savings as well as longer times between relamping with the new system.

Figure 55e. Silly place to attach extra lighting.

Figure 55f. An example of a good choice of fixtures for a period interior: Compare this style to that in Fig. 55d.

Low-voltage wiring There are several advantages to using *low-voltage* (12-V) instead of *high-voltage* (U.S. 120 V; European 220 V) wiring and fittings.

1. Less energy is utilized.
2. Openings and fittings are smaller and less obtrusive.
3. Less heat is generated (thus reducing air-conditioning load).

Lamp life and energy use As a rule of thumb, *life expectancy* increases, and *energy use* decreases in the following order:

1. Incandescent
2. Fluorescent
3. HID (high-intensity discharge)
4. High- and low-pressure sodium

Users should understand that for other than incandescent, constantly turning units requiring a ballast on and off *does not* increase life. In fact, it reduces it. Once turned on, fluorescents and HID lamps are better left on.

The last two selections, while cost-effective, are least acceptable in historic locations. High-pressure sodium may be color-corrected to some extent, but low-pressure sodium cannot. In both cases, the fixtures themselves do not yet lend themselves to such use. New types of lamps and bulbs which give better light with less energy use are being developed all the time. The client should keep abreast of the latest available.

A word should also be said about selecting the proper lamp and bulb color and shape for the particular fixture. A plain round bulb where a flame shape is needed cancels out the most expensive fixture. Also, if two different types of lamp are installed in the same fixture, this makes the mistake that much more obvious (Fig. 59).

Likewise, yellowish warm white fluorescent may not be suitable where color-corrected deluxe cool white is the choice to make. Of course, sometimes it is not the fault of maintenance personnel because the purchasing department may not have done its job in stocking all the types needed.

Electrical savings and payback are highly predictable by tracking lighting costs. Flexibility rather than automation is more practical.

Example

In the December/January 1986 issue of *Energy Management Technology Magazine,* there was a report about a 2-year retrofit of the New York Metropolitan Life Insurance Company's 96 floors and 3.75 million square feet of lighting space. A conservative 25 percent of the annual lighting bill was recouped by this exercise.

"Modular powerline carrier (PLC) technology was used. It

Figure 55h. An example of a good choice of fixtures for a period interior: If the original lighting scheme can be retained, as in this late-1920s space, the solution is at hand.

Figure 55i. An example of a good choice of fixtures for a period interior: This early-1930s lighting cannot be improved on.

Figure 55j. An example of a good choice of fixtures for a period interior: Lacking any other ideas, a floor lamp of the period can be used.

required minimal building disturbance to the 31-floor 1932 building, the 14-floor 1960 structure, and the famous 700-foot Metropolitan Life Tower, built in 1909.

"In addition to saving money and having better control, the owners wanted the ability to set "theme" lighting—variable lighting levels in specific areas (lobbies, art gallery, tower), according to changing requirements. Also, the valuable Art Deco paintings and marble surfaces of the 1932 structure and the Tower had to be protected from damage during installation.

"The system selected was easily installed by Metropolitan's own staff on a convenient two-stage schedule, and it delivered

Figure 55g. An example of a good choice of fixtures for a period interior: The original fitting suits this 1920 interior.

Figure 56. Notice the blackening around each fixture; this indicates heat buildup

a rapid payback on investment.

"PLC technology operates by transmitting command signals over a building's existing alternating current (AC) wiring. Therefore, it does not require costly or damaging construction (to run new wiring) or dedicated control circuits, leaving the architectural integrity of the building intact.

"The control system operates as a flexible network of devices in which command units (manual or programmable) transmit coded command signals [CCS] over existing AC wiring to specially coded relay modules configured as switches and receptacles. These modules detect their own codes and respond by turning their respective loads on or off.

"To illuminate seasonal lighting, a CCS manual controller was pressed to transmit a coded signal (C1) over all AC wiring in the three-building complex in seconds. Every switch and receptacle receiver controlling holiday lighting had been set previously to the same C1 code. Each, detecting its own signal, switched on its specific load. This simultaneously lit two giant lobby Christmas trees and 12 trees and other displays in ground floor atrium windows, and washed the 700-ft Tower with green and red floodlighting.

"The computer is easily operated or reprogrammed by office personnel. A hard copy of each schedule can be printed.

"In order to install a PLC system in a high-rise building, there must be an inspection and testing of its electrical distribution systems. Many older buildings work off a 120/208-V three-phase system.

"Additional phases of the work will enable additional energy savings (by turning off office equipment such as desktop computers, copiers, typewriters, and coffee machines at night). There is also the capability to extend programmable control for HVAC. [*Author's comment:* Air-conditioning can be turned

Figure 57. Almost-invisible fishing line was used to support fixture arms which bounced too much when lowered for relamping.

Figure 58a. Retrofitting original incandescent fixtures to HID: The special insert to hold the ballast.

Figure 58c. Retrofitting original incandescent fixtures to HID: An interior view of the bulb.

Figure 58b. Retrofitting original incandescent fixtures to HID: Putting the ballast into the fixture.

Figure 58d. Retrofitting original incandescent fixtures to HID: The marked difference in the light.

down at night, but never off, because the initial surge to start it up again in the morning would take more energy than was saved the night before. Also, additional current would be needed to cool down a now-overheated area.]

"At all times, an employee working late (or early) can use the wall switch module to manually override programmed schedules and turn on lighting, etc., in his/her space. In the evening, special light levels are programmed to serve the cleaning crew."

Maintenance   At all times, design for *ease of maintenance.* Urge *scheduled* relamping. This will reduce cost of getting

ladders or erecting scaffolds for individual fixtures. It will also ensure better lighting at the level originally designed. Refer to ASHRAE/IES (Illuminating Engineering Society) procedures for further information.

Example

A large municipal zoo was celebrating the gift of 70 elephants. In anticipation of the fund-raising party for the occasion, special lighting of the animals' area was arranged. The fixtures selected were intended for HID lamps to be burned in an *upright* position. This fact was not indicated on the fixtures or the lamps.

Consequently, the lamps were installed facing downward instead of up. The gathered group of spectators was mystified when the switch was pulled and they saw a herd of *blue* elephants. The light was altered from the expected color of metal halide because of the incorrect installation.

Accidents such as this could be easily avoided if lamp manufacturers would follow the lead of fuse manufacturers. They furnish *rejection-type* fuses which can be installed only in the correct way. Lamps and bulbs should have this same *notched feature.* Moreover, the fixtures should be plainly marked in *raised lettering* how the lamps should be placed.

Example (Fig. 60)

An 1868 four-story brownstone town house was converted into a contractor's office. When the company moved in, in 1939, things Victorian were considered worthy only of the trash heap. In fact, people had to be paid to take away carved pier mirrors, woodwork, and other decorative features, items which would command large sums today. Then, it was expected to drop ceilings from the 15-ft height, paint over the rich wood, and generally "modernize." In 1987, after years of putting up with stifling rabbit-warrens of offices, poor lighting, hot/cold pockets, lack of space, very few outlets for the increasing array of office equipment, and blowing fuses every time an electric heater was plugged in, it was decided to do some major work to correct all of the unmatched, jerry-built changes that had "growed like Topsy."

Starting with the basement, everything that had to be cor-

Figure 59a. Incorrect shape bulbs in antique fixture; flame type would be more suitable.

Figure 59b. Relamp all like bulbs at one time.

Figure 59c. Make installation convenient to relamping. This high fixture in the background has never been relamped because it requires an expensive scaffold.

rected or added was noted on a legal-sized pad. Pictures were taken of the offending features. Six months was spent on deciding space requirements and provisions for equipment before the first nail was hit. The floors and stairs were covered with plywood and the doors were removed for refinishing and safekeeping during construction. Etched glass was covered. All wiring was chased into solid masonry walls and the plaster repatched.

From a depressing melange of disorganization, some order was designed. Instead of squinting, the office and engineering staff could finally see what they were doing. In the first-floor administrative offices, the original gas pipes were the spots where copies of a wall sconce were placed. While doing an

800-room hotel, the contractor convinced a manufacturer to reproduce Victorian fixtures needed for this building. They, and other designs taken from original pattern books, are now in the catalog.

The actual room lighting comes from HID fixtures placed on the cubicle partitions and painted out. The over-desk lighting which came with the furniture was completely changed to throw light toward the front of the desk. When even this correction was not enough for some operators, fluorescent gooseneck desk lamps served for electronic typewriter use. The computer terminals were placed to receive minimum glare.

Since there never had been a central ceiling fixture in this double parlor, none was used now. Very small emergency lights

Figure 60a. The rehabilitation of a Victorian townhouse: Total confusion—poor lighting and HVAC, cramped space.

Figure 60b. The rehabilitation of a Victorian townhouse: Same space as shown in Fig. 56a with improved lighting, acoustic treatment, and private workplaces.

Figure 60c. The rehabilitation of a Victorian townhouse: Ornamental doors with concealed wiring for security. The top rail of the door was removed, and space chiseled out for wire.

Figure 60d. The rehabilitation of a Victorian townhouse: Installing the door opener.

were installed unobtrusively in strategic places, and painted out.

With full carpeting on the floors, heavy-duty acoustic material on the partitions, and triple acoustic material on the now-restored ceiling, the resounding noises formerly endured were eliminated. All wiring from panelboards is projected against electrical surges. There are ample outlets for clocks, radios, computers, calculators, terminals, printers, and telephones at each station. On every floor, there is a television monitor for viewing callers and to release the secured doors to allow entry.

It was a logistical puzzle to color-code every piece of furniture and other equipment for transfer to another floor while construction was under way. The first floor went to the third and then returned to the first. The second floor went to the third and then back to second, whose occupants were split up, with half finally going to the third floor. Everything happened on a Saturday, so that Monday morning, the staff could go right to work. The movers were in constant attendance and transported heavy filing cabinets with great cheer.

The change was so great that visitors who have not been in for a while universally exclaim "Wow!" when they enter. Almost every day, an employee can be seen giving a friend the $5 tour. The best part about the job was that it was done under the 20 percent investment tax credit (ITC), and a considerable sum was deducted from federal taxes for 2 years. What is more, the project won BOMA's[35] first "In Pursuit of

[35] Building Owners and Managers' Association.

Figure 60e. The rehabilitation of a Victorian townhouse: Original hardware back in place on door.

Figure 61a. Unsuitable choice of fixtures: Fluorescent and ornamental plaster do not mix.

Figure 61b. Unsuitable choice of fixtures: The light source should always be concealed.

Figure 61c. Unsuitable choice of fixtures: Too many downlights, and inappropriate for early-nineteenth-century space.

Figure 61d. Unsuitable choice of fixtures: Emergency lights—wrong color, too big, plugged in on wall, all ruining historic room.

Excellence Award" for being the best office building in the city in the "Historical Category."

The plasterers, carpenters, painters, and plumbers exchanged tips with the electricians, so that all these tradesmen now know a lot more about the other's craft, to all their benefits. The then fifth-year apprentice is now a journeyman and is in great demand for older buildings.

His current project is a 1906 head office which had suffered tremendous fire damage. When asked if he could move some monumental lighting fixtures, he knew a few tricks of the trade learned from the old-timer on the previous job, to do it quickly and without damage.

Unsuitable fixture installations (Fig. 61)

Fluorescent industrial fixtures should never be attached to Victorian ceiling medallions.

Indirect lighting must have the light source *concealed*. Baffles should be used.

The less fixtures and holes in the ceiling, the better.

Emergency lights should never be installed on period walls without concealing the battery pack (behind the wall or elsewhere). Their location should be as unobtrusive as possible. The small fixtures should be selected in preference to the large (Fig. 61d).

EXTERIOR LIGHTING

The success of *son et lumière* (sound and light) shows in Europe has proven the economic reason for illuminating important buildings. Not only does this action indicate the cultural attractions in a city, but it also enhances security. The cost of lighting up the top of a 51-story Art Deco skyscraper is only $25 per night, using off-peak electricity rates!

Obviously, since every building is different, a competent

lighting designer should be used to specify the best solution for the particular circumstances.

When it comes to floodlighting the exterior of buildings, there are two basic schools of thought: illuminating only the *ornate tops of structures* (which automatically eliminates many modern square boxes with no architectural interest) and lighting the *entire property,* from top to bottom. Of course, this presupposes a sufficient vantage point from which to view. The Channel Gardens of New York's Rockefeller Center offer such an opportunity. Otherwise, the beholder will be too close to the glare of the fixtures themselves to appreciate the sight.

Another factor to consider is where to locate the floodlights conveniently while avoiding the possibility of vandalism. If it is difficult or too expensive to install lighting on the building itself, choices include making use of street lighting poles, burying units in surrounding landscape, or striking an arrangement with adjoining buildings. In any case, however the lighting is installed, *be careful to conceal wiring and baffling the light source.*

Here is a procedure for *small-scale* area focusing.

1. Team size (total personnel 2 to 8)
   a. Electrical contractor or consultant
   b. Plant specialists (if landscaping is involved)
   c. Chief focuser
2. Time
   a. From mid-September to mid-March
   b. All work to be done *after dark*
   c. Use of an astronomical twilight chart
      (1) Latitude of project
      (2) Specific time zone
3. When to start
   a. After all preliminary wiring completed and fixtures have been set in approximate location
   b. After all lighting equipment has been tested for proper functioning
   c. After all accessories (lenses, lamps, etc.) are on site
   d. After all related equipment (lifts, ladders, fastening, lamps) is on site
4. Length of focusing session (3 to 8 hours per night)
5. Actual focusing:
   a. Aim for effect desired.
   b. Balance brightness.

   c. Document final settings and lamps.
      (1) Mark "as-built" plan with specific lamp for each fixture.
      (2) Note direction in which each fixture is aimed; designate specific planting (if landscaping is involved).
      (3) Note additional accessories needed.
      (4) Note areas which will change with plant growth.
6. Communication to team:
   a. How equipment should be set up
   b. Order
      (1) Ground-mounted fixtures first.
      (2) Ground downlights second.
   c. Assignment of tasks
      (1) Direct the aiming.
      (2) Physically adjust the equipment.
      (3) Coordinate accessories and/or tools.
      (4) Document the final design.
   d. Assignment of time schedule for each area

Note: When mounting height is under 20 ft, set fixtures in approximate locations with ladders. For mountings over 20 ft, use tree specialists' equipment. Obviously for high-rise buildings, suitable safety equipment must be used.

Suggested tools are

Heavy gloves (to handle hot lamps)

Welders' glasses (for bright lamps in the dark)

Materials for taking notes

Flashlights

Spare louvers, lenses, lamps

Sufficient hand tools for the entire team

Walkie-talkie radios for easier communication

Caution: All wiring and equipment must be suitable for humidity, wind, and rain (or snow and/or ice). All installations must take these conditions into account.

All conduits and pipe placed under excavated earth must be properly marked and access to each provided. The garden manager must be consulted before any excavating is to occur in landscaped areas.

CHAPTER TEN
ACOUSTICS AND VERTICAL TRANSPORTATION

There are two M/E topics that could have a great impact on the interiors of older real estate: acoustics and vertical transportation.

ACOUSTICS

The reason for inclusion of acoustics in this book is because there are so many former 1920s and 1930s movie palaces being turned into nonprofit performing arts centers throughout the United States. However, each type of presentation requires different sound delivery, from legitimate theater to opera, lectures, ballet, classical and rock concerts, and movies. The acoustics of a house cannot be all things to all disciplines, and only a compromise can be afforded. Therefore the acoustic installation can range from tightly woven parachute silk hung horizontally over the performing area, to multi-million-dollar equipment.

In all cases, care must be taken not to permanently scar the interior finishes when stringing cables or hanging the very heavy equipment from the auditorium ceiling. Often, the roof structure has to be reinforced before modern theatrical gear is introduced.

Acoustics is a subject reminiscent of the famous Victorian song "The Lost Cord." What did they do then that isn't being done now? From roughly 1875 to 1900, many theaters were designed whose acoustics, in the absence of electronic amplification, were extraordinary. In the amazing 4600-seat Auditorium Building built in the late 1880s by Adler and Sullivan

in Chicago, a person speaking on the stage can be heard at the top of the house, a block and a half away, without mechanical assistance, as though standing next to the listener. "Progress" has eliminated the use of traditional architectural design and natural materials in favor of expensive equipment which usually sends the listener out into the street with a blinding headache from the excessive noise.

SPECIAL TREATMENT FOR CONCERT HALLS[36]

In addition to acoustic criteria for noise-producing equipment, there is also the need for constant relative humidity (50 percent) to keep musical instruments in tune. Because of the potential for moisture migration within the building, particularly during intermission, when the doors of the concert hall are open to the lobby area, it is necessary to humidify the entire building.

Using *thermal storage,* generating chilled water during off-peak periods results in lower operating costs by taking advantage of lower utility rates.

During the cold-weather months, finding a method to recycle heat to augment the building heating system is another energy-saver. Acoustic considerations include the following:

Isolation joints are used for the mechanical equipment room.

All supply, return, and exhaust air ducts are acoustically lined.

---

[36] Adapted from Anthony M. Cottone, P. E., "Featured Performer; Thermal Storage," *Heating/Piping/Air Conditioning,* August 1990.

Ductwork serving noise-critical spaces is physically separated from that serving noncritical spaces.

Special air nozzles were designed without directional vanes and volume control devices to supply air to the main auditorium.

Electrical switchgear is installed on a floating "jack-up" slab to prevent the transmission of hum and vibration into the building structure.

There is separation of power and sound conduit throughout the building to reduce the possibility of electrical interference.

Plumbing fixtures and roughing are fitted with vibration isolators.

Constant volume systems with zoned reheat are used to service noise-critical spaces and areas with a high population density.

Variable-air-volume (VAV) systems with hot-water heating coils at the VAV terminals are used for administrative areas, dressing rooms, and storage spaces.

Double-walled internally insulated fan casings were used to attenuate noise.

Duct silencers were provided where further noise reduction was wanted.

Air distribution In a concert hall, integrating the acoustic requirements and air distribution with the architectural design is a challenge. The optimum noise level to be maintained within the concert hall is the threshold of hearing when compared to the noise criteria curves. To obtain this, grilles and volume dampers are not permitted at the air outlets serving the hall.

These special air terminals consist of a straight duct section internally lined glass fiber and a perforated metal inner liner, terminating at a plain duct opening without volume dampers, directional vanes, and grilles. Volume adjustment is accomplished via interchangeable bellmouth openings installed at the nozzle inlet. The nozzles are supplied with air through large acoustically lined plenums to ensure even distribution.

All acoustical testing was conducted during night and early morning hours when the ambient background noise was at a minimum.

Example (Fig. 62)

William Cavanaugh[37] writes: "Today there are other factors which did not come into play at the turn of the century. Among them are the noise and vibration of modern HVAC, the use of non-naturally-occurring materials like fibre-glass instead of plaster, and the general outside sounds of traffic and airplanes, in addition to the non-traditional design of a building."

WHAT AFFECTS ACOUSTICS

1. Size of the hall
   a. Cubic volume.
   b. Distances from stage to listeners.

Figure 62. Mid-nineteenth-century Mechanics Hall, Worcester, Massachusetts.

   c. Hall width and height.
   d. Cubic volume of a hall and its interior finishes, which determine the *reverberation* characteristics, i.e., the degree of persistence of sound (music or speech) after the source stops. (Excessive persistence is unfavorable for speech events, rendering them unintelligible.)
2. Low level of background sound
   a. The location of the hall relative to outside noises (basement or upper floor) has an effect.
   b. Natural ventilation eliminates the need for mechanical air-moving fans, if that is possible.

Historic halls Many designers of historic halls instinctively created space with the following features:

1. There was a quiet ambient sound condition with little or no intrusive interfering sound.

2. The desired sounds were delivered to all listeners with adequate loudness, with adequate blending of music sounds yet not excessive persistence such that speech sounds were blurred.

3. The hall was free of discreet echoes, focusing, and other undesirable acoustical phenomena.

[37] Adapted from William J. Cavanaugh, Senior Partner, Cavanaugh Tocci Associates, Sudbury, Mass., "Mechanical Air Handling System—A Case History of Mechanics Hall," *Technology and Conservation Magazine*, Fall 1980.

4. The hall was of a "shoebox" design
   a. Finished in hard sound-reflective materials (plaster or masonry ceiling and walls, wood floors).
   b. [*Author's comment:* There is also the "Bayreuth" design which is effective. It uses an expanded stage apron over the orchestra pit.]

5. The seating capacity of the hall was relatively small (up to 2700 seats).

SUBJECTIVE ATTRIBUTES IN MUSIC ACOUSTICS

The reader is directed to L. L. Beranek's *Music Acoustics and Architecture* (John Wiley & Sons, New York, 1962) for the 18 attributes listed for music acoustical quality.

Of all the 18, *intimacy* has been found to be the single most predominant attribute. This is where the early reflected sound arrives at the listener's ear after the direct sound. In Mechanics Hall in Worcester, Massachusetts (constructed in 1857), intimacy rates highly because of the relative narrowness of the space.

Interior design fabric   Sound-absorbing materials of aisle carpeting and seat upholstery must be chosen wisely. Whether the house is full or empty affects sound and selection of amplification hardware.

Location of equipment   In the case of Mechanics Hall, the decision had to be made regarding where to put the fans, motors, heating, and refrigerant equipment: in the remote basement and lower levels of the building or in the attic space directly above the main hall created by the building roof truss system?

The former location would be costly because of lengthy duct runs and need to use some of the valuable commercial space at the lower levels which have direct access to the street. In the latter location, extraordinary noise and vibration control would be required; this entailed the following:

1. Create a new separate room within the attic with a "beefed up" floor structure (gypsum concrete floor slab poured over a reinforced existing wood floor).

2. Fan equipment was mounted on massive concrete inertia pads which were resiliently separated from the building structure by means of steel spring vibration isolators.

3. All supply and return-air ducts serving the main hall were internally lined and fitted with special duct silencers to reduce fan-generated noise transmission to acceptable levels in the hall. Particular attention was given to regenerated noise at the linear supply diffusers concealed along with the side balcony fronts. Exit velocities were kept low (250 ft/min) and air volume control dampers were relocated away from the grille discharge face.

4. To control intrusions of external noises, all doors to the main hall were fully gasketed and the lobby and public circulation areas were acoustically treated with sound- and "footstep"-absorbing carpeting.

5. A resilient suspended ceiling in the hall below provided the desired degree of sound insolation between the two performing spaces and permits their simultaneous use for most events.

Here is yet another case where something that was inherently good to start with was preserved and brought to twentieth-century standards of comfort and safety. (End of section adapted from Cavanaugh.)

ELEVATORS[38]

Currently, there are three major categories of elevators:

1. *Hydraulic*—least expensive and suitable for low-rise, heavy-duty use

2. *Geared motor*—for mid-rise operation

3. *Gearless and/or variable-speed motor*—for high-rise, energy-conserving service

The gearless motor can last indefinitely. The variable speed accommodates for sudden changes in traffic without requiring a larger-sized motor which may be underutilized most of the time.

Over speeds of 2000 feet per second, cabs may have to be pressurized for human comfort, but the difficulties of depressurization at each floor and lobby are not yet resolved. Ordinary travel time now ranges between 200 and 500 ft.

At least one supplier, Otis Elevator, maintains warehouses and machine shops that can either furnish obsolete parts from stock or manufacture anything dated 1852 or after from original prints and casts. *This means that existing equipment can be kept working safely and efficiently in older buildings.* Also, modular controllers are available which can be inserted in the often tight spaces which formerly made replacement difficult. Extensive research is going on all over the world, from Germany to Japan on miniaturization of machinery and better use of electric power.

The architect Craig Morrison suggests that if a new addition is made to an historic building needing an elevator, that the elevator be put in the new wing, to avoid resorting to variances in the original section of the property.

Michael Farinola advises: "The restoration of elevators with significant historical value follows much the same consideration as the building they reside in. Before any steps are taken, you must first decide if you wish to merely 'preserve' the aesthetics or take on the formidable task of full 'historic landmark' restoration" (Fig. 63).

He recommends the following steps as a general guide to either type of restoration.

IDENTIFYING THE EQUIPMENT

The identification of the manufacturer of the elevator can be the most important step, especially if you want to restore the elevator to its original status. Most manufacturers used a system of numbering the elevator, usually found on a metal tag mounted on the controller, machine motor, and the elevator cab crosshead. If the manufacturer is still in business, ask for any details of the original installation which may help you to

---

[38] Courtesy of Michael Farinola, Otis Elevator.

Figure 63. A turn-of-the-century elevator. New, thin, unbreakable glass is now available to allow for retention of the original open metal cab.

decide how to proceed. Some inquiries may reveal if the elevator was installed after the building was erected, or whether it was ever modernized.

CODE AND OTHER AUTHORITIES

Almost all states in the United States use the American National Standards Institute (ANSI) A 17.1 Safety Code for Elevators. Pennsylvania and a handful of other jurisdictions are exceptions, using their own versions. The governing code authority (the governmental body which is responsible for enforcing the code it has adopted) for each state varies; in Pennsylvania, it is the Department of Labor and Industry, Elevator Division, located in Harrisburg. In New Jersey, the state delegates responsibility in each municipality for enforcement of the ANSI A 17.1.

Under "grandfathering" the building owner is usually only required to adhere to the code that was in force at the time the elevator was installed. However, you may have to bring the elevator up to current code requirements if your restoration is only the aesthetics *and* you are upgrading (modernizing) the controls. You may still be able to petition for a waiver under some circumstances.

SURVEY OF EQUIPMENT

At this point, with the type of restoration chosen, and the code issues addressed, you are ready for a site survey. This should

be done by the manufacturer or any competent qualified elevator contractor. Remember that restoration work is not your typical repair job; therefore, keep in mind there is a direct correlation between the thoroughness of the survey and the quality of the work performed.

The areas to be surveyed should be

1. *The machine room*—where the machine, generators, governor, selector, and controllers should be checked for repairs or replacement. The main line switch should also be checked for safe and proper operation.

2. *The hoistway*—where door hangers, rollers, interlocks, limit switches, car-door operator, counterweight, and main guides and rails, in addition to hoist ropes (cables), are located. Safeties and traveling cables are inspected for retention, repairs, or replacement.

3. *The pit equip*—where the final limit switches, safety plank, buffers, governor tension sheaves, selector tape, and clearances are checked for required adjustment, repairs, or replacement.

4. *The fixtures*—usually retained because they are part of the aesthetics; include the hall buttons, hall lanterns, and position indicators.

5. *The entrances*—also usually retained because of aesthetics. Some hoistway door entrances are quite elaborate. [*Author's comment:* Strawbridge & Clothier in Philadelphia

Figure 64a. Original elevator doors, first third of twentieth century: Metal.

Figure 64b. Original elevator doors, first third of twentieth century: Marquetry.

and The Chrysler Building in New York are good examples of art deco design in metal and marquetry.] (Fig. 64)

6. *The cab*—the focal point of any restoration. The most popular is the birdcage type of the late nineteenth century. [*Author's comment:* The new, thin, fireproof glass developed in Europe can now allow these open units to stay in use.]

Other types of cabs (item 6) worth keeping are wood inlaid and a variety of mahoganies, oak and steel. Since most cabs prior to 1940 were custom-built by or through the manufacturer, it would be helpful if they were still in business. Some companies keep patterns or layouts of the original design which would prove most useful.

START OF WORK

Before work has begun, make sure all material is *on site* or in storage so that downtime is at a minimum. Also, most reputable elevator contractors will provide a schedule with milestone dates so that you can coordinate with other trades.

These "checkpoints" are

1. Date of contract
2. Date of all approvals
3. Date of final material shipping
4. Date of job being manned
   a. Removal of existing equipment (not retained)
   b. Installation of machine room equipment
   c. Installation of hoistway equipment
   d. Installation of cabs and entrances
5. Date of final inspection and acceptance
6. Start of 3 months' free service (minimum) to ensure that

the equipment will operate reliably over time and to its design capability

SUMMARY

It is imperative to remember that this is a *general overview* of conservation work. As no two buildings are alike, so, too, do elevator systems differ. Proceed carefully and verify each decision on more than one level. While not every situation, equipment type, or code requirement can be addressed in this brief piece, the aforementioned should prove useful in generally any instance.

Mr. Farinola also suggests using *repeated vertical space* that can be spared for a new elevator, such as closets or bathrooms which can be relocated elsewhere, and stairwells (if their loss does not compromise code requirements). (End of section courtesy of Farinola.)

Since the well hole cost is 25 percent of the entire price for a new elevator, many architects chose to use an outside window or door location, since this only needs a less expensive truck-mounted rig for drilling. Of course, the façade must not be disturbed by the addition of an elevator shaft, so the selection must necessarily be done on a side elevation. Hydraulic elevators placed internally require a skid-mounted rig, which is more expensive.

For the past 15 years, a relatively new material has been used effectively by structural engineers to create a shaft. These are *Avany blocks,* which have grooves to accept rods for additional stability (Fig. 65).

Whenever boring a shaft for new elevators, great care must

Fig. 65. Avany blocks being used to create a new elevator shaft.

be taken not to create cracks and other structural damage to the surrounding areas, which would be irreversible or costly to repair. The electrical and plumbing contractors must completely remove all pipes and wiring in the way of the new installation (Fig. 66).

Retention of the original ornamental doors is the optimum. If that is not possible, at the very least, the existing design should be silk-screened on to the new flat doors, to retain the feeling of the lobby (Fig. 67).

If the use is for concerts, springs and vibration-eliminating material should be used to minimize the operation noise.

A radically new type of elevator, developed by Nippon Otis, promises to offer operating costs equal to or less than the cost of the standard rope or hydraulic elevator, while eliminating the need for either an equipment penthouse or a hydraulic-pump room.

It is similar to a conventional rope elevator in that it has wire ropes running from the cab over sheaves at the top of the shaft to counterweights. But instead of a drive motor at the top of the shaft, the new design has a *linear induction motor* (LIM) incorporated into the counterweight to provide the vertical movement. Future versions of the elevator may eliminate ropes entirely.

Dumbwaiters Many nineteenth-century buildings made use of dumbwaiters. If this facility is not already in place, it

Figure 66b. Installing additional elevators in a Victorian theater: Moving pipes, cables, ducts in the way of new shaft.

is possible to have a free-standing dumbwaiter going up within a staircase without affecting the historic bannister. It can be as simple as a hand-operated cage with fail-safe cord attachment and buzzer and light combination to indicate floor. The side panels are selected to suit the building style. Most importantly, it is *reversible,* and can be removed without compromising the stairs (Fig. 68).

Escalators Using the same care in selecting space, modern moving stairs can be installed in older buildings successfully (Fig. 69).

Recently, spiral escalators have been developed in Germany. Their use in existing constricted space is immediately obvious. In addition, the position of the motor in conventional moving stairs may now be positioned in the middle of the straight run, instead of at the top, to make better use of electric power.

New materials not requiring the constant lubrication of metal parts now used, have also been developed.

In fact, all types of people-moving mechanisms are on the horizon, which could service museum complexes and other historic tourist attractions to better advantage. They include moving sidewalks (even up a grade), and train cars that run on air instead of rails. We may be approaching the visions of Buck Rogers, Flash Gordon, and all those other science fiction characters from the comic books of over 60 years ago.

Figure 66a. Installing additional elevators in a Victorian theater: The side-street entrance for the new location.

Figure 66c. Installing additional elevators in a 1930s museum: Framing out for the shaft.

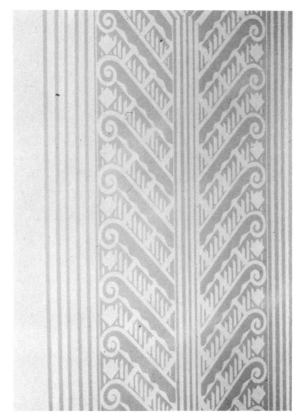

Figure 67. The original elevator door design silk-screened on new flat doors.

Figure 68a. Installing a reversible dumbwaiter within an historic stair: Wiring for bell and buzzer.

Figure 68b. Installing a reversible dumbwaiter within an historic stair: The completed unit with Victorian metalwork enclosure.

Figure 69. An escalator installed in an 1868 department store.

CHAPTER ELEVEN
SCHEDULED MAINTENANCE

According to an article in *Heating, Piping and Air Conditioning Magazine*,[39] preventive maintenance programs exist in less than half of commercial and institutional buildings! This indicates there is a vast opportunity out there for companies to sell scheduled maintenance, whose cost is much less than that of replacement of the entire building's systems. In fact, the low level of the entire retrofit market penetration indicates a huge potential for those seeking an expanded market.

To indicate that no design is successful unless the *preventive maintenance* is *built in,* picture the fate of the very high floodlight mounted over a swimming pool. Even a very high dive would not reach the fixture to relamp it. The only way to keep the space illuminated was to drain the pool and erect a scaffold. This was not well received by the client.

As pointed out in the engineer's experience when he returned to the building he had originally worked on, the design professional has little contact with the aftercare of the project. Consequently, there is little feedback if changes to the engineer's customary methods are needed.

Sir Bernard Feilden[39a] says: "A maintenance appraisal should be included in the Royal Institute of British Architects (RIBA) Plan of Work. If this were done, and architects visited their buildings, after the glossy photographs had been published, we might get a better building technology.

"Historic buildings are a laboratory experience. They can teach architects how buildings are used and abused, how they react to their environment, and where design might have been improved, for time is the shrewdest of fault-finders. This digression is meant to emphasize the importance of learning the lessons implicit in the aftercare or maintenance of buildings and its importance to designers, especially those who think themselves original and avant garde, but do not understand the wisdom of the ancients.

"Generally the architect will only be concerned with major repairs and the aesthetics of preservation, whereas the maintenance staff come into action only when something breaks down.

"The cleaners who look after a building and come into direct contact with every part of it do not know how to recognize symptoms of incipient problems or to whom they should report. Indeed, large intermediate areas are neglected because no one has been allocated specific responsibility for them. Most building maintenance, as practiced, is concerned with tactics, with solving a particular problem, often in vacuo, without considering its relationship to the building as a whole. What is required is a coordinated strategy involving the owner and users of the building, the maintenance staff, and the daily cleaners, all of whom can, by constant vigilance, provide an early warning system.

"William Morris, in his Manifesto of 1875, establishing the Society for the Protection of Ancient Buildings, enjoined: 'Stave off decay by daily care. Historic buildings differ from new ones in that they are expected to last for ever—definition of "for ever" being "as long as it is wanted".' Electrical and mechanical services, on the other hand, generally have a safe life of about 20 years. Thus the skilful installation of up-to-date services in historic buildings deserves careful study, as a usable structure may be said to be only as up-to-date as its services. Ancient monuments such as ruined castles and abbeys do not have such problems.

"Efficiency in maintenance depends on

---

[39] by Bob Korte, Editor, March 1989.

[39a] in *Conservation of Historic Buildings* (Butterworths, London, 1982).

1. Correct diagnosis

2. Effective remedies

3. Good workmanship

4. Good management

"The less *emergency maintenance,* compared to preventive and corrective, the better. Obviously, to accomplish the task, access to all parts of the building have to be provided. Install electric lighting within roof spaces and socket outlets for handlamps to view difficult places such as the underside of parapet gutters. All concealed spaces should nevertheless be kept clean and in good order to encourage a high standard of *preventive maintenance.*"

Cyclical Maintenance for Historic Buildings, by the late J. Henry Chambers, covers this subject in depth. He advocates preparation of a maintenance manual documenting frequencies of work. His examples of typical routines are

1. Daily
   a. Check fire-detection and security systems.
   b. Check heating plant, controls, and temperature and humidity recorders.
   c. Check boilers and pumps.
   d. Feel heating pipes and radiators for air locks or leaks.
   e. Check fuel tanks.
   f. Check the heating feed tank.
   g. Change defective lightbulbs.
   h. Check panelboard breakers if power is out somewhere.

2. Weekly
   a. Change or clean air filters of the heating or air-conditioning plant or (pipe) organ with humidifier.
   b. Check all thermographs, humidigraphs, and other recording instruments. Change charts and make reports. Correct faults in calibration.
   c. Check loudspeaker and microphone units in public-address equipment.
   d. Check all automatic fire-alarm and security devices.

3. Monthly
   a. Lubricate and adjust all mechanical drives and bearings, e.g., pulley belts, flexible drives.
   b. Check all log books.

4. Quarterly
   a. Check humidifiers.
   b. Service sound-reinforcement systems.
   c. Clean light fixtures.
   d. Have technical supervisor conduct a maintenance inspection of one-third, one-fourth, or one-fifth of total fabric.

5. Semiannually
   a. Sound fire alarms.
   b. Give staff fire-fighting practice exercises.

6. Annually
   a. Overhaul entire electric plant. Change fuses (if any), bulbs, and tubes, especially where these are not easily accessible.
   b. Inspect boilers and controls, overhaul boiler, clean main stack, and renew firebricks. Maintain feed tanks and ease ball valves.
   c. Clean out ducts and fan-assisted heaters, etc.
   d. Service lifts (elevators).
   e. Overhaul air-conditioning plant.
   f. Test lightning conductors and earth resistance.
   g. Ask fire brigade to test occupants and plant in mock fire-fighting exercises
   h. Test all fire extinguishers and refill if necessary.

7. Quinquennially (every 5 years)
   a. Have architect or surveyor make a full report every 5 years.
   b. Change tap washers, as a matter of preventive maintenance.
   c. Have specialists clean out sanitary equipment to avoid infections.
   d. Check lightning conductors.
   e. Inspect and test electric insulation and installation.
   f. Check on all mechanical wear, wear of electrical contacts, corrosion, and any signs of abnormal deterioration.
   g. Inspect and test the heating and cooling installations.

Sir Bernard says, "In Denmark and England, quinquennial inspections have been conducted for parsonage houses and parish churches for many years, with great success. For large buildings or a series of buildings, this quinquennial inspection becomes the basis of a 30-year *rolling program* for preventive maintenance. Skilful management of building maintenance while respecting the principles of conservation is a high-level occupation which deserves respect. Contracts with specialist contractors are a necessity to carry out proper preventative maintenance."

Here are a few low-cost domestic (U.S.) rules of thumb for scheduled maintenance compiled by Building Conservation International:

1. *Relamp* all similar fixtures on a *regular* basis, not when one burns out. The proper lamps or bulbs must be used. They must match in size, shape, color, and wattage with all the others in the same type of fixtures.

2. Exercise emergency generators *regularly.*

3. Specially focused lamps must not be knocked out of kilter by a thoughtlessly wielded broom handle. Maintenance staff should be attentive to the correct focus.

4. No elevator should exist without a *proper maintenance contract.* Older manually operated elevators can be maintained to give safe and dependable service, and with attention can last indefinitely at lower cost than automatic elevators. This does not mean having the resident maintenance person do the job.

5. Clean the air-conditioning filters regularly.

6. Have the heating and cooling systems checked every season before using.

7. Monitor iron plumbing pipes.

8. Check the sewer pipes if they are aged.

9. Check washers in faucets to save water.

10. Check wiring older than 30 years.

11. Clean all water filters regularly.

CHAPTER TWELVE
CASE HISTORIES OF M/E INSTALLATIONS

THE NEW YORK PUBLIC LIBRARY[40] (Fig. 70)

This Beaux Arts building had so many changes, additions, and renovations that the original interior design was virtually gone. Mrs. Vincent Astor made it her project to collect the money to return this major cultural institution to its former grandeur. Room by room, it has been reclaimed. The Fine Arts collection must be housed in special environmental conditions. Therefore, the restoration of that space had to be carefully done. One can see from an early photograph compared to another taken 60 years later that this would muster all the resources of the restoration team.

In addition to the original lighting fixtures which remained, ugly new ones were added. Air-conditioning ducts were inserted in the skylight. The room was painted institutional green and debris piled high in it.

The first lighting fixtures were cleaned, rewired, and reused. The skylight was relit to resemble daylight. The space above the room was adequate to conceal both lighting and air-handling units.

Security and environmental controls were cleverly concealed in the walls and ceilings and also under stationary furniture.

The cost had to be kept at a point which was equal to the amounts contributed, yet exemplary work was done.

THE RAINBOW ROOM, ROCKEFELLER CENTER, NEW YORK[41] (Fig. 71)

Since its opening in the 1930s, this has been one of the most popular dining and dancing rooms in the United States. It was always noted for its elegance. Although no major changes had been made, the fabric itself was getting shabby. While other spaces on the 64th and 65th floors were changed drastically, including altering the floor levels, the Rainbow Room had to stay exactly the same.

While it was closed for this work, all kitchen equipment was replaced. The original crystal chandelier and wall sconces were rewired and reused. The same aubergine silk lined the walls. The lighting under the glass banisters was renewed. The revolving parquet dance floor was made to work again. Decorative dome lighting was restored. There was already existing space for the systems, so it was a matter of retrofitting carefully. The reopened room is still so in demand, it takes 6 weeks to get a reservation.

THE FRANKLIN INSTITUTE, PHILADELPHIA (Fig. 72)

This science museum was built in 1930. To accommodate increased attendance, new elevators and a dining room had

[40] Courtesy of Lewis Davis, FAIA, of Davis, Brody & Associates, New York.

[41] Courtesy of Hugh Hardy, FAIA, Hardy, Holzman, Pfeiffer, New York.

Figure 70a. The Fine Arts Room of the New York Public Library: What had happened in 50 years—added lighting fixtures, air-conditioning ducts sprouting out of the skylight. (*Photograph courtesy of Davis, Brody & Associates.*)

Figure 70b. The Fine Arts Room of the New York Public Library: Concealed HVAC and lighting in space above the skylight. (*Photograph courtesy of Davis, Brody & Associates.*)

Figure 70c. The Fine Arts Room of the New York Public Library: Completed room, with original lighting fixtures, plus security, environmental controls, and museum lighting. (*Photograph courtesy of Davis, Brody & Associates.*)

Figure 70d. The Main Reading Room of the New York Public Library: Using space behind paneling. (*Photograph courtesy of Davis, Brody & Associates.*)

Figure 70e. The Main Reading Room of the New York Public Library: Wiring under original tables. (*Photograph courtesy of Davis, Brody & Associates.*)

Figure 70f. The Main Reading Room of the New York Public Library: Completed. (*Photograph courtesy of Davis, Brody & Associates.*)

Figure 71. The Rainbow Room, Rockefeller Center, New York, put back to the way it was 60 years ago.

Figure 72a. The Franklin Institute, Philadelphia: Available spaces to provide lighting for floor below.

Figure 72b. The Franklin Institute, Philadelphia: Exploratory demolition to search for space.

Figure 72c. The Franklin Institute, Philadelphia: Available space in the walls.

to be created. Aside from finding a thin electrician to crawl into the tight quarters, there was no problem in executing the work, especially after the same crew had just finished two previous jobs from the same period.

FIDELITY MUTUAL INSURANCE COMPANY, PHILADELPHIA (Fig. 73)

This purpose-built office building, erected in the 1920s, had been empty and abandoned for 20 years before it was resurrected. The lobby wall sconces were stolen and held for ransom when news of the planned restoration appeared. Because the architect, Mary Werner DeNadai, of John Milner & Associates, had done her homework, the restoration documents included photographs of the original units. These fittings were reproduced at a much lower cost than the "light-nap" money demanded.

The original design and materials were so extraordinary that they made the project an enjoyable experience, and an award-winning one as well. The entire crew showed its respect for its charge by treating it thoughtfully and carefully, so that it is once again a showplace.

All the necessary and requested systems were installed *inconspicuously*. The project came in on time and on budget, which was the best reward of all.

Figure 73a. The former Fidelity Mutual Insurance Co., Philadelphia: Original photograph from 1924. (*Photograph courtesy of Mary Werner DeNadai, AIA, John Milner & Associates.*)

Figure 73b. The former Fidelity Mutual Insurance Co., Philadelphia: Abandoned room after 20 years. (*Photograph courtesy of Mary Werner DeNadai, AIA, John Milner & Associates.*)

THE LOTOS CLUB, NEW YORK (Fig. 74)

The architect, Bert L. Stern, AIA, and mechanical engineer, Salvatore Farruggia, of Syska & Hennessy, were part of the restoration team. For the life-safety system, they retrofit the interior spaces of this late-nineteenth-century private club with hard-wired smoke detectors tied back to a central panel. The two large spaces, the ballroom and the library, are fitted with beam-type detectors, while the private dining room has conventional detectors. Every introduction of code-satisfying equipment was unobtrusive.

The smoke beam system has an operating range of 32.8 to 328 ft (10 to 100 m). The transmitter-receiver is normally located 6 to 20 inches (15.24 to 50.8 cm) below a flat ceiling or below the bottom of structural beams perpendicular to the line of sight. Stratification of smoke below ceiling level may necessitate locating the projected beam at a lower level where smoke interception is likely to take place.

On smooth ceilings parallel beams should be spaced 60 ft (18.3 m) or less from each other and no further than 30 ft (9.15 m) from any parallel sidewall. Other spacings may be determined depending according to ceiling height, airflow characteristics, and response requirements.

Mounting surfaces should be rigid, and the detectors should

Figure 73e. The former Fidelity Mutual Insurance Co., Philadelphia: Penetrations in ceiling for air-conditioning, life-safety, and lighting fixtures. (*Photograph courtesy of Mary Werner DeNadai, AIA, John Milner & Associates.*)

Figure 73c. The former Fidelity Mutual Insurance Co., Philadelphia: Restored room. Paneling was intact. Lighting fixture was rewired and cleaned. Air-conditioning ducts carefully inserted. (*Photograph courtesy of Mary Werner DeNadai, AIA, John Milner & Associates.*)

Figure 73d. The former Fidelity Mutual Insurance Co., Philadelphia: Elevator lobby as found. When news of the rehabilitation was made known, the original lobby wall sconces were stolen and held for ransom. Since a photograph of the units was found, new units were fabricated at a lower price than what was demanded, and the "hot" ones could not be unloaded because everyone knew where they came from. Here is an example of how research saves money. (*Photograph courtesy of Mary Werner DeNadai, AIA, John Milner & Associates.*)

Figure 73f. The former Fidelity Mutual Insurance Co., Philadelphia: Completed lobby. (*Photograph courtesy of Mary Werner DeNadai, AIA, John Milner & Associates.*)

Figure 74. The ballroom of the Lotos Club, New York. (*Photograph courtesy of Burt L. Stern, AIA, Architrave.*)

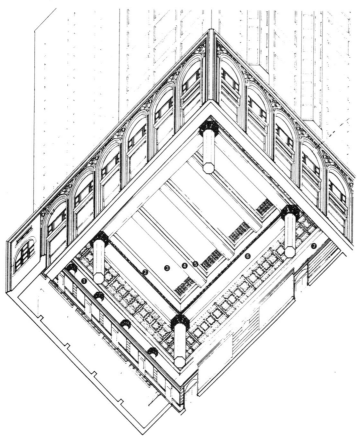

Figure 75a. The Trading Room, Chicago Stock Exchange: Daylight originally lighted art glass through lunettes and skylights with prismatic glass.

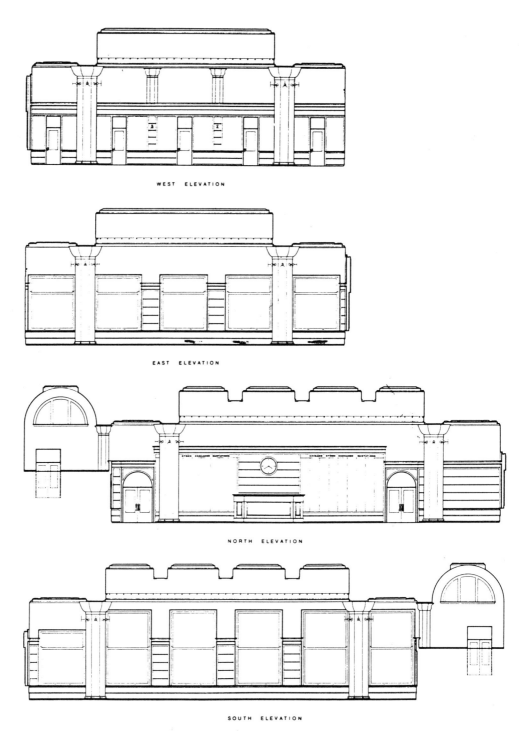

WEST ELEVATION

EAST ELEVATION

NORTH ELEVATION

SOUTH ELEVATION

Figure 75b. The Trading Room, Chicago Stock Exchange: Original room probably had cast-iron radiators and natural ventilation. Carbon filament bulbs were used for lighting. Spot lighting was placed above art glass for evening light.

be located where they will not normally be interrupted by day-to-day facility operations.

THE TRADING ROOM, CHICAGO STOCK EXCHANGE (Fig. 75)

"If one had to choose for preservation an architectural interior of unequaled beauty that represented ideas formative to the course of modern architecture, the Trading Room would top one's list. From the time of its completion in 1894 until its demolition in 1972, the Chicago Stock Exchange Building stood as an eloquent example of the contributions of Dankmar Adler and Louis H. Sullivan to the formation of the tall, metal-framed commercial building. This space has been preserved and re-constructed in the Art Institute of Chicago by the office of John Vinci."[42]

CONCLUSION

It is hoped that all the examples of case histories, from both sides of the Atlantic, for both private and governmental owners, demonstrate the ability to bring historic buildings up to date profitably as far as conveniences are concerned, while respecting the uniqueness and beauty of the original design. Future generations will benefit from the economic and cultural concern given to the retention of architectural heritage.

[42] From the booklet on the Trading Room published by the Art Institute of Chicago, 1989, by John Vinci, with a foreword by Pauline Saliga.

APPENDIX A
PRELIMINARY WORK
PRIOR TO CREATING
CONSTRUCTION DOCUMENTS

O = owner, SE = structural engineer, C = contractors, A = architect, P = professionals

Who?	Does what?
O + SE + A	1. Check for structural soundness
O + A + C	2. Stabilize the building
O + A + P	3. Thoroughly explore the site
	4. Find available spaces
	5. Determine scope of work
	a. Corrections to existing systems
	b. New installations
	c. Provisions for future needs
O	6. Engage the design professionals and consultants
O + P + A	7. Design considerations for thorough planning:
	a. Historic research
	b. Investigate code compliance and variances
	c. Provide flexibility of design
	d. Investigate best tax situations for funding (if income-producing)
	8. Decision on jurisdictions, time schedules, and coordination
	9. Special preconstruction requirements for restoration
	a. Protection of exterior and interior
	b. Special safety and fire precautions
	c. Establish housekeeping rules
	d. Require documentation of work done

Who?	Does what?
A + P + O	10. Develop a list of competent bidders
	11. Put the job out to bid or negotiation
	12. Let contracts
	13. Have general meeting of all participants of the team to explain goals and expectations
A + P + C	14. Actual construction
	a. Good use of interstitial spaces for concealment of new systems
	b. Use of innovative tools, materials, equipment, and instruments
	c. Care in penetration of original fabric
	d. Protection of exterior and interior
	e. Provision for easy maintenance
O + P + C	15. Development of regular maintenance program

APPENDIX B
BASIC GUIDELINES FOR PREPARATION OF CONSTRUCTION DOCUMENTS[43]

For bidding and/or construction:

1. Use standard scales ($\frac{1}{16}$, $\frac{1}{8}$, $\frac{1}{4}$ inch, etc.) consistently (avoid $\frac{3}{16}$, $\frac{3}{8}$ inch, etc.).

2. Orient plans consistently throughout the set, ideally with north up, including site, floor, detail, and structural, mechanical, and electrical (SME) plans.

3. Do not include drawings in the project manual or specifications.

4. Avoid drawings smaller than 11 inches × 17 inches, or larger than 30 inches × 42 inches. All drawings in bid set should be the same size.

5. Documentation of alteration work should clearly distinguish between new, existing-to-remain, and existing-to-be-removed. If demolition is extensive, separate demolition drawings may be required.

6. *Avoid duplication of structural, mechanical, and electrical information on architectural drawings. (Provide cross-reference where necessary.)*

7. All drawings should have a number, a date, a scale, and a north-pointing arrow on all plans.

8. Where possible, include details and sections on the same drawings on which the detail or section is designated. Details, sections, elevations, etc. should be clearly identified and cross-referenced if possible.

9. All openings should be uniquely numbered for consistent identification and/or coordination of doors, windows, frames, hardware, etc.

10. The recommendation for order of working drawing elements should be as outlined in Appendix A.

11. The Joint Committee recommends that the latest edition of *Architectural Graphic Standards,* by Ramsey and Sleeper, be followed for material indications, abbreviations, dimensioning, and graphic symbols.

12. Revisions to the documents should be clearly identified and dated on drawings and noted in drawing index.

13. Architects should also include names, addresses, telephone and (if available) fax numbers of owners, consultant, etc. Also, north-pointing arrows should be included on all plan drawings and all revisions should be clearly marked and revision dates shown.

It is recommended that the order of working drawings should be as follows:

Cover sheet

Three-dimensional sketch

---

[43] Joint recommendation of Philadelphia Chapter, AIA-Phila. Builder's Chapter Associated General Contractors of America, June 13, 1990.

268

APPENDIX B

Basic Guidelines
for Preparation of
Construction
Documents

Drawing index

Owner/design team/contractor (where appropriate, addresses and phone numbers)

Symbols, material indications

Dimensioning and other graphic systems

Abbreviations

Project location plan

Code information

Site information

Site plan (cross-reference M/E site plans)

Zoning information

Civil engineering

Landscaping

Subsoil information

Basement and/or foundation plan(s)

Floor plans—removal (where appropriate), new work

Elevations

Building sections

Wall sections

Exterior wall details, window schedules

Interior elevations and details

Casework and built-ins

Finish schedules (if possible, place on floor-plan sheets)

Door schedules (if possible, place on floor-plan sheets)

Color schedules

Specialties, equipment, furnishings, special construction

Conveying systems

Structural systems

Mechanical [Construction Specifications Institute (CSI) Section 15] systems

Electrical (CSI Section 16) systems

APPENDIX C
CHECKLIST FOR ENGINEERED PLUMBING AND FIRE-PROTECTION SYSTEMS

Source
Transmission
Outlet

1. Domestic hot- and cold-water systems
   a. Flow in pipes
   b. Friction loss
   c. System arrangement
   d. Street pressure
   e. Pumped and gravity systems
   f. Fixture units and sizing
   g. Sizing water heaters
   h. Hot water circulation versus heat tracing
2. Drainage and vent systems
   a. Sanitary drainage arrangement
   b. Storm drainage
   c. Flow in pipes, sanitary and storm systems
3. Plumbing equipment
   a. Pumps and controllers
   b. Potable water
   c. Waste water
   d. Tanks—pressure, atmospheric
   e. Water heaters, preheaters
   f. Sumps/ejector
4. Plumbing fixtures
   a. Selection of fixtures and supports
   b. Water and drainage requirements
   c. Low-consumption fixtures
   d. Handicapped fixtures

5. Field inspections and testing requirements for plumbing systems
   a. Site inspection as it relates to plumbing specifications and construction documents
   b. Field observations and engineer's recommendations
   c. Shop drawings—purpose, review process, and execution
6. Sprinkler system design
   a. Combined fire suppression protection (FSP)/sprinkler system
   b. Pipe sizing methods
7. Sprinkler system types
   a. Wet
   b. Dry/preaction/deluge
   c. On/off
8. Specifications
   a. General: scope of work
      (1) Codes
      (2) Qualifications
      (3) Manufacturers
   b. Products
      (1) Piping materials
      (2) Valves
      (3) Fixtures
      (4) Equipment
   c. Execution
      (1) Product installation
      (2) Tests
      (3) Equipment connections

270

APPENDIX C

Checklist for
Engineered
Plumbing and
Fire-Protection
Systems

9. Sprinkler system design
   a. System arrangement
   b. Hydraulic calculations
   c. Fire Codes NFPA 13
10. Gaseous agent fire-suppression systems
    a. Advantages and disadvantages of Halon and CO_2
    b. System arrangement
       (1) Detection devices
       (2) Alarm devices

   c. Piping
   d. Tanks
11. Plumbing and fire-protection codes and standards
    a. City code
    b. BOCA[44] (or other regional) code
    c. NFPA[45] Standards 13 and 14
    d. Pipe sizing (sanitary, water, and storm)
    e. Plumbing piping material

APPENDIX D
RELATED DATA

Many experienced conservation professionals refer to the 18th edition of the Kidder-Parker *Architects' and Builders' Handbook* [John Wiley & Sons, New York, 1931 (1st ed. 1884)]. It has been used by architects, structural engineers, and contractors since the nineteenth century.

This standard reference work on building construction contains not only valuable guides on how structures were put together and the properties of material used but also *related data* which all members of the team need to know to get the job done.

Such miscellaneous items included:

Data on specific gravity and weights

Data on wire gauges and metals

Data on nails and screws

Data on excavating

Data on stonework

Data on bricks and brickwork

Methods of estimating quantities of brickwork

Data on lime

Data on sand and gravel

Data on lathing and plastering

Data on lumber and carpenters' work

Data on building papers, building felt, quilts, and insulators

Data on paint and varnish

Data on window glass and glazing

Memoranda on roofing

Memoranda on tiling

Data on asphaltum

Data on mineral wool

Methods of estimating the cost of buildings

The quantity system of estimating

Dimensions and data useful in the preparation of architects' drawings and specifications

Data on athletic fields and courts

Data on mail chutes

Data on refrigerators

Recommendations for construction of cooling rooms and large refrigerators

Data on mechanical refrigeration

Data on tower clocks

Data on library book stacks

Data on classical moldings

The classical orders

Roman alphabet

Data on lightning conductors

Data on vacuum cleaning

Data on waterproofing for foundations

Data on force of the wind

Data on wind stresses in tall buildings

Data on horsepower, pulleys, gears, belting, and shafting

Data on chain blocks, hoists, and hooks

Data on bells

Symbols for the apostles and saints

Documents of the American Institute of Architects

Glossary and architectural terms in building codes

APPENDIX E
THE AUDITORIUM BUILDING, CHICAGO

Figure 76 is a vintage vertical section of the Auditorium Building, Chicago, by Adler and Sullivan (1890). This was one of the first multiuse buildings, housing a hotel, office block, and 4600-seat theater. It was a structural and acoustic marvel. The theater lighting influenced Radio City Music Hall, New York, and it was one of the earliest to have air-conditioning. Its hydraulic elevators were only recently replaced, not because they were inoperable, but too "slow" for the school which now is the occupant. Innovative ideas, such as using space under stairs and imitation fireplaces for ventilation, and means to close off upper levels of the theater for a more intimate setting, have been copied widely.

The entire heavy mass floats on concrete rafts designed by the brilliant engineer Dankmar Adler. Louis Sullivan's distinctive decorations are still standards to follow.

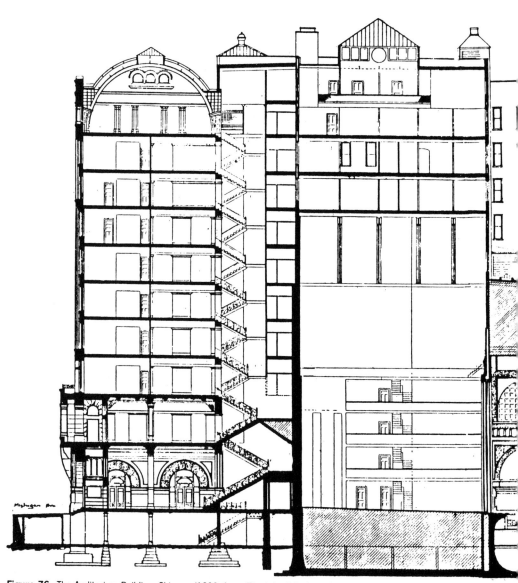

Figure 76. The Auditorium Building, Chicago (1890; from *The Inland Architect*).

APPENDIX E

The Auditorium Building, Chicago

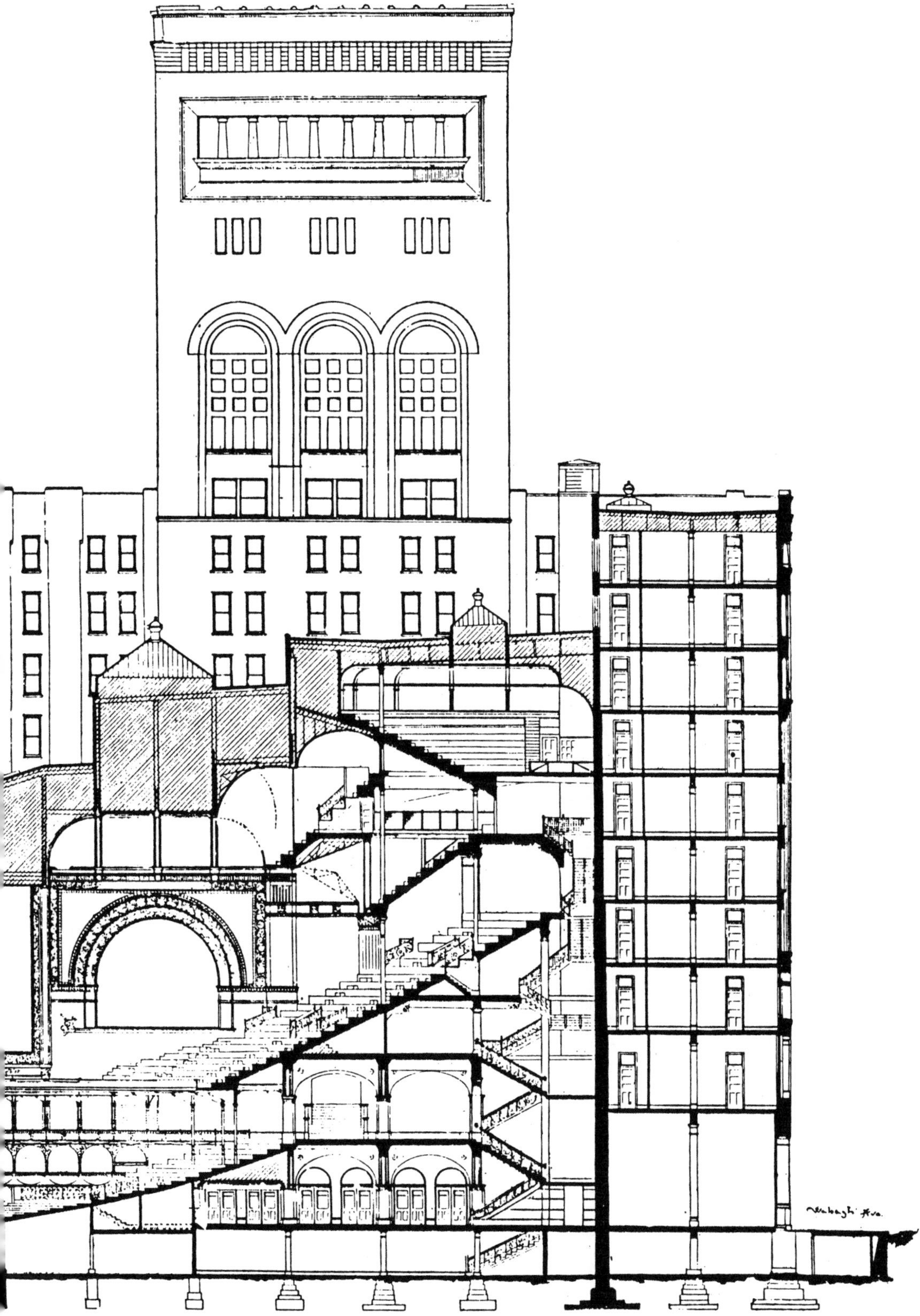

APPENDIX F
TIPS ON HANDLING FIBER-OPTIC CABLES AND COMPONENTS[46]

The glass fiber is typically only 0.005 inch in diameter; a human hair is about the same size. The fiber is placed in various layers of plastic coverings to protect it and provide strength for bending and pulling. The resulting cable is about $\frac{1}{8}$ (0.125) inch in diameter.

Necessary accessories include inspection microscopes, continuity checkers, and scribe and polishing tools.

A checklist for the installer

Do protect the end of the connector. Keep the connector end covered with a dust cap while handling it. Cover the end with tape if the dust cap is missing.

Do keep the optical interface clean. A piece of dirt is larger than the beam of light that carries the signal. Use a clean, lintless cloth dipped in denatured alcohol to gently widen the ends of the optical connectors. A blast from a can of clean pressurized air will remove any residual dust and dirt. Materials used to clean camera lenses are usually acceptable. If the system has failed after the connector has been disconnected, a good first step is to clean the ends of the fiber-optic connector.

Do have respect for the fact that this transmission medium is glass. It does chip, scratch, and break if handled improperly. It does not need to be handled like fine crystal, but it cannot be treated, or mistreated, like copper cables.

Do make repairs in the proper manner. Replace damaged cable and connectors with identical components. Optical fibers require special connectors which require special tools. Make sure you've received the proper training on installing and making repairs to fiber-optic components and cables.

Don't look directly into the optical cable or connector, or you may damage your eyes.

Don't step on, place heavy equipment on, push wheeled carts over, or otherwise crush the optical cables. The glass fiber inside the cable is protected by plastic coatings and strength materials, but these will not protect the fiber from heavy concentrated loads.

Don't bend the cable at right angles or kink it. Optical fibers are remarkably flexible. However, temporary loss of light or permanent breakage of the fiber will result if the cable is bent too tightly. The allowable bend size will depend on the type of cable being used, but a safe rule of thumb is, don't bend the cable over a radius of less than 4 inches. Most connectors have strain reliefs to prevent small bends from occurring as the cable exits the connector.

Don't overtighten optical connections. Some connectors use threaded nuts to hold them in place. These should be tightened with light finger pressure only, unless the instructions specify otherwise.

---

[46] Adapted from an article by Mike Peppler, AMP Inc., in *CEE News Magazine,* November 1990.

APPENDIX G
THE SECRETARY OF THE INTERIOR'S STANDARDS FOR REHABILITATION (REVISED 1990)

The Secretary of the Interior is responsible for establishing standards for all national preservation programs under Departmental authority and for advising federal agencies on the preservation of historic properties listed or eligible for listing in the National Register of Historic Places.

The Standards for Rehabilitation, a section of the Secretary's Standard for Historic Preservation Projects, address the most prevalent preservation treatment today: *rehabilitation.* Rehabilitation is defined as the process of returning a property to a state of utility, through repair or alteration, which makes possible an efficient contemporary use while preserving those portions and features of the property which are significant to its historic, architectural, and cultural values.

The Standards that follow were originally published in 1977 and revised in 1990 as part of Department of the Interior regulations (36 CFR Part 67, Historic Preservation Certifications). They pertain to historic buildings of all materials, construction types, sizes, and occupancy and encompass the exterior and the interior of historic buildings. The Standards also encompass related landscape features and the building's site and environment as well as attached, adjacent, or related new construction.

The Standards are to be applied to specific rehabilitation projects in a reasonable manner, taking into consideration economic and technical feasibility.

1. A property shall be used for its historic purpose or be placed in a new use that requires *minimal change* to the defining characteristics of the building and its site and environment.

2. The historic character of a property shall be retained and preserved. The *removal* of historic materials or *alteration* of features and spaces that characterize a property shall be avoided.

3. Each property shall be recognized as a physical record of its time, place, and use. Changes that create a *false sense* of historic development, such as adding architectural features or architectural elements from other buildings, shall not be undertaken.

4. Most properties change over time; those *changes* that have acquired *historic* significance in their own right shall be retained and preserved.

5. *Distinctive features,* finishes, and construction techniques or examples of craftsmanship that characterize a property shall be preserved.

6. Deteriorated historic features shall be *repaired* rather than replaced. Where the severity of deterioration requires replacement of a distinctive feature, the new feature shall match the old in design, color, texture, and other visual qualities and, where possible, materials. Replacement of missing features shall be substantiated by documentary, physical, or pictorial evidence.

7. Chemical or physical treatments, such as *sandblasting,* that cause damage to historic materials shall not be used. The surface cleaning of structures, if appropriate, shall be undertaken using the *gentlest* means possible.

8. Significant *archeological* resources affected by a project shall be protected and preserved. If such resources must be disturbed, mitigation measures shall be undertaken.

280

APPENDIX G

The Secretary
of the Interior's
Standards for
Rehabilitation
(Revised 1990)

9. *New additions,* exterior alterations, or related new construction shall not destroy historic materials that characterize the property. The new work shall be differentiated from the old and shall be compatible with massing, size, scale, and architectural features to protect the historic integrity of the property and its environment.

10. New additions and adjacent or related new construction shall be undertaken in a manner that if removed in the future, the essential form and integrity of the historic property and its environment would be *unimpaired.*

Note: To be eligible for federal tax incentives, a rehabilitation project must meet all 10 Standards. The application of these Standards to rehabilitation projects is to be the same as under the previous version so that a project previously acceptable would continue to be acceptable under these Standards.

Certain treatments, if improperly applied, or certain materials by their physical properties, may cause or accelerate physical deterioration of historic buildings. Inappropriate physical treatments include, but are not limited to, improper repointing techniques, improper exterior masonry cleaning methods, or improper introduction of insulation where damage to historic fabric would result. In almost all situations, use of these materials and treatments will result in denial of certification. In addition, every effort should be made to ensure that the new materials and workmanship are compatible with the materials and workmanship of the historic property.

Guidelines to help property owners, developers, and federal managers apply the Secretary of the Interior's Standards for Rehabilitation are available from the National Park Service, from State Historic Preservation Offices, or from the Government Printing Office. For more information, write: National Park Service, Preservation Assistance Division 424, P.O. Box 37127, Washington, D.C. 20013–7127.

APPENDIX H
BUILDING CONSERVATION INTERNATIONAL'S GUIDELINES FOR MECHANICS

At all times, the mechanic working on a building must realize that shelter is a basic human necessity, and that life safety is uppermost. Therefore, every member of a construction crew must be constantly aware of the consequences of every action taken while on the job.

1. Thorough knowledge of older building technologies (how structures were put together)

2. Knowledge of properties of natural and synthetic materials (especially stone, wood, metal, glass, and plaster)

3. Ability to diagnose the correct cause of the problem

4. Habits in good housekeeping on the job to protect the building, the materials, tools, and equipment, as well as the workers

5. Constant awareness of safety and threat of fire

6. Alertness against theft of the building's historic components

7. Care in penetrating irreplaceable original fabric (material) of the project

8. Knowledge of where to research historic details pertaining to the job

9. Basic knowledge of architectural styles and materials used with them

10. A flexibility to move when conditions change unexpectedly

11. Inventiveness—an open mind to the problem's solutions

12. Scrupulous documentation of whatever innovative procedures were done

13. Thorough knowledge of applicable codes and ability to present a well-prepared case for variance, *as long as life safety is uppermost*

14. Attention to detail at every level

15. Desire to upgrade personal knowledge continuously

16. Awareness of the latest in tools, materials, and equipment to get the job done

17. Willingness to do detective work to find existing space within which to conceal modern systems

18. Willingness to coordinate with everyone else involved

19. Willingness to plan ahead before starting any work

20. Scheduling of every item in proper order to save duplication of effort

21. Ability to anticipate results of actions, to avoid unnecessary costs due to lawsuits for public liability or property damage

22. Ability to handle labor fairly but efficiently.

23. Always reading specifications and instructions carefully

24. Inspecting deliveries for quantity, catalog number, and condition before accepting them

282

APPENDIX H

Building
Conservation
International's
Guidelines for
Mechanics

25. Taking pride in work, which is a source of personal satisfaction

26. Thinking it is *fun* to face the challenge

27. Neatness in handling and care of both personal and company tools

28. Meticulous cleaning up the area after working on it

29. Always seeking for the simpler, less expensive solution

30. Never doing irreversible procedures to the historic fabric of the building

31. A passing knowledge of adjacent trades and their impact on the craft in question

32. Arriving on the job *prepared* with proper tools and materials

Anyone with all these qualities should be singled out from the crowd. There must be a means of identifying this competency for prospective clients. Only those who don't know that they don't know would oppose this selectivity.

In the words of Local No. 98 International Brotherhood of Electrical Workers, "A laborer works with his hands; a craftsmen, with his hands and mind, but a Building Conservator works with hands, head and heart."

BIBLIOGRAPHY

There is really no definitive book on how to deal with mechanical/electrical systems in older buildings while keeping the architectural integrity of the structure. Most of the information given in this book, deceptively simple as it seems, is the result of suggestions from practitioners with years of practical experience in the field, and original research from the archives.

American magazines useful to the industry include

Building Design and Construction

Electrical Construction and Maintenance

Electrical Contractor

Contractors' Electrical Equipment (CEE)

The Construction Specifier

Commercial Renovation

Heating/Piping/Air Conditioning

Consulting/Specifying Engineer

Technology and Conservation

The following publications were used in researching this book:

Kidder-Parker Architects' and Builders' Handbook, John Wiley & Sons, New York, 1931

Construction Specifications Institute (various)

The Builder (1880–1930)

The Inland Architect and News Record (from 1879 on)

Engineering Record (1879–1930), from the collection of Jane Mork Gibson

Historic American Building Survey/Historic American Engineering Record (HABS/HAER) collections of the National Park Service

Bernard M. Feilden, FRIBA, *Conservation of Historic Buildings,* Butterworths, 1982

Alan C. Parnell, FRIBA, *Building Legislation and Historic Buildings,* English Heritage Architectural Press, 1987

The British publications used in this book were obtained from the following organizations:

Irish Georgian Society

The Thirties Society

The Georgian Group

Society for the Preservation of Ancient Buildings

National Trust of Great Britain

English Heritage

SAVE Britain's Heritage

Research facilities were used at

Chicago Historical Society

Art Institute of Chicago

Boston Public Library

New York Public Library

284

BIBLIOGRAPHY

The Athenaeum of Philadelphia

Library of the British Museum

Library of English Heritage

Library of Hampton Court Palace, England

Medieval collection of Terry Every, Carpenters' Company, London

In 1990, as United States Chairman of Professional Education in Building Conservation for ICOMOS (International Council on Monuments and Sites), the author conferred with representatives from all member countries about the need to improve curricula, training, and work experience for everyone who does this type of work as a vocation. They have generously shared their technical knowledge.

INDEX

ABOUT THE AUTHOR

Gersil Newmark Kay is Chief Executive Officer of M. Newmark & Bro., Inc., Philadelphia, Pennsylvania, the second-oldest commercial electrical contracting firm in the city. She is a second-generation contractor with extensive practical experience. Mrs. Kay is also the founder of Building Conservation International, a technical nonprofit educational organization which researches and teaches the techniques of historic building conservation. She started the Continuing Professional Education course "Profitable and Practical Building Conservation" at Drexel University, Philadelphia, and is a well-known lecturer in this country and abroad. Mrs. Kay was the recipient of the first President of the United States' Award for Historic Preservation, for excellence in building conservation education. In 1990, she served as United States Chairman of Professional Education for ICOMOS (International Council on Monuments and Sites), and helped develop guidelines for improved curricula in this field.